The
CAMERA
NEVER
BLINKS

Books by Dan Rather

THE CAMERA NEVER BLINKS
by DAN RATHER with MICKEY HERSKOWITZ

THE PALACE GUARD
by DAN RATHER and GARY P. GATES

The CAMERA NEVER BLINKS

ADVENTURES OF A TV JOURNALIST

by
DAN RATHER
with MICKEY HERSKOWITZ

WILLIAM MORROW AND COMPANY, INC.
NEW YORK   1977

Library of Congress Catalog Card No. 77-76017

ISBN 0-688-03184-6

BOOK DESIGN   CARL WEISS

TO

JEAN GOEBEL RATHER,

AND HER PARENTS,

HILDA AND MARTIN.

TO

ROBIN AND DANIEL.

AND

TO THE MEMORY OF

MY MOTHER AND FATHER.

CONTENTS

The
CAMERA
NEVER
BLINKS

HOUSTON: HOME AGAIN

> Q. . . . Thank you, Mr. President. Dan
> Rather, of CBS News. Mr. President
> . . . (*Applause, mixed with jeers.*)
> THE PRESIDENT: Are you running for some-
> thing?
> Q. No, sir, Mr. President, are you?
> —OFFICIAL GOVERNMENT TRANSCRIPT
>
> *March 19, 1974*
> *Houston, Texas*

THE ADVERTISING brains at the White House had put the President of the United States on the road. This was their newest Watergate strategy. The problem, as they saw it, was not that Richard Nixon had broken the law or lied. The problem was the people who called attention to the problem. They had seen the enemy and it was us: the Press. The time was ripe, they believed, for a counterattack—what General Alexander Haig called "a breakout."

The plan was for Mr. Nixon to bring yet another tailored, self-serving case to the people and sell it hard. On friendly ground, before audiences that were handpicked, fielding questions under the most promising conditions. The approach was one favored by politicians long before Nixon, creating the illusion of taking big risks where few existed. The press would tag along, literally, like the guys sweeping up after the elephants.

The President and his staff opened the show in Chicago before a convention of business people. The performance went off socko for them. Afterward I saw General Haig, Nixon's chief of staff, and he was ecstatic. Ron Ziegler, the press secretary, wore the beaming smile of a small boy who had just seen a Bruce Lee Kung Fu movie. They thought they had found the answer, a way out—over the head of the special prosecutor, around the flanks of the news media.

It was a strange time. For the past eight months the President had talked to the country mostly through his lawyers. He had all but taken diplomatic asylum in the White House, resorting to television to assure the American people that he was not a crook. In his words, we had "wallowed in Watergate" for two years.

His public relations people were doing now what they did well, setting up the staged news conference, the kind designed to win sympathy, not to give information. It had seemed to work in Chicago.

Houston was to be the third such appearance within a week. At the outset, my White House colleague, Robert Pierpoint, and I were opposed to being a part of the act. The President obviously had a right to defend himself. He was entitled, if he could, to pick his spots and stack the crowds and screen the questions. But the press, we felt, should not serve as his stooges. My instinct was to sit this one out.

Nixon's advisors had gone through a period in which they wanted to believe—and sought to convince others—that Watergate was nothing but a Washington disease. True, it tended to devour us there. The story was on our doorstep in the morning, on our TV screen at night, at the next table wherever one had lunch. Relief was just beyond the Potomac, his advisors thought.

On a Tuesday night, March 19, the National Association of Broadcasters would meet in Houston. A news conference had been arranged as part of the President's appearance. Behind the scenes some heavy maneuvering was going on. The White House wanted the questions to come from the audience, from the station managers and salesmen. To their credit, Bill Walbridge and other leaders of the NAB insisted that news people should be included. There were telegrams and phone calls back and forth. A compromise was suggested. Local news directors would be on the program.

Then someone said, well, we can't exclude the White House regulars, can we? They should be among the mix. After some resistance the President's aides agreed.

At CBS we debated among ourselves—Bill Small, the Washington bureau chief, Walter Cronkite and the correspondents, Eric Sevareid, Pierpoint and myself, among others, what position to take. There were shades of gray. We thought we could envision what would happen. The news conference was to be held in Jones Hall, a center for the performing arts, a graceful building with colonnades and an Italian marble exterior. It seated three thousand and the White House would "paper" the crowd, which is to say that in addition to NAB delegates a number of tickets would be reserved for local Republicans and friendly guests. The news people would be arranged on the stage, facing the President.

What we finally concluded was this: The appearance had the feel of a political rally, but we could not be sure until we got there. We were among the ones who had been harping, for all these many months, that Richard Nixon needed to face questions. This gathering had been labeled a news conference, and even though we suspected it might not be, eight months had passed since his last one. How could we ignore it? Nor did we want to appear disrespectful to the local news directors.

So with misgivings I went to Houston. For me, the trip was mildly ironic. The city had been my home. My father had moved us there from Wharton, Texas, when I was less than a year old. I spent my boyhood in Houston, most of my schooling, my salad days in journalism. And took a wife. We still had kinfolks and old college chums and friends there. But this was business, not fun, and I didn't look forward to it.

People were choosing sides and I was aware—I would have been a fool not to be—that I had become a part of that division. Not by design but as a consequence of my job. It was not an easy feeling. There was a sense of having traveled a bad road too long. This was what it had come to, from the bungled break-in at the Watergate, to Judge John Sirica's hard line and James McCord's letter and John Dean's charges, to the unraveling of the coverup, to this vaudeville show that was to be Nixon's last call.

Along the way I had acquired a reputation, as *New York* magazine put it, as The Reporter the White House Hates. Given the time and the temper, it is true that some people saw that label as a distinction. I wasn't so sure. The reputation was not one I had sought or courted or even now fully understood.

In a way it disappoints me that I am not in better touch with those feelings. But, in fact, by being drawn into the fevers of Watergate I felt I had in some ways failed at my job. My job is to inform, not persuade. At the same time I don't want to come across as some kind of Pollyanna. I do not subscribe to the idea of the reporter-as-robot. I can't walk into a room and say to you, look, every day that I went to the White House I left my emotions behind me. But one test of the professional is how hard he tries and how well he succeeds in keeping his own feelings out of a story. I tried.

By March, 1974, I was not fully convinced, myself, of the absolute guilt of Richard Nixon. I knew well his basic argument: Whatever he approved, whatever he covered up, he did not for himself but for his country. As a citizen I had trouble with that defense. The list of facts that didn't match was growing. But as a reporter I had to lecture myself. No one had yet shown me any undeniable evidence of criminal involvement on the part of the President. No one had yet produced the "smoking gun," which was concealed, we now know, among the tapes Nixon had refused to release, for reasons the tapes explained all too clearly.

That morning, as we landed in Houston, the President had been dealt a double blow. James Buckley, the Conservative senator from New York, had called upon Nixon to resign "to save the office of the presidency itself." Buckley had suggested it would be an act of courage and statesmanship.

On this same day tape recordings, obtained through the courts, now made clear that Nixon knew of the hush money paid to the Watergate conspirators and, in fact, had approved it. He had now given three different versions of his meeting with John Dean, one on national television, and had retracted or amended all three. The special prosecutor, Leon Jaworski, had that day charged H. R. Haldeman with lying when he quoted Nixon as saying, of the proposed bribes: "It would be wrong."

It seems odd to remember the joy among the President's defenders when the existence of the secret White House taping system first surfaced. Surely, they gloated, Nixon had held back the tapes to ambush his accusers. Now he would spring the trap. It had been his word against that of John Dean, the boyish, prim-looking young lawyer, who said he had warned his boss that "Watergate is a cancer on the presidency." There had been an effort after his testimony to picture Dean as the mastermind behind the break-in. No one who really knew anything about the White House could believe that accusation. Dean was just what one fellow staffer described him: a pilot fish, the little fish that swims beside the sharks.

But nothing had worked. With each new development—another Nixon aide implicated; new tapes and edited transcripts and eighteen-minute gaps and expletives deleted—Richard Nixon's support leaked away like sawdust from a torn sack. Since the beginning the White House had tried to treat Watergate as a public relations problem, not a criminal case. If the story wouldn't die, they saw it as proof of television's "liberal bias." How often Nixon and Spiro Agnew had sent that train of thought rumbling down the track.

Yet I think people ache to hear those in power confess to being human. They ached for it then, they ache for it now. What a relief it would be to hear those at the apex of leadership say, just once, on a major matter of policy or judgment: We blew it, we made a mistake. We have not heard such a confession in high places, although John Kennedy may have come close on the Bay of Pigs. The lack of candor hurts us all. It hurt Richard Nixon, in fact, wounded him mortally. In the end his refusal to tell the truth, to level even with his own family and friends, brought him down.

And that was why the White House caravan had kept moving, now to Houston. The man whose political career had been resurrected after no less than six crises, by his own count, had found a crisis he could not manage.

The evening of the NAB program, producer Bob Mead and I walked the few blocks from our hotel, the Hyatt Regency, to Jones Hall. I knew well that part of Houston, although the skyline changes constantly. The city is like a friend who, every time you see him, has a new hairstyle or moustache. Long ago Houston had been dubbed The Land of the Big Rich. In another era Texas oilmen played poker in the lobby of the Rice Hotel, where fortunes were won or lost on the turn of a card. Howard Hughes was a quiet Houston schoolboy. So was Walter Cronkite. Lyndon Johnson once taught speech classes there, at old Central High. Leon Jaworski and John Connally practiced law not many doors apart. I know of few other cities where men and events tripped over so many roots. It was in Houston that candidate Kennedy met the Baptist ministers, and President Kennedy promised to land a man on the moon.

When I was growing up, the whole city suffered from an inferiority complex. Dallas had the better stores, more class, all the culture. Houston just had oil, money and hard grabbers. The Astrodome and Jones Hall and the Space Center helped change the image of my hometown. But Houston was still a city where the folks favored an underdog, a role that suited Richard Nixon. Only in America could the man who held the most powerful office in the land become an underdog.

These were some of my thoughts as I strolled into the lobby of Jones Hall with Bob Mead, a good companion and the producer I most often sought when the news was on the road. I called Mead "deputy dog," a private joke between two kindred spirits. Bob is a smooth-looking fellow, a sharp dresser, regarded by some at CBS as too "Hollywood" when he first joined the network. But Bob came up the hard way. He had talked his way into a news job after working nights as a bellhop. I liked his "can do" hustle. We understood each other.

Once in a newscast I referred to Gerald Warren, the White House deputy press secretary. Mead's ear picked up one of my Texanisms. "You said 'deppity,' " he corrected me later. "The word is *deputy*. As in deputy dog." We had a rehearsal on the spot and from then on deputy dog was Bob's title.

As we moved to the stage I told him I had made up my mind not to ask any questions. The local news directors had flown in from around the country, most of them from the South and Southwest. It was their hour, and unless I heard something that drove me to my feet, something that demanded a follow-up, I intended to sit it out. Even so, I had prepared a list of questions, had worked on them on the flight from Washington and in my hotel room. Reporters often fiddle with questions the way some people work on crossword puzzles. To kill time.

On the stage two monitors were assigned to call on reporters, an option usually left to the President. The press had insisted on this procedure, an attempt to allow more independence in how people were recognized. One of the monitors was Ray Miller, the news director at Channel 2, the NBC affiliate in Houston. I had known Ray since 1955, when I broke into radio. He is among the best I have ever seen at aiming a question, direct and crisp. By contrast, I was then a blathering, inarticulate zero. I had trouble mustering the courage to ask a question of someone like Roy Hofheinz, then the city's mayor, later the genius behind Astrodome and a formidable character in his own setting. His son, Fred, was elected mayor of Houston in the mid-1970's.

Ray Miller was a tough competitor, never unkind but all business. He was not about to give you any helpful hints or let you see the date on the dime he put in the pay telephone. We knocked heads a few times and I learned from him. No one ever accused Ray of being in show business. Integrity, ethics and hard work were the only fish he sold. He has a Franchot Tone look about him—lean, neat, brisk, sometimes grim. You tended to forget Ray has a smile until you saw him flash one.

I guessed that Ray was one of those who fought to open the news conference to the White House regulars. Indeed, the trappings of a political rally did develop. The county Republican party had papered the house, handing out passes to the faithful. People walked in wearing Nixon pins and carrying small stuffed elephants. To the mild confusion of the press, applause and cheers greeted the President's answers. When a newsman rose whose name was known, a slight but audible stir could be heard. A press conference is not a church service, but this was something new.

And, finally, there did come a moment that drove me to my feet. Nixon had answered a Watergate question by saying that he had complied fully with the demands of the grand jury and the special prosecutor's office. An alarm went off in my brain. I looked at my watch and judged that time still remained for not more than three or four questions. I also had a sense that the news conference had not gone well. (Later *Newsweek* reported that the proceedings "resembled a softball game at the annual company picnic . . . with soft, fat questions.")

Based on what I thought to be the facts, and on a statement released only two days before by the special prosecutor, I could not let that answer pass. It begged for a follow-up. I raised my hand. At the same time so did Tom Brokaw, of NBC, and Tom Jarriel, the ABC correspondent—like myself a Houston product.

When Miller nodded in our direction I assumed he had called on Brokaw. Tom started to stand, as did the reporter sitting behind him. But Miller shook his head, indicating no, not you, or you. Then he took a half step forward and pointed straight at me. I motioned with a thumb against my chest and he mouthed the words, *yes, you.*

I had no way of knowing exactly what was in Ray's mind. But I would wager that, one, he sensed the news conference *had* taken on the aspects of a pep rally; two, he felt there were questions that needed to be followed; and three, he thought, We do not want to be accused of ignoring Rather because of any past difficulties with Mr. Nixon.

So with time running out, knowing that not everyone could be recognized, he came right to me. In the scheme of things life turns in a lot of funny circles. Ray Miller had been a competitor of mine in the 1950's. Now he had passed over Tom Brokaw, whose network represented *his* station, and he passed over Tom Jarriel, who had once worked in Ray's own newsroom, to allow me to question the President.

Depending on your point of view, he may not have done me a favor. If I had not been recognized, I would not have found myself up to my ears in another controversy.

The form at the news conference was simple: the reporter rose, announced his name and company and asked his question. Once in front of the microphone, I attempted three times to do so. But the moment I said, "Mr. President . . . thank you, Mr. President. Dan Rather of CBS News," a noise seemed to fill the room, loud and hollow, as though I were hearing it through a partition.

I suppose we are all alike in that we tend to hear selectively. There was some applause. Boos welled up in the very next wave. I know they did. I know the television audience heard them. I can only tell you that I did not. A number of people said to me later, "Well, you couldn't have been listening very closely if you didn't hear the booing." And I must not have been, because I was surprised to read and hear about the booing and to learn that people had sort of kept score.

But one reason I did not hear had to do with my concentrating on why I was standing there: to ask a direct question and try to get a straight answer. That was my job. Period. I attempted to blot out the rest.

Keep in mind that we were dealing in milliseconds. When the President said, *"Are you running for something?"* I thought to myself, Well, I don't quite know what he means by that. If I had been allowed half a day, or even half a minute, to think, my response *might* have been different. But in those sandspecks of time I only had long enough to think, Well, you don't want to stand here simply mute. And so I said, *"No, sir, Mr. President, are you?"*

This exchange, a magazine writer assured me later, would become a classic of television journalism. He meant that in a way complimentary to me. But I cringed to think so. No, I don't have exciting memories of that moment. But I would not take back what I said, if only because I do not believe in replaying events. What might have happened did happen. What I do regret is this: I do not want to be judged on such asides. I am painfully aware that one person in a thousand remembers the main question that I asked that night, or how the President answered. But many can tell you in some detail about the phrases that flashed between us.

People often refer to the scene as "the time Dan Rather asked the President if he was running for something." Their recollection is not that I was reacting to his prod, but that I had initiated the exchange in an insulting way. There is a difference of opinion about whether I had insulted the President. I didn't feel then that my words were disrespectful. And I don't now. His question called for an answer, and I wanted to respond in kind, in a way that could be taken in whatever spirit the President had intended.

Part of my retort was simply a reflex. Nixon made a habit, in a tight spot, of diverting the question or asking the reporter to repeat himself. By doing so he accomplished two things. He had more time to think and he put more heat on his questioner, who might even forget what he wanted to ask. I saw President Johnson do that once and I marked the tactic then as one to guard against. A reporter posed a complicated question. LBJ gave him The Stare, then said flatly, "Well, first of all, I don't think you can even repeat that question." And the guy couldn't. He just froze. The room erupted with laughter.

I have gotten in hot water before for saying this, but I strongly believe that in our system no citizen has to face any leader on bended knee. He is not standing before a monarch, or a descendant of the sun god.

What I really wanted to do—*all* I wanted to do—was to ask my question, which had two parts. After the applause and the boos subsided I eventually did. The first part had to do with Nixon's insistence that he had cooperated fully with the grand jury and the special prosecutor. I asked him to reconcile that statement with his refusal to appear before the grand jury and the fact that Leon Jaworski, in a letter to the Senate, charged he had not received all the tapes he requested. In short, the President had not done what he had just told a national television audience he had done. His words did not match the known facts.

My basic question, the one I had worked on in my hotel room but had not expected to ask, was this: Since the Constitution clearly assigns to the House of Representatives any impeachment investigation, how can the House meet its constitutional responsibilities while you, the person under investigation, are allowed to limit its access to potential evidence?

And Mr. Nixon replied, "First, with regard to the first part of the question, Mr. Rather, what I was referring to with regard to cooperation was that Mr. Jaworski, at the time he handed down the indictments, said that he had the full story on Watergate. You reported that on CBS, I think, as other reporters, quite properly.

"Now, as far as the hearing before the grand jury was concerned, I respectfully declined to do so, and I would advise no President of the United States to appear before any grand jury. That would not be in the best interests of the presidency of the United States.

"Now, if you would repeat your second question . . . ?"

RATHER: "Well, the second question had to do with the House impeachment investigation. I pointed out that you had sought to limit, to define the limits of that investigation, what evidence they have access to and what evidence they should not have access to."

NIXON: "Well, Mr. Rather, referring to the House of Representatives, just like the President, it is bound by the Constitution. The Constitution says specifically that a President shall be impeached for treason, bribery, or other high crimes or misdemeanors. It is the Constitution that defines what the House should have access to and the limits of its investigation, and I am suggesting that the House follow the Constitution. If they do, I will."

The next question from the panel had to do with food production.

As I returned to my seat I had no inkling that anything dramatic had taken place. I had not known what was in the President's mind when he asked if I was running for something. If he intended to throw me off balance, I hoped he had not done so. If he meant his comment in a joking, friendly way, I hoped my answer would reflect the same. But I did know his earlier false statement had had to be challenged. That was part of my job.

A few minutes later, when the questioning was over, I walked to one end of the stage to say hello to an old friend, Don McClendon, who was one of the sound engineers that night. We had worked and traveled many miles together when I first started with CBS. Don is a straight-talking fellow, blue-collar, and I mean that in an admiring way. We shook hands. Don said quickly, "I know you haven't had time to think about what just happened, old buddy. But you ought to get out of here and do that because this could cause you a heap of trouble."

Those words startled me. Up to that instant I had no inkling of the turmoil ahead. But as I turned away from Don McClendon, a tall, lanky blond man made a beeline for me. I saw him coming at me out of the corner of my eye. He grabbed my shoulder, which is not my favorite way of being approached. In what I took for a Tennessee accent he said, "That was a most disrespectful thing you said to a great President and I resent it. Your remark was disloyal and un-American and I hold you personally responsible."

I was speechless. I walked away and he followed me. He was heavily into a disloyalty speech. Then the crowd moved on, I was swept up the aisle and he faded away. Out in the lobby Tom Brokaw and Tom Jarriel both made a point of saying, "You handled the President's question well." This is a business where a misstep by a rival can make your heart leap like a fawn. But they meant what they said and I was grateful. Still, the message had begun to soak in: I had not heard the last of this night. By the time I returned to the Hyatt Regency, pink phone slips were spilling out of my box at the desk.

The next morning the President was to tour the Space Center at Clear Lake, half an hour's drive from Houston. Reporters were waiting in the bullpen, behind the ropes, for his arrival, when Pat Buchanan strolled over. Buchanan had a few society notes to lay on us from a reception held for Mr. Nixon after the press conference.

Pat was one of the White House speechwriters and p.r. policy men, a conservative hard-liner. We never liked each other, but I respected him because he would say to your face whatever he said behind your back, and not all of them did. Once he had said to me, "You know, I don't have any use for you, Rather, but my wife keeps telling me I'm wrong about you."

There was a story behind that declaration. Buchanan had married an attractive young woman who worked at the White House. We ran into each other one day in a Georgetown pet shop called "The Friendly Beasties," during my son Dan's exotic-pet period. I was helping him pick out a pet snake. She recoiled in some horror as I said hello, at the same time trying to explain that the snake wrapped around my arm was to be Daniel's, not mine. I could imagine what a source of fun this might be for the fellows at the White House. "Where's Rather?"

"Out walking his pet snake."

But Mrs. Buchanan apparently had concluded that any father who spent time with his son, who in fact would help him shop for a pet reptile, couldn't be all bad.

I don't believe she ever convinced Pat, however. When a gaggle of reporters pushed against the ropes to hear what he had to say, as though it were feeding time, I hung back. Not my scene. I could hear Buchanan telling them about the reception, how well the President was received, who the guests were.

Then he sort of stood on his tippy-toes, raised his voice and over the heads of the other newsmen threw out the word, "Oh, yes, and Arthur Taylor, the president of CBS, was there."

He was just making a point.

Not all the Nixon people were quite sure how to weigh what had happened the previous night. Ron Ziegler seemed to make a special effort to say to me, "Listen, the President did not consider that disrespectful."

"Have you talked to him?" I asked.

Ziegler said, "I'm saying to you that he did not consider it disrespectful."

A week passed before any heavy reaction set in. The headline in the next morning's edition of the Houston *Post,* March 20, 1974, said:

"Nixon Repeats Vow Never To Resign." Our exchange appeared only as several lines in a transcript that covered two full newspaper pages.

Then the clamor began to build. In the Houston *Chronicle,* Ann Hodges, the television critic, came to my defense. "To put the incident in perspective," she wrote, "it is necessary to underscore that what occurred here was not a press conference but a carefully controlled and staged TV spectacular. A Happening, with a very vocal and receptive audience out front."

In an interview in *Broadcasting* magazine Tom Jarriel described the scene as a "prostitution" of the news conference format.

Meanwhile the White House mail had been sorted and counted. Through a mutual friend I received a message from a member of the Nixon staff. "Tell Dan they *think* they've got him." Okay, whoa, I can see someone rubbing his eyes, wondering why a Nixon man would send a friendly warning to Dan Rather. We often forget, and as a reporter I have to keep reminding myself, that people and events are seldom as easy to define as black and white. One must allow for light and shade.

This source was on the inside. He felt affection for Nixon. He remained loyal to the end, even made the final move to San Clemente. He wept the day the helicopter picked up the Nixons for the last time on the White House lawn. But he was one of those who went through the personal torment of having to juggle his duty to the President with his conscience over what he knew Watergate represented.

What the message meant was clear. Nixon aides, and perhaps the President himself, had decided the incident had exposed the hostility of the press, all to the President's advantage. They thought they could make me a symbol of that antagonism. They could put me on the defensive. At the very least, I would become gun-shy.

They were wrong. Events had gone too far. Time was too short, the evidence too strong. A case of burglary and wiretap had grown into bribery, perjury, abuse of power for criminal ends, the subversion of the CIA, the FBI and the IRS. It couldn't be held back much longer. In a slight way that night in Houston only exposed the frustration, the treadmill that Watergate had become for most of us. But the high drama was nearly over. Richard Nixon, who repeated his vow that night never to resign, would indeed resign in less than five months.

I had some uncomfortable days around CBS, but one of the things that helped was a letter, among thousands, received by Richard Salant, my boss. This one was from Ray Miller. It said, in part, "I have been around here a long time: I was the person who recognized him that night. And let me tell you, what I think you need are more, not fewer, Dan Rathers. For whatever that may be worth."

To me, it was worth a ton. And I appreciated Ray's sentiments all the more because, indirectly, Ray had gotten me in trouble at San Clemente, when the President had held his last press conference, in August, eight months before. That was part of the Houston story because the President and I had tangled then. It was the time of my "all-due-respect-to-the-office" question and Mr. Nixon's rebuttal, "That would be unusual."

I had cribbed that technique, in a manner of speaking, from Miller. He once moderated a panel show in which he frequently reminded the viewer, "Please keep in mind that the question does not necessarily reflect the view of the questioner, but is a reporter's way of getting a story."

That lesson had stayed with me. And that was what I meant, and all I wanted to convey, when I prefaced my San Clemente question to the President. A correspondent walks a fine line between respect for the office and doing his job. The footing was not always easy in the Watergate months, given the nature of the questions that had to be asked. But let me leave no doubt. I was raised in a home where the White House was considered a shrine. The presidency is an important part of what holds this nation together and I do not take lightly what the office represents.

At the same time no reporter wants, or can afford, to be a sycophant. The incident in Houston may have focused on the role of the press in an era when the press made news as well as covered it. If so, I might persuade myself that the uproar did indeed serve a purpose.

One of the harder tasks in life is to deny with sincerity a description you know to be flattering. But the picture painted by one magazine of "the test of wills" between the hard-nosed young reporter and a besieged President was a bit much. If that reference is unacceptable, so was the image offered in some of my mail that I was a "far Left, radical, wild-eyed, bomb-throwing Bolshevik."

I don't believe I have suffered from an identity problem, though I may have caused a few. Which brings me to another memory I have of that night in Houston. I felt confused, out of sorts, annoyed at letting myself be used as a prop in a stage show, with a studio audience clapping and booing as though it were a vaudeville act. I knew we had just been through a set performance by the President. I had felt at the start it was wrong to be there. And, having come, I had landed myself in a contest I didn't understand, whose consequences I could not measure.

As I hurried out of Jones Hall I realized I was being chased by a fat woman waving a stuffed elephant at me. She pursued me up the aisle and into the lobby, yelling after me in a very fishwifey way, "Boy, Dan Rather, he really told you off!"

I tried to ignore her, which proved impossible. She had the kind of voice that would frighten the pigeons in a park across the street. People stopped in their tracks and watched. I was almost out the door when she shouted again, "Boy, he really told you off." For a moment I hesitated. Just frustration, I guess. As I did, she blared out, "Why don't you go home, Dan Rather?"

And for the first time that night I laughed out loud. I had the delicious pleasure of turning around, slowly, and saying to her, "Madam, I *am* home."

Chapter 1

A LITTLE LEARNING

THE DREAM begins, most of the time, with a teacher who believes in you, who tugs and pushes and leads you on to the next plateau, sometimes poking you with a sharp stick called truth.

Mine was named Hugh Cunningham and he taught journalism in 1950 at Sam Houston State Teachers College. With an enrollment sometimes as low as 700 and no pretensions, Sam Houston blended quietly into the red clay and piney woods of East Texas. Traces of the Old South still existed in that part of the state, where cotton, though never king, was about all anyone had. Cotton, lumber and a few scraggly cattle.

With a population of five thousand, Huntsville had grown up around the school, a lean, scenic town with a colorful history. General Sam Houston had built a cabin there and came back to it to die. So the school was named after the liberator of Texas, the hero of San Jacinto and the first elected president of the Lone Star Republic.

For whatever interest it may hold for historians, until the 1920's the official name of the college was the Sam Houston Institute of Teaching. When freshmen started wearing sweatshirts with the school's initials the state legislature hastily passed an act and renamed it.

How Hugh Cunningham happened to wind up there, with a master's degree from the Missouri School of Journalism, young, with a mind that could light up a room, I do not know. But it was a break for me. Otherwise I would not have lasted in college longer than three weeks and most likely would not have gone on to whatever career I have had. That may be putting too much on one man's conscience, but I owe a debt to Hugh Cunningham.

Actually, my ticket to college was to have been football. Based on my size (I weighed one-fifty), and my talent, which was marginal, there was no reason, other than my own ignorance, for me to think that the gridiron would become my salvation. But I had started at end in my senior year at Reagan High School in Houston and I had shown I could catch a pass. There was nothing to indicate I was a gifted athlete, nothing to feed the hope that it would pay my way through college, except that it was the only hope I had.

So near the end of my last high school year I dropped by the gymnasium to see the coach, a man named Lamar Camp. Football coaches tend to be a major influence on a young man's life. Coach Camp had kept me in school when I wanted to drop out and get a job, the choice people in my neighborhood often faced around the tenth grade.

"I want to start looking for a college," I told him.

"That's fine," he said. Coach Camp was a taciturn man.

"It occurs to me that it might help if I had a letter from you," I replied.

He stared at me for several moments. I thought he hadn't understood what I meant. Finally he just said, "Look, you're not going to play college football. You're not big enough. You're not fast enough. You're not good enough."

There was no misunderstanding what *he* meant and I was absolutely crushed by it. I went home, in a daze, to decide if college was so important after all. Neither of my parents had finished high school. My father, Irvin Rather—known to his friends as Rags—had worked as a pipeliner for twenty years, which meant that he dug ditches for a fair amount of his lifetime. He met my mother, Byrl, at the Travelers' Hotel in Victoria, where she worked as a waitress, fresh off the farm, sending money back home every week to help her family through the Depression.

Mother later passed a high school equivalency test and took a few night classes at a junior college. But, basically, they were not people who understood what a college education represented, other than as something a lucky few people strived for, a goal. Their immediate concern was to feed and clothe three kids. I was the oldest, born on the last day of October, 1931, at Wharton. Then came Don and Patricia, six and eight years younger.

I don't intend for this to sound like another version of Up from Poor. We were not poverty-stricken, but money was always tight. My father felt that if I finished high school that would be achievement enough, as indeed in the 1940's it was. As far back as our heirloom Bibles recorded, no one on either side of our family had ever attended college.

Yet, in a curious way, I developed my passion to become a reporter through my father. That was all I could ever remember wanting to do, to work for a newspaper. I never thought of broadcasting as a career until I was nearly out of college. But radio did intrigue me. As a boy in Houston I listened to the broadcasts of the roller derby at the City Coliseum. Sometimes as I walked to school I would reconstruct in my mind my own roller derby play-by-play. I was, vicariously, the greatest roller derby describer who ever lived.

At home I was surrounded by newspapers. My father was an impulse subscriber, a voracious reader, and a man of sudden angers who would leap from his chair and cancel whichever paper had offended him. We went through every newspaper in town, the *Post,* the *Chronicle* and the *Press,* which was part of the Scripps-Howard chain and known locally for its muckraking policies. There was a constant harangue about newspapers in our house. My father would read something in the *Press* that riled him and he would shout, "Mother, cancel the *Press.* We're through with that paper forever. I don't want to ever see it in here again."

At one point we were down to the *Christian Science Monitor* and the St. Louis *Post-Dispatch,* which arrived in the mail, usually a week late.

Out of that cycle, somehow, grew my interest in the news, how it was gathered and reported and in what form it reached our home. I had always written for the school papers, usually on sports, and in the summer of 1948 had worked at the *Press* as a *gofer.* That, of course, was just below a copyboy. I'd go for coffee or cigars or egg rolls, or whatever the reporters needed.

I was still determined to get to college and my mother, bless her, was adamant that I should make the attempt. I considered myself fairly streetsmart. I had been to sea briefly one summer, at sixteen, worked on an oil rig, and dug pipeline ditches. But no money had been set aside for my schooling. It was that way with most families.

So I picked out the nearest small school with a full, four-year enrollment, and that happened to be Sam Houston State, seventy-five miles northeast of Houston. I knew nothing else about it, but I hitchhiked to Huntsville and asked around for the football coach. I found him in the basketball gym, a little crackerbox the students used to call the Tarpaper Tabernacle. He was watching a game, his head swiveling from side to side, and the entire time I talked to him he never once looked me in the eye.

I said, "Coach, I'm Dan Rather. I'm from Houston, Reagan High School, and I'm a football player."

He said, "Uh-huh," and in a very fishlike way he shook my hand.

This meeting was my introduction to Puny Wilson, who had been a great football player at Texas A&M in the days when the All-America selectors did their picking from the Ivy League. According to local legend, Puny Wilson also had the distinction of being the only football coach in the nation who actually, honestly, had a degree in basket weaving.

When he was in college peach growing was the rage in East Texas towns eager for new income. The peach crops created a demand for baskets in which to ship the fruit. So the Agricultural and Mechanical College of Texas offered an undergraduate certificate in basket weaving, and Coach Puny had one.

He was a disillusioned man long before that day in 1950 when I approached him in the gym. Fourteen straight losing seasons will do that to a coach.

My conversation with him was painful, punctuated by long silences. I explained to him that I would graduate at midterm and could enroll for the next semester, which was to begin the fifteenth of February.

He said, "Well, spring training starts March sixth and I'd be glad to have you come out."

That was all I needed to hear. It was an invitation to try out for the team and, in my mind, that was tantamount to a scholarship. I was ecstatic as I hitchhiked the seventy-five miles to Houston. When I told my mother the news she was jubilant. Then my dad came home and he thought it was madness. One, there was no money to cover my living expenses. Two, my football tryout did not sound like a very solid arrangement to him. And, three, there was a lapse of maybe three weeks between the start of classes and spring training.

The final jolt came when I informed my father I intended to major in journalism. That was not a word he could define and it was never clear to him how I thought I could make a living at it. He understood newspapers. But if one was going to college, it was to become a teacher or an engineer or a lawyer.

The days passed very quickly, and what my mother instinctively knew was that if I didn't go off to school immediately, I would never get there. She was simply very determined about it. She had never been on a university campus, but her feeling was that once I enrolled something would work out.

In February, 1950, Mother took me to Huntsville on the Greyhound bus. We had a car, a 1938 Oldsmobile, but there was some doubt as to whether it would hold together, so we rode the bus. In my lifetime I have not made many more exciting trips than that one. We went first to the office of the dean of men, where I mentioned, proudly, that I was a candidate for the football team.

The dean replied that he didn't know anything about that, but registration ended that week and I needed $25 to enroll and $15 for student fees. My mother had brought along two $25 U. S. Saving Bonds—bought during the war and not yet worth their full value—and while I waited in the dean's office she went into town and cashed them.

There was just enough money to cover all the fees, and when I was enrolled I could only guess what my mother felt. I don't know if anyone who didn't live or grow up during the war will understand what my mother had done. But a family paid $18.75 for a savings bond and waited ten years for it to mature and pay back $25. You cashed one only in an emergency.

Again, this isn't meant as Humble Beginnings nostalgia. That was simply the way it was. Next I found a boardinghouse a block from the campus and the manager agreed to give me a month's credit.

I had a great sense of satisfaction about the whole process. Really, I was very little different from the farmers' sons and daughters who were enrolling that day, the youngsters who had been valedictorians in Roans Prairie and Sundown and North Zulch, who carried whatever they owned in cardboard boxes wrapped with rope. Or the workmen's kids from Beaumont and Dallas and Houston, who lacked the money or the grades to get into the bigger universities. I felt at home, walking the grounds in my blue jeans, open-neck white shirt and tennis shoes.

Later, when I signed up for classes, I paid my first visit to the young journalism professor, Hugh Cunningham. He had started the department and only had five or six students enrolled. That suited him fine. His idea was to work with a small number of young people and turn out a handcrafted product.

Where journalism was concerned he had a jealous nature. "Why are you here?" he demanded. "Do you know why you want to major in journalism?"

I said, "It's the only thing I've ever wanted to do."

He said, "What makes you think you can do it?"

I kind of bristled. "Well, I *know* I can."

With that reply, he barked out a half dozen facts and he had me sit down and write a news story for him. Now that I think about it, I was in the odd position of having to try out for the journalism department even before the football team.

From that moment Cunningham took me under his wing. When he heard about my football plans he threw up his hands.

"That's crazy," he said. "You don't want to be a football player. You'll get killed."

"There's no other way I can stay in school," I said. "This way I'll get a scholarship."

He laughed out loud. But he didn't push me about it. Possibly he knew it would do no good. Sometimes we ought not to be talked out of our mistakes. But I had to survive the next three weeks before the football practices started, and during that time Cunningham literally fed me out of his own pocket. In the meantime he kept lining up part-time jobs for me. I became a correspondent for the local Huntsville *Item,* which neither then nor now would be mistaken for one of America's distinguished newspapers. I was to string for the wire services—calling in basketball scores, mostly—and I also received ten dollars a month for cranking out publicity about the college. He had put together a package that would allow me at least to tread water.

In addition, I held a series of odd jobs, none of which lasted very long: I waited tables, pumped gas, worked at the Zesto Tastee-Freeze stand. It was a dollar here and a dollar there and then it was time to report for football. Just as Cunningham had warned, I damned near got killed. To begin with, we had played two-platoon football in high school and I knew nothing about defense. Beyond that I lacked speed and couldn't block.

As if my other handicaps were not enough, Puny Wilson had a fearful prejudice toward city boys. He was a big, rawboned ol' country boy himself and he typed me—this was laughable—as just another pampered, big-city dude. His idea of a gut check, of putting a youngster to the test, was to stick the candidate at defensive end and run one power sweep after another in his direction. In the first two weeks of practice I did not distinguish myself. Cunningham used to drop by the practice field, a cow pasture really, and he would stand there, shake his head and cover his eyes when the herd rumbled over my body.

Finally it dawned on me that Coach Puny was trying to make me quit. One afternoon as I limped toward the showers he ambled over, dressed as usual in a T-shirt, football pants and army surplus boots. He splattered a missile of tobacco juice amid the sand and cockleburs, rubbed the stubble of his beard, then put his arm around me. It was the first human gesture he had shown me.

"Son," he said, "I watched ya out thar the whole time t'day. And I wanna tell ya sumptun' I hope'll stay with ya the rest of your life. You're little." Pause. "And you're *yellow!*"

Well, I set about trying to prove he had at least the last part of it wrong. The proof was to be that I wouldn't quit. I played day after day, getting my bones smashed. Finally I went to see him and asked about my scholarship. Coach Puny was a tough, no-nonsense man, about fifty, and this time he didn't try to belittle me. I think he sensed that I really wanted to stay in school and that I needed help. For all I know, Cunningham may have put the fix in. Anyway, Puny said, "There's no way you can get a scholarship. But if you want to come back out in the fall, practice starts August fifteenth." (This was the same routine we had gone through before, but I accepted it, again, as an invitation.)

But I realized he had a heart when he told me I could drop around to the Bearcat Den—that was where they fed the football team—and take my meals on weekends. Coach Puny knew the boardinghouse, where I was eating on credit, closed its kitchen on the weekend.

I struggled through that spring and, in spite of everything, the odd jobs and the strange meal arrangements, Hugh Cunningham managed to capture and hold my attention. He was about five nine, slight, with dark hair combed straight back. An intensity poured out of him like water from a fire hose.

His idea of teaching journalism was to get you away from the classroom. He didn't believe the reporter's craft could be taught in school, and when he did, it was only because the state required it. The college had to have a curriculum. There had to be a Journalism 101. But Hugh Cunningham didn't really give a damn about any of that. He wanted us out in the field. "Write stories," he kept hammering at us. "Go interview the college horticulturist. Go downtown. Hang around the courthouse. Ride with the police. I don't want to see you the rest of the afternoon."

I learned long ago that the term *a good teacher* is redundant. While the phrase *a bad teacher* is a contradiction in terms. Rare is the teacher who fully understands what a tremendous difference he or she can make, but

Cunningham was one of them. He picked the courses his students needed to get a degree, and he set their standards. Often he lectured me: "Coming out of a school this size, with no reputation at all, your only chance is to make virtually straight A's.

That admonition I took to heart. I studied as hard as I could without actually feeling pain. Before breakfast, in the afternoons and at night I worked at money-paying jobs. Classes were crammed into the morning hours. Homework was done in snatches of time during the day and after midnight. In between and all about was the school paper. With Cunningham and Cecil Tuck, we put out the *Houstonian* twice a week. Tuck was another of Cunningham's prize students. He eventually went to Hollywood and has done well writing for television. He helped to discover and promote Glen Campbell, among others. Cecil was in much the same financial shape as I was, maybe worse. He stayed in school that semester by writing bad checks and then scrambling to cover them. Truth to tell, we often covered for one another with criss-crossing hot checks. We always paid our bills, but some semesters it took longer than others.

Meanwhile, Cunningham kept preaching experience to us, that you learned to write by writing. Cecil and I would compose stories and mail them to the Houston *Post*. Heaven knows, most of the time no response came and none was really expected. We would just send them off into this great vacuum. We'd do a feature story on a football player, or a teacher, or some campus character. Once, we sent out a piece on the lady who maintained Sam Houston's home. That was the big bone. The story was published and we were very proud. (You could get that feature printed almost every year. Even today. There is something about Sam Houston still having a housekeeper that seems to impress big city editors.)

Cecil was a major presence at the college. He was sloppy and fun and we hit it off from the beginning. He came from a sawmill town near Jasper and for that place, and for those times, he was an authentic free spirit. I believe he still holds the Lone Star Conference record for gin consumed by a third-string linebacker. He would occasionally show up for football practice under the influence, as they say, and he did not take many things seriously, including Cunningham.

Hugh was always torn. He knew he was a gifted teacher, knew how much of himself he was putting into us. But at the same time he wanted to be on the cutting edge of journalism. He was always taking summer jobs at newspapers like the Atlanta *Constitution*. He saw things in us and tried to express them in the way a father would, but he finally gave up trying to convince Cecil.

He couldn't talk to Tuck the way he could to me. Cecil would fall asleep or say, "Aw, come off that shit." So Cunningham would say to me, with a wrenching earnestness, "You can do it, Dan. You can go all the way." Keep in mind that for Hugh Cunningham, getting a job with the Houston *Post* was going all the way. A byline in the Houston *Chronicle* would have given him raptures. That was going all the way.

Cecil Tuck was country down to his toes. I never knew how or why he wanted to be a reporter. But we came along at the same time, and for the next three and a half years Cunningham tutored and pushed us. It was a fine relationship. I cannot imagine any student, anywhere, having a more meaningful one.

All that summer of my freshman year my major concern was winning a football scholarship in the fall of 1950. I still saw no way to stay in school without it. I landed a job during the summer working on a pipeline gang, digging ditches, as my father had done for so many years. I was able to save almost two hundred dollars and that relieved some of the pressure.

Still, it wasn't enough to get me through the school year. The money I had earned only meant that I could pay my bill at the boardinghouse and not mooch off Cunningham. So when football practice started in the fall I was there, drawing a uniform. The coaches looked at me with a weary respect. I was like a bastard cat you keep throwing off the end of the dock, and by the time you drive home he's waiting on the doorstep. But I stuck it out, long after all the others who didn't have scholarships had quit, and one or two more had given theirs back.

Before the first game I went to Coach Puny again and asked him where I stood. I think he may have been getting used to me. He still wouldn't give me a scholarship, he said, but I could suit out for the games if I wanted. I believe part of him wanted me to make it. We had a fine passer that year named Cotton Gottlob, and he knew I could catch the ball. There was always the possibility that the eight ends ahead of me might get hurt.

I worked out every day, letting the power sweep roll over me in waves, and I suited out for the first three games. Finally, in a fit of conscience, Coach Puny Wilson called me in and said, "Son, take my advice, give it up. It's useless for you." And that was it. I can remember walking out of his office and into the rain. Tears streamed down my face. It was one of the few times in my life I can remember crying.

My pride was involved. I had put so much of myself, emotionally, into it. And there was the feeling that I wouldn't last through the school year. All of that just came down on me.

Hugh Cunningham picked me right up. "It's the best thing that ever happened to you," he said. "You'd have wound up coaching or crippled or both. You don't know how lucky you are."

The next thing I knew he had obtained a job for me at the radio station in Huntsville, KSAM. It was Kay Sam to all who knew the station, what was known in the trade as a teakettle. Kay Sam had an operating power of 250 watts, the lowest allowed by the FCC. It was a three-room shack with a tower in the back, an oversized outhouse with an antenna sticking out the top. Our signal did not even carry to the city limits of Huntsville. We used to sell advertising to merchants over in Madisonville, fifteen miles away, and nobody in Madisonville could hear the station after six o'clock.

Kay Sam was basic, good ol' boy radio. We used to sell time on the pitch of a dollar a holler—the idea being that advertising spots cost a dollar each—but we often cut the price to forty cents.

The station was owned and managed by a Baptist minister known as Pastor Lott, Ted Lott. He was a journalist at heart. He loved the stories, the newscasting. He took a genuine liking to me, but I also filled a need for the station. He wanted to know if I had ever done any play-by-play of football games, and I said no, but I was sure I could.

He said, "Well, let me hear you. Go ahead, do some."

So I sat there and made up a game in my head, using the players from Sam Houston and a mythical opposing team. Altogether I did five or six minutes, and it wasn't difficult. It was not unlike the times I had invented a broadcast of the roller derby on the way to school or other occasions when I would amuse myself with the play-by-play of an imaginary football game in which I would be the hero with two seconds left on the clock.

When I walked out of the station Cunningham was gleeful. "Now that does it," he said. "If you really do a job for him, that's going to keep you in school and you'll have no more worries."

Kay Sam became my scholarship. Almost as important, it was the kind of place where you could make a lot of mistakes. At one point, in the same week, I was broadcasting the junior high, high school, college and black high school games. I did not lack for air time. I also put together the newscasts and on occasion covered executions at the state prison for the wire services. The town was so small then that a myth had grown up around the executions. You were supposed to be able to tell when they threw the switch to the electric chair because all the lights in Huntsville would dim for a few seconds. I have never been certain that was so, but it was pretty romantic stuff, and I must say I believed it at the time.

By now I was knocking down seven dollars a month acting as sports information director for the college and forty cents an hour at KSAM, plus a talent fee for the football games, usually ten dollars. I actually came out of Sam Houston State with a little money squirreled away.

Pastor and Mrs. Lott became major influences on my life with their many kindnesses and, of course, by continuing to provide my best paying job.

My survival was due to Cunningham, and he would not sit still for a thank-you. He was like a man cleaning out an attic so he could see what was there. He wanted you to get on with your future, go to class, make your grades and, when you had the time, read the Chicago Great Books Series. Hugh wouldn't classify himself as an intellectual, not then and I suppose not now. He probably would have laughed at the idea. But he had a restless mind and a decency impossible to overstate.

He was also a very tough editor. He would keep kicking material back to his students. It was not uncommon to have to rewrite a story as many as a dozen times before it suited him. And when it came to the student paper he was a lion defending the cubs. Once, an executive whose company published a house organ walked through the journalism offices. Cunningham instantly indexed this outlet as a job resource, a place where one of his graduates might break in, writing for the company publication.

The visitor was politically conservative and he questioned Hugh about a couple of items in that week's student paper. Looking back, it was ridiculous, but he wondered if these stories didn't smack of Left-wing socialism. Now, communism might have been big in the eastern academic circles, but it hadn't reached Huntsville yet. Socialism was still our big threat.

Cunningham simply threw him out. No fuss, no ceremony. And Hugh himself was by no stretch of the imagination a liberal. But this was ground where strangers were not welcome. He cared so much about news gathering, and the integrity of it, that he would tolerate no compromises. Later Hugh's principles would lead him into difficulty with the college.

Cunningham's practices might strike someone at Columbia University, or Northwestern, as quaint, but each semester when we returned to school he required us, in class, to repeat out loud the journalist's creed: "A public journal is a public trust . . ." It was like the Boy Scout oath and he took it seriously. In a way it was beautiful. Not very sophisticated, perhaps, but then he was not dealing with sophisticated minds.

Without my really being aware, I had the best of two worlds. On the one hand, I had Cunningham drilling into me the fundamentals—who, what, when, where, why and how. Get it, get it right, get it fast. Over and over again. "I want to know *exactly* what was said," he told us. "Treat it fairly. Write it fast." He often emphasized the need for quality writing, but he knew that reality was a city desk clamoring to meet a deadline, caring less if you made the language pretty.

That approach, I would learn in time, was tailor-made for broadcasting. Meanwhile I was working at a radio station where nothing was closed to me. I could do anything I was big enough to try. This led to some comic crises, but it was the richest kind of training.

One of Pastor Lott's best clients, and one of my major assignments, was the Gospel Hour from eight to nine at night, with the air time bought and filled by the local black funeral home. This period usually served as my break time, with the exception of those nights when the Gospel Hour's anchorman failed to appear and I had to fill in, faking a deep, East Texas black accent, or what I thought was one. I owed much to the early work of Amos 'n' Andy.

I would also sing occasionally on the air, although I no longer remember whether I did so for my own amusement or because of a sponsor's requirement. But for the most part it was lonely work and at night I usually had the station to myself. I put in a lot of hours there, studying in between records and newscasts and commercials. Once in a while one of the coeds from the school would drop by during the Gospel Hour— the only show that ever allowed me an hour of privacy—and we would slip out to the back room and go off to paradise.

Youth will have its way, but I am here to tell you that you have never tried to make out until you have known passion in the back of the Huntsville radio shack while the Gospel Hour was on the air. You have to know that I calculated my break time with great care. A lot of disc jockeys can dredge such memories from their small-town days. If you ever worked nights at a one-man radio station, you needed a diversion to pass the time. That *was* the standard diversion, but with the Gospel Hour pouring out of the speakers, a new dimension was added.

In truth, KSAM was a one-man operation simply because you could not operate the station with less. On the weekend I put us on the air at six in the morning and kept the broadcast going until midnight. I answered the phone, repaired the equipment, mowed the lawn and painted the tower.

Long-playing records—those of one artist in particular—were all that saved me from working nineteen hours without food. The artist was Pastor

Lott's brother, in spirit if not in fact, who sold Bibles out of Del Rio, Texas. The pastor's brother had recorded several religious albums featuring such favorites as "The Old Rugged Cross." He would pick a guitar and preach a little between songs.

At 6 P.M. each Saturday and Sunday I would put on one of those records, hop into the "Mobile News Unit" (a 1937 Plymouth pickup truck) and drive to the Dairy Bar two miles away. There I would order two hamburgers to go and get back to the station before the record had stopped playing.

One night I decided to alter the routine a little. I listened to a few bars of the opening hymn, hustled into the truck and headed for the Dairy Bar. A new waitress, a freshman at the college, had started working there and I noticed she had nice legs. So I said to myself, well, it doesn't matter much whether you take the hamburgers back or eat them here, so long as you get back to the station before six thirty. I sat there, made small talk with the girl and watched the big diesel trucks roll by on Highway 75 to Dallas.

I had been at the Dairy Bar about twenty minutes when the phone rang.

"It's Pastor Lott," she said, handing me the phone across the counter. The pastor was in a very unpastoral mood.

"Young man," he roared, "have you heard my radio station any time lately?"

"No, sir. You see . . . well, I got detained here."

"Well, you get your butt where you can hear it. Then you get back to the station . . . fix it . . . and you're fired."

Click.

I rushed out to the truck and turned on the radio. The voice of Pastor Lott's brother came through loud and clear. "GO TO HELL!" he thundered. "GO TO HELL . . . GO TO HELL . . ." And he had been thundering it for about twenty minutes.

The record was stuck.

Anyone who has ever lived in a small town can appreciate the impact of twenty solid minutes of "Go to hell" on the local radio station. Especially when the station is owned by "a man of the cloth," as some of the townspeople referred to Pastor Lott.

Luckily for me, the Christian ethic prevailed. Pastor Lott found it in his heart to forgive me, especially after Hugh Cunningham reminded him that finding dependable help for forty cents an hour wasn't easy, not even in Huntsville.

I could not foresee that there was another ordeal yet to come. It would involve, of all people, Fulton Lewis, Jr., whose nightly broadcast from Washington in the 1950's was carried by more than three hundred stations, many of them in small towns. A lot of people thought it was less a newscast than a platform for Lewis's Right-wing political views.

Believe me, you could sell time in Huntsville, Texas, for Fulton Lewis. It was a participating program; that is, the network (Mutual) took the first position and the local station could sell the next two. Three times during each ten-minute broadcast Lewis would say, "I'll be back after these important words," and take a one-minute break. There was a two-beat pause. Then I would cut away for our own commercial message: "The Huntsville National Bank is proud to present Fulton Lewis, Jr. Put your money in a local account, don't go to the big city of Conroe . . . etc., etc. Now, here again is Fulton Lewis, Junior."

We had sold one of the spots. For the other, if you didn't cut away after the two-beat pause, the staff announcer in Washington would read a sustaining spot, a plug for the Red Cross, or whatever. That night I ran our one local spot, and was off in the back filing records when I heard Lewis say, "I'll have more news after these important words."

And the next important word anyone heard was *"horseshit."*

I thought to myself, holy smoke, what's this? I raced into the control room, not believing what I had just heard and wondering if the obscenity had gone out over the air.

Immediately, the phones started ringing off the wall. In a small town everyone knows everyone else, and people were calling in to say, "Dan Rather, I am mortified at you for using such language on the air." Fortunately for me, Pastor Lott couldn't get through because the phones were jammed. He decided to drive to the station, but by the time he got there the network was already carrying a brief apology. What had happened was that Lewis or someone at his side had thrown the switch before his announcer had the copy ready, and when the announcer said "horseshit" he didn't know his microphone was on.

Of course, a good many people in town refused to believe that explanation. Over the next few weeks it became a mini-scandal locally, with people arguing over whether Rather had said it or Pastor Lott, and had we tried to cover up by blaming poor Fulton Lewis. The funny thing was, Pastor Lott would never use such language, not even if he had to describe what came out of the rear end of a horse.

Thanks in part to such incidents, Cecil Tuck and I came to be considered a little avant-garde around the college. For one thing, we made our own way. A lot of students did that, of course, and there was no particular credit in it. But the school paper gave us certain entrées, and Cecil even ran for the student council. We roomed together after our freshman year off campus, which required special permission, and we had such good times, such a sense of *joie de vivre,* that it spilled over into occasional fist fights. All part of the image.

You have to understand how small the school was; how small the town. One summer we had five hundred students and I knew nearly every one of them by name and hometown.

There was no social life as such. The *Sans Souci* of Huntsville was the Texas Café. If you took a date to the Texas Café and ordered the chicken-fried steak, well, you were a man of means. Few students owned cars. Nobody owned a new one with the exception of a wealthy girl from Beaumont, who was a sensation on campus.

In our senior year Cecil and I bought a 1939 Ford for sixty dollars. After a good deal of tinkering we sometimes were able to get the heap to run, after a fashion, but that really wasn't why we bought it. We figured if we could just get the car to the dormitory, we'd have a place to bring a girl after the movie. That old Ford didn't have to run.

Once, I did get it cranked up, which turned out to be a near disaster. We had driven off to Elkins Lake to count the stars and now I was returning my date to Elliott Hall, which was at the foot of a hill. The car had no brakes and there was no tread on the tires, but we would use the clutch for slowing down. Coming down the hill this night, the clutch went out. I couldn't get the gears to work. We were gaining speed.

The women students had an eleven o'clock curfew, and at three minutes to eleven the lights outside the dorm would start blinking to signal that their time was up. Couples would straggle out of the brush, and they would appear in various stages of dishevelment. That was the scene as my car came careening down the hill. My whole life, such as it was at twenty-one, flashed before my eyes. My only hope, I decided, was to jump the curb and ram into the low stone wall that encircled the campus. Just kamikaze right into the damned wall.

At the last minute my headlights picked up the fact that there were still a dozen or so couples clustered in front of the wall, stealing one last goodnight kiss. I hit the curb, veered away, knocked over a fireplug and came to a halt against the front of the dormitory. Water sprayed everywhere. It was a miracle that no one got splattered against the building like some kind of bug. My date wasn't even hurt.

There followed a long session about that incident with the dean, who tried to impress me with how dangerous the situation had been. I agreed wholeheartedly, while pointing out that it was unavoidable. I could not be held responsible for students necking against a wall.

The wonder was that I ever finished school. The Weeper—that was Cecil's nickname—did not. He was sort of handsome, in a chunky way, but he could give you an expression so sad he would touch the heart of a Greek statue. Tuck was always in financial hot water and he was forced to drop out with one semester to go. I knew it was coming the day Cecil climbed to the top of the water tower.

Huntsville, like Rome, was built on a series of hills. There was a water tower, eighty feet high, down by the gymnasium, and one night a girl came running from that direction to get me. "Dan, Dan," she squealed, "you gotta come. Cecil's on the water tower. And he's drunk and he doesn't have his clothes on."

You have to get this picture. Hunstville was a small town that hadn't changed in character since the days of the Republic of Texas. Here was a crowd gathered down below while my friend, Cecil Tuck, stood on top of the tower and shouted, "PISS ON THE WORLD." And, sure enough, he did.

I climbed those eighty feet to the top of the tower to coax him down. Over the years I have thought many times about that moment, and Cecil. As his talent grew and he became respectable, I always hoped that he would not lose that nerve or spirit. Many do. He never did.

Between us, I regret to say, we were responsible, at least indirectly, for Cunningham's leaving Sam Houston State. By 1953 the McCarthy era was in full swing, and the Korean War had almost devastated the campus of able-bodied males. The administration hurriedly arranged for the formation of an ROTC unit, which provided a shelter of sorts for those students who needed, or wanted, to avoid the draft. They drilled in makeshift uniforms, in shirts that didn't match their pants. Cecil and I wrote pieces in the student paper poking fun at the ROTC's ragtag army. I must say that Cecil's stories were much funnier than mine. He was always much better when a story called for a light touch. This was a comical subject, in some ways, but the humor was lost on the school's officials, who had gone to considerable lengths to bring in the ROTC and, really, for good reasons.

Now here was the school newspaper making fun of what the college had done. So Cunningham was called on the carpet, a form of bullying that he took badly. He was told to exercise more control over his department. He said it was a matter of principle with him to teach his people independence. "I give them guidance," Hugh said, "and help them with their writing and editing, but they decide what goes into the paper. I don't decide that for them."

This may have been very small potatoes in the context of where we were and the times we were in. But Cunningham did not take the scolding lightly. Not long afterward he left. He wasn't around when I graduated, but he had given Sam Houston State a journalism school, against what odds only Cecil Tuck and I could fully appreciate. He had said to us several times, almost in despair, "You know, I feel guilty because I really should be encouraging you to go to Texas. It's the only university in the state with a journalism department worthy of the name, and you are good enough to make it there."

I never felt that I suffered for having attended Sam Houston. Among other reasons, I had opportunities that would not have been available at a larger school. One of them was the closeness that could develop with a professor like Hugh Cunningham. He stayed in teaching—it was and is his life—and has taught for years at the University of Florida. He encouraged us to think, and read, and form opinions.

On our own time he had us reading the work of people such as Elmer Davis. Then he would grill us with questions in that Gatling-gun style of his. "For the working reporter," he demanded, "what's the most important thing Elmer Davis said?"

There was silence in the room. None of us knew.

"Don't let the bastards scare you," he said.

Out-Take

1

WORDS

When I was a small boy in Houston my family lived on Prince Street, on the last block of a colorful section called The Heights (no one referred to them then as *suburbs*). But these homes, once so fine, now had the look of peeled paint and sagging porches. The wide streets were ideal for drag races. The neighborhood had grown tough.

The city had begun a series of programs for so-called underprivileged children, a term my father fiercely rejected. Indeed, we were not. He had a job. He felt contempt for the idea of accepting charity. But one of the programs was a day camp, and I went to it.

I was not yet eleven. We met at the Heights Park on 19th Street, near the movie theater (we called it The House of Fantasies). A counselor, a woman, was always there, trying to interest us in going to the public library. One day I gave in. She arranged for me to get that small yellow passport to another world, a card that allowed you to check out books. She accompanied me on my first trip to the central library. I can remember being astonished at the sight of all those books, shelf after shelf.

She would sit with me on the bench as I waited for my bus, the 8th Street shuttle, and once she said, "You know, your only way out is to read. Sooner or later you're going to think about getting out of where you are. And whether you think of it in vicarious terms or literally that's the best way out. To read."

I looked the word up later. That was when I learned the meaning of *vicarious*. For years it was the longest word I knew.

She frequently recommended books for me to read. One of the first was on Paul Bunyan. I long ago forgot her name, I am sorry to say. But she opened up that world to me. Today, when I speak to college journalism students, one of the early questions is certain to be: But how do you start? Where?

And the answer is so simple. With reading, with books, with words. Education starts there. So does good writing. How do you know when you have had enough education? You don't. It goes on every day. The trick is to get all you can without feeling actual pain.

Most of the good advice I have received about writing came back to that. My college journalism teacher, Hugh Cunningham, once told me, "If I had my way I'd just put you off with the Chicago Great Books Series and let you read them, cover to cover."

Then there was Alexander Kendrick, my predecessor in London when CBS sent me overseas for the first time. Kendrick was a chronic reader. He was, in fact, a *scholar-correspondent,* as Ed Murrow defined the term. At one of our first meetings he said to me, "You should read two or three books a week." I thought to myself, if I do, I won't have time for anything else. I soon learned that Kendrick did.

Kendrick also read every newspaper in town. He had them sticking out of his topcoat pockets. His way was not to move on a story until he had done his homework. A reporter needs to keep reminding himself of that. As with a lot of fundamentals, you tend to get sloppy about them.

Alex was a large man, over six feet, stoop-shouldered, lumbering, with thick glasses. With all the books and newspapers and fine type he must have read in his lifetime, I didn't wonder that he had a slight eye problem. He read everywhere, in badly lighted trains and subways and hotel rooms. In London he and his wife used to go to the bookshop every Saturday, every week, to browse and to buy. He read some things for fun, he said, but mostly because he felt they contained information he needed to know.

I still don't read as much as I should. But I try. And I often think of Kendrick and Cunningham and the lady in the park.

A CHILD OF THE STORM

WITH THE EXCEPTION of my wife, Jeannie, the lady who had the most influence on my career was named Carla. She had a nasty temper and no redeeming virtues, but she was responsible for my breaking into network television. If you think that is a good thing to have happen to you, then I suppose I owe much to her.

Carla happened in September, 1961, at a time when the CBS affiliate in Houston, Channel 11, KHOU, was wrestling with that demon known as the ratings. In a period of one year we had moved from third to first and were struggling to stay there.

I was the news director and the anchorman at 6 P.M. and 10 P.M. But the key man in our coverage was a chunky, genteel Pennsylvanian named Calvin Jones, the program director. Jim Richdale ran the station and, like most station managers, was more attuned to the commercial side of the business. But the beauty of working with Richdale was his willingness to say, okay, you're the news director. *You* tell me what to do about the news.

One of the most important ingredients for any news department is live, local coverage. Yet it amazes me how many stations never seem to learn that. Simply put, to attract and hold viewers you must develop a reputation for jumping on a major story early, staying close and leaving last. Cal Jones and I worked hard to establish such an identity. It wasn't easy, given what they had going at Channel 2, the NBC affiliate. Ray Miller, a skilled and seasoned reporter, led their staff. He was backed by Jack Harris, who understood earlier than most local managers that a station would be judged by the quality of its news. The third station, Channel 13, ABC, was less effective. Good people, poor equipment.

In Texas when you reach September you are nearing the end of the hurricane season, probably the second most interesting season in the state —after football. I had received my early weather training on radio, over KTRH (owned by the Houston *Chronicle*). You become a kind of weather buff when you work for a station with a power of 50,000 watts, which enabled us to cover most of the Gulf Coast. In fact, KTRH billed itself as The Voice of the Golden Gulf Coast, reaching all the way down into that good, black farmland through Wharton and Victoria.

We had many times stayed on the air all night covering hurricanes, or the threat of them. KTRH had carried the first reports of Audrey, which had blasted through Cameron, Louisiana, in 1957, killing nearly five hundred people.

So I had a working knowledge of big storms and what they were, and of the Weather Bureau setup. Which meant that I knew such an elemental thing as the fact that the Galveston office was better prepared than Houston's to give information. Galveston had installed a radarscope—a WSR-57—and that equipment was still relatively new in 1961.

On Tuesday, the fifth of September, the U. S. Weather Bureau began tracking a low-pressure system in the Caribbean, east of the Yucatán Peninsula. When the first reports moved on the wire that the storm had crossed the Yucatán, I mentioned to Cal Jones, the program director, that this was a story we needed to watch. Reared in the East, Cal didn't know a hurricane from a handcart. He said, in effect, what the hell is this? The burgeoning storm was more than a thousand miles away. All the weekend forecast indicated was partly cloudy.

Frankly, we had been husbanding our budgets on the weekends, as most local stations do. But I said to Cal, "We really have to watch this thing. If it blows across Yucatán, then gets loose in the Gulf of Mexico and starts building again, it will be the most dangerous kind of hurricane. Any time a storm crosses land and gets back out over open water, it generally turns into something terrifying."

To his everlasting credit, Cal said, "Okay, if you think so," and we made some standby arrangements. Cal's interest was now teased. He has a continually inquisitive mind. He had learned to fly at a late age, which tells you, I think, something about his sense of adventure. On September 7 the Weather Bureau officially designated the storm as a hurricane and attached a name: Carla.

That night Cal called me and said, "You know, I've been studying your hurricane. It is growing in force and there's a little rumble about it on the wires. But, God, there is no way of telling where the storm's going."

Then I quoted a little local mythology, and that's all it was: "Well, Cal, there are two or three places that just seem to suck hurricanes toward them. One is the Sabine River, on the Louisiana border. Another is the mouth of the Mississippi. And a third is the Corpus Christi area, around Matagorda. For no known reasons and, again, this is the myth, if a hurricane is going to hit, these places often catch the brunt of it."

Cal said, "You've named three places and two of them are in our coverage area. I think we ought to start gearing up."

Jones was a strong believer in live coverage which, as I say, is the mark of a really good local news station. Quickly, he said, "Let's assign someone downtown to the Weather Bureau. And let's think about moving our mobile unit down there."

I said, "That doesn't make much sense because Galveston has the best radar."

There was a slight note of pain in Cal's voice. "Yes, but Galveston . . ."

I had raised a minor problem of place and image. Channel 11 had been a Galveston station once and was still trying to shed that identification. We were fighting to make it a HOUSTON (in large letters) and galveston (in small letters) station.

Cal went on, "Let's not get involved with that."

But I insisted. "If we're going to do it, then we have to go to Galveston because of the radar unit. That way we can track the storm."

We went back and forth and then I knew his wheels were spinning. "Do you mean, if this thing hit," Cal asked, "we could actually see it on radar?"

"Yes, of course," I said.

"Then why couldn't we pick it up on our cameras?"

I said, "You mean, put the radar picture on television? Well, that's not impossible, though it seems unlikely. I doubt that the Weather Bureau would allow it."

But the prospect excited him. At first I thought his idea was crazy. But even the long-shot chance of being able to see a hurricane, on television, struck Cal as worth a dice roll.

Jim Richdale, the station manager, wasn't so sure. We were looking at a cost of around two thousand dollars to take the mobile unit to Galveston and set up for the weekend. But Jim was less concerned with the budget,

I think, than the pace we all had been keeping. The entire news staff worked marathon hours. We rated stories on a scale of one to five and I had a standard rule about any story three or better. When an important story broke I wanted to be called at home, whatever the hour. That meant a lot of calls in the predawn. My main helpers, Bob Wolf and Bob Levy, often worked eighteen or more hours a day.

We had reached a point where the effort was paying off. We had gone through a stage of leaning hard on what we, among ourselves, referred to as Fuzz and Wuz, meaning a liberal use of film showing both the police (the Fuzz) and dead bodies (the Wuz). Emphasis on that sort of coverage weighed on my conscience at times. But Houston was big on fires and car wrecks and murders. They had proved to be ratings-builders. And at every local station I ever knew about, the station manager was looking down your gun barrel each rating period. "Hey, we're beginning to gain. Another three points and we knock them off."

So we were first now, and Jim Richdale was telling the staff, "If we can just hold our news department together and not let them burn themselves out or get hired away, we're going to be all right."

This time he said to Jones, "Let's cool it for the weekend and take a long look at this thing on Monday."

Cal passed it on. "The storm is still a helluva way out there. We still have time. By Monday we'll be fresh and ready to move if we need to."

"No," I said. "If we're going to go, let's go now. I have a feeling about this, Cal." One of the rules of journalism is, you never *report* your hunches. Doing so can prove fatal. But this doesn't mean you can't play them. "I've been thinking about it, and your idea about the radar is terrific. We ought to get down to Galveston and we ought to throw everything we've got into this thing." I added that our competition would not think of making this move. While they were sitting out the weekend we could be rolling. "If it lands anywhere on this coast, we'd be holding aces," I concluded.

Cal called Richdale and talked him into it. We began to gear up. By late Friday we moved our mobile truck to Galveston and connected our microwave relay equipment. In what turned out to be a lucky stroke for us, the U. S. Weather Bureau had sent down its Chief of Observation, Vaughn Rockney, a hurricane expert. The moment I saw him I knew we had made the right call. No one else knew he was there.

Over the years weather people have been generous about working with newsmen, even to the point of doing live reports at their desks. Part of the job, after all, is to reach the masses and help them tolerate the caprices of nature.

I hit it off with Rockney, a burly, informal man with a round, open face and a high forehead. I asked him if, conceivably, we could get a picture of the hurricane from the radar scan. He hesitated. "Well, yes, if it got close enough, we might," he said, "but what we have to think about is whether or not that's a good idea. What you're talking about, you'd be putting an awesome-looking monster on the screen. Panic is a possibility."

There had been pictures of hurricanes before, of course. Newspapers and magazines had printed stills of the hurricane eye taken from a weather plane. There even had been some film of it. Yet nothing really compared to sending a live picture of a hurricane into your living room, dropping it in your lap and saying, here it is.

This was a question many of us in television journalism would face over and over again, in other forms, on other levels: Should we show John Kennedy's head being blown apart? Should we turn an electronic camera on the war in Vietnam and bring the scene live and bloody into the viewer's home? We never did—not live combat, as it was happening.

So Rockney and I talked over mugs of coffee with the steam rising from them in the middle of the Galveston Weather Bureau. I don't want to overstate the dilemma, but in that room we pretty well had the eternal contest over the public's right to know: The journalist licking his chops and saying, hoo boy, if we could see that baby live! And the participant, a prudent and intelligent man, asking, would that be a good thing?

There is a thin line between seeing an event live and seeing it even one step removed, on film. That difference isn't easy to convey to those detached from the business of collecting news. Understandably, they do not share the newsman's urgency of feeling. And, in this case, the hurricane was still beyond our range, if not beyond our imaginations. It was not even raining yet, although the air had the heaviness, the gray-gold color that portends a coming storm.

I said, "Well, one problem with a hurricane is to get people to believe how dangerous it is. Your office is always talking about getting out that word. If this one is as big as we think it is, you and I both know we are dealing with one of the classic hurricanes, maybe the biggest, most dangerous of this century." As it turned out, in terms of pure mass the hurricane was the biggest.

We still did not know the full dimensions of the storm, but once Carla sped across the Yucatán and well out into the Gulf, we knew she was building. Ships several hundred miles from the center were reporting un-usually high waves. An average-size hurricane does not do that. A hurri-cane moves in a counterclockwise direction and high tides begin on the sweep side. The height and fierceness of the waves and tides can indicate the size of a storm.

Vaughn listened quietly as I argued my case. If Carla was as big and potent as she appeared to be, it was going to require a lot of shouting to alert people. "You and I both know," I said, "that since the war this coast has been settled by a lot of people who didn't grow up here. We have a chance to save lives, save property and, first of all, avoid panic by showing this thing early. That will get their attention."

I may have mentioned the tired old story about the farmer who was observed hitting his mule across the nose with a two-by-four, explaining, "First you have to get their attention." The radar pictures would be our two-by-four.

It was never clear to me whether Rockney received permission from Washington or if he needed any. He ducked into a private office and when he reappeared he said, "Let's do it. It's a damned good idea."

They kept a very small camera in the Bureau for in-house monitoring of major storms. So we plugged a line into their camera and positioned it in front of the radar console. By noon Saturday, September 9, 1961, Carla had moved in our direction and, at one point, veered straight toward Galveston Island. It seemed almost certain that we would be in the hurri-cane's path. Our coverage was now making an impression.

Carla was getting closer. That night we picked up the picture for the first time, 250 miles from the coast, and carried it on the air. There were no trumpet flourishes, but we felt a sort of controlled elation. We were able to say, in effect, There it is, folks, never before seen on television, live, an actual hurricane.

It came up from the bottom of the screen in the shape of a half moon, white against black. Then, as it rose, you saw the eye, like the hole in a doughnut, with the swirl around it. At that point Carla was 400 miles wide, the eye 50 miles across.

It was Cal Jones's idea to show Carla superimposed on a map of the Texas coast and the Gulf of Mexico, roughly in proportion. When I said, "This is actual scale, there's the state of Texas, one inch equals fifty miles," you could hear people in the studio gasp. Anyone with eyes could measure the size of it. The picture took your breath away. The storm actually covered much of the Gulf of Mexico.

Using a pointer, I tapped the screen, like a flight commander picking out targets. "Here's the coast, here's Carla. Keep in mind that a hurricane operates in a counterclockwise fashion. That means this entire upper Texas coast, as well as the Louisiana coast and parts of Mississippi, Alabama and Florida are going to catch the waters driven up by this hurricane, and that the underside will be the least damaged by floods."

We kept pounding home that point. People possess the popular misconception that hurricane winds always represent the greatest danger. There is danger, of course, any time you are caught in a two-hundred-mile-an-hour blow. But the most destructive force can be and often is water—abnormal tides, tidal waves, flooding rains.

As the U. S. Weather Bureau's chief observer, Vaughn Rockney had the authority to order a mass evacuation. By Sunday afternoon he had used his authority to order the evacuation of Galveston and all the coastal lowlands. It was the largest peacetime removal in the history of this country, involving over 350,000 people and inspired in part by a single news camera pointed at a radar screen. All that day and into the night cars drove bumper to bumper heading west, on the causeways and highways and farm roads. Whenever the traffic stalled, people slept in their vehicles or by the sides of the road, catching quick naps until the procession could continue.

Carla struck the coast early Monday morning, the main force of the storm howling across Port O'Connor, a few miles south of Galveston. In the next three days a total of twelve persons died, half of them in the tornadoes that were spawned in Carla's wake. Sad enough, but a remarkably low number given the history of such disasters. More than six thousand had died in the great Galveston storm of 1900, which led to the building of a seventeen-foot seawall.

The Weather Bureau said later that strong early warnings had minimized the loss of life. We were a part of that. The very authority of our radar picture, of seeing Carla's eye on the screen, had convinced people, "Hey, we better get out of the way." Property damage ran into the millions of dollars even in Houston, fifty miles inland.

By noon Monday our crew of ten had been on duty for seventy-two hours and rations were short. For the next two days we existed mainly on candy bars. Twice we lost our picture. The first really brute winds, of about seventy-five miles an hour, knocked out the main transmitter on Sunday. We went to emergency power until an engineer named Racy Sanford climbed the tower and, as it swayed in the winds, replaced a hook in the microwave dish.

We had broadcast continuous reports for thirty-six hours when the video went out again at midday Monday. Even then we still had sound and stayed on the air, describing from Galveston what was happening while the studio in Houston ran up charts and maps.

Perhaps this is the place to note that a certain legend has developed over the years about Hurricane Carla. The legend has been kind to me but it has been vastly overstated.

The impression that I was "up to my ass in water moccasins" grew out of a flattering quote from Walter Cronkite, referring to the aftermath of the storm. Snakes, like every other living creature, head for the high ground when water rises. So what little high ground remained in Galveston was, indeed, infested with snakes. But I was no more up to my ass in them than anyone else.

Then there was the story of my having rescued a drowning horse. One writer suggested that no horse had done so much for a man's career since Roy Rogers and Trigger. Let me try to set the record straight.

It is true that we showed not one but two scenes of horses being led to safety. Horses do get trapped in a storm, left behind by people who don't think the water will ever get that high. The next thing you know the horse is locked in a corral, unable to break free.

Before and as the hurricane struck and at intervals during the storm's fury we simply poked a camera out a window of the Weather Bureau, which was on the fifth floor of the Post Office. Panning around, you could see quite a lot of Galveston Island. Among the things we tried to develop were small, electronic photo essays of people and animals in the face of danger. We had a poignant shot of a man carrying what was left of his possessions in a pillow case slung over one shoulder. He was leaning into the wind, up to his hips in water, trying to force his way up the street. You could measure his progress in inches. We just stayed on him, without commentary, for six or seven minutes.

Once, our camera caught a horse in panic, thrashing from one side of a pen to the other, aware that something was wrong. The first chance I had I walked down to a lower floor and shouted out the window to the people in another building that a horse was trapped near them. Someone swam over and opened the gate. I had about as much to do with the animal's rescue as King James had to do with writing the Bible.

Actually, the scene most people saw on national television was described by Roger Mudd, who had been sent down by CBS with a camera crew out of Chicago. Their presence was unrelated to our Channel 11 coverage. Roger's crew flew into Houston and drove to Victoria, ninety miles to the south. At some point on the coastal highway a cameraman noticed a horse stranded in a corral, the water rising all around and turning it into a small island. He waded out and led the horse back to the road. They filmed the scene, Roger narrated it and the CBS Evening News, with Douglas Edwards, showed the rescue to the nation.

Years later Dick Salant, the president of CBS News, in an interview, told the story as though it had been some exclusive of mine. He knew that I had been hired as a result of Carla, had seen a good deal of our live coverage and, possibly, had gotten Roger's coverage confused with mine. Right horse, wrong jockey.

The story has been retold and reshaped until it is said that I leaped from a second-floor window, landed on the horse's back Hopalong Cassidy-style, rode him out and jumped over a wire fence. All of which has a nice, romantic, cowboy ring to it, and I only regret that it didn't happen.

At other times I have received credit for repairman Racy Sanford's climb to the top of our microwave relay tower. Again, I did not. Sanford did. It was one of those foolish, courageous things that go beyond the reason. It also kept us on the air another six to eight hours.

For my part, the truths of Carla were strong enough. We were marooned for the better part of three days, at the peak of the storm, in a building where the water eventually reached the second floor. It was not without risk. Even after the winds calmed and the tornadoes had passed through, an amphibious vehicle had to bring us out. Days passed before anyone could travel by car. There are times when you cover such a story when you wonder later if you really knew what the risks were. The only answer I can give is that you do and you don't.

Among other citations KHOU received the Sigma Delta Chi Award for distinguished service in journalism for its coverage of Hurricane Carla. The plaque hangs today in the office of Cal Jones, who now owns a small, creative ad agency in Houston.

It seems curious to me even now that Carla would lead to my going to the network. That could not have been what they meant by an eye for an eye.

CBS News, I knew, had monitored nearly everything we did (while one hundred radio stations, including four local ones, had carried our audio signal). There was a hint over the phone, even during the mop-up, that people were impressed in New York and I might be offered a job.

Perhaps because I didn't take the rumors all that seriously, the idea did not exactly overwhelm me. When the offer came I turned it down. It wasn't a case of my being timid or without ambition. But at that moment I was right where I wanted to be, doing what I wanted to do.

There are times when career decisions take on all the anguish of a moment from "Let's Make a Deal." Do you stay with the box or do you go for what's behind the curtain? I had been in local television only two years. I still found myself thinking, I have to get out of broadcasting and get back to what I set out to do, which was print journalism, the newspaper business.

I had become sidetracked at a point after Sam Houston, after a semester of teaching, after six months in the marines. My tour of duty was short and undistinguished. The war in Korea had ended and the doctors discovered I had suffered from rheumatic fever as a boy.

During that summer I worked at the Houston *Chronicle,* part time, and in the fall I was hired at KTRH by Bob Hart, the radio news director. For me the hard decision had been to leave radio and go into television. At KTRH I had met Jean Goebel, fell in love and married her. She was a secretary, a pretty, lively woman with a smashing smile and gentle eyes. Her energy and vitality attracted me. She worked long hours with endless enthusiasm and encouraging words for everyone. There was a don't-give-up, we-can-do-it quality about her. And she, more than anyone I'd ever met, understood my hopes and dreams. Jeannie and I still laugh about it. With the hours I worked, where else would I have met my future wife?

There were many nights when I wouldn't leave the station. To someone who doesn't know the business, such zeal may seem incredible. It was real. And I enjoyed every second of it. I went to work at five in the morning. My eight-hour shift was over at 1 P.M., and spanned the so-called morning drive time, the best news audience, between 7 A.M. and 9 A.M. But my schedule didn't cover the afternoon drive time. So I would come back— frequently I didn't even leave—and do the evening news, for which I eventually got a little extra money. I did it because I wanted to be there.

I was doing the one thing I had always visualized myself doing. Not the broadcast part, but the reporting, covering City Hall, the courts, the police station. I was learning. I made ghastly mistakes, but I think I learned from them.

Looking back, I was sometimes a source of amusement to the veterans in the *Chronicle* city room, where we often did live newscasts. We considered that kind of broadcasting rather innovative. Since KTRH was owned by the paper, we were provided a carbon of every story that came across the city desk. They'd stack them on a spike, and I would come in before the newscast and go through them. It was good exposure for the *Chronicle* and good for us because it gave us the edge on some news stories.

I was blessed with not having what is known in other parts of the country as a standard Texas accent. What I did have I never worked to get out. Instead I had to work, hard, at pronouncing certain words. Once my boss, Bob Hart, sent me to a speech teacher to learn to say *posts,* the plural of *post.* I could not say the extra "s." She taught me in the course of one afternoon.

Another time a fairly big local story broke about a heroin case. I was in the *Chronicle* city room, telling this story in a fairly excited fashion: "Houston police today captured a large cache of her-OYNE . . ." As I read through the story I pronounced the word the same way about three times, a not uncommon colloquialism.

But by the third or fourth reference the church editor of the *Chronicle,* a large woman with a robust voice, could stand it no longer. She rose from her desk and started walking toward me, shouting across the room, the words booming louder into my live microphone as she drew closer, "Not her-OYNE, you idiot! It is HER-OH-in! HER-OH-in! HER-OH-in!"

During those years I spent a lot of time poring over dictionaries. I was not a good speller, which was one reason I didn't make it in the newspaper business. And poor spellers are frequently poor pronouncers.

I was not unaware of my weaknesses when I took over the late-night newscast at 10 P.M. Nighttime radio, of course, was then a much bigger influence than it is now. The ten o'clock news on KTRH was a listening tradition in Houston, with a large audience. I really labored over that broadcast. It was my first fifteen-minute program and I did it all, news, sports and weather. I would usually close with the next day's forecast, on the order of, ". . . sunny and bright, with light, var'ble winds." Leaving out the "i."

A woman began to call, the moment the newscast was over.

"Is this Dan Rather?"

"Yes."

"Dammit, boy, the word is var-EE-able. Has another syllable in there. Look it up." Very schoolmarmish. After two weeks of repeated calls I finally got the word right. The first night I was able to say it distinctly on the air, instead of "var'ble," she called and said, with great zest, "Congratulations! You finally got it."

I never did learn the lady's name. She never identified herself. But a full year later we lost the network line one night and someone rushed into the newsroom and said, "You're needed in the studio. You have to fill—meaning kill time—while we get the network back up." We had an emergency format for such times and they shoved the script in front of me. "We regret that network programming has been interrupted. In the meantime we bring you Music in Mini'ture."

Phone rang. Same woman. "Dammit, boy, the word is minny-a-choor. Minny-a-choor. It has another syllable. Look it up." I found it encouraging that I hadn't heard from her in a year.

Those were learning experiences. Eventually, with the help of a lot of people, I made myself a reasonably good newsreader. I like to think I had some talent for news gathering. But I had very little for announcing.

So I had begun to establish myself in Houston and now had a job as news director at Channel 11 that fulfilled me. I felt a special joy in helping to build a losing team into a winner and you only feel it, really feel it, the first time it happens. Carla had been a big strike for me. In some ways it was as satisfying as anything I have ever done. We had brought Channel 11 from third to first and now our ratings had begun to zoom. I could see that for a while things were going to be golden.

But my closest friends pounced on me when the word got around that I had refused the CBS offer. One of them, Dick Perez, said, "I can't believe that CBS offered you a job and you're turning it down. You're crazy. If you do that I'm going to have you committed." We went off to lunch at a tamale stand near the station and talked.

In an odd way Dick Perez represented the real world to me, as network television never could. I had not been at KHOU very long when he appeared one day, wearing a taxi driver's cap. In fact, he did drive a taxi. He was shaped like a beer keg, five seven and two hundred pounds, curly-haired, bouncy and hardly lacking in Latin *macho*. He talked his way into the newsroom, still wearing his cap. He stuck out his hand and said, "Rather, my name is Perez and if you're smart enough to hire me, I'll make you a star."

We both laughed. Then I cut him short and said, "Okay, not a bad opening line. Now what do you want?"

He said he had been a cameraman in San Antonio, at KENS, one of the stations that had pioneered Fuzz and Wuz news. They had won their ratings race with it. If there were a drowning, a suffocation and two murders in San Antonio overnight, they would get the film and run it at length with a dramatic, March-of-Time narration. The approach has been successful and, as a result, in Texas broadcasting circles, a station manager would look at his ratings and call in his news editor. "We're running third," he'd say. "Look at KENS. They shot right to the top. What are they doing over there?"

I told Perez I did not have the money to hire him. Nor did I have the time to check whether he had actually worked at KENS. And if he had, I didn't necessarily consider his employment there a recommendation.

He broke in and said quickly, "Well, I didn't work there long and I didn't work there regular."

As it happened his timing was right. Channel 11 needed more news people. We just couldn't afford them. We then had a two-and-a-half man staff, with only myself and Bob Wolf, a cameraman, assigned full time. The *half* was Bob Levy, a swing man who wrote and edited copy and did eight other things around the station.

We had just ordered our first film processor, which came in a crate, with an instruction booklet that read like an army training manual. Between us we assembled and installed the damned thing. Wolf did most of it. Things mechanical fascinate me, but I rarely understand them.

To get the processor I had struck a bargain with Jim Richdale. If he bought the machine, he would not have to hire a lab man to operate it. We would learn to process the film ourselves. Now here was this tubby taxi driver, off the street, asking for a job in film.

I hired Perez on a pay-as-he-filmed basis, three cents a foot for whatever we used and we'd replace the film. He went to work on his own, part time, and he was sensational. All hustle. He quickly convinced me that he was much better than a stringer and I put him on the staff.

Dick Perez was not someone with a lot of formal education. But he was a head-down, ass-up, I-can-do-it kind of guy. He was valuable to us in helping to define what our newscasts would be. He was always pressing for more police-beat stuff. So were Bob Wolf and Robert Levy. In their hearts they wanted to go the Fuzz and Wuz way because they knew it would help us in the ratings.

But they were better than that as people and as journalists. They were constantly saying to me, "Look, let's strike a balance here. Do some Fuzz and Wuz and some of that high-falutin stuff you like." Finally we did add a dose of Fuzz and Wuz and it was helpful to our ratings. We'd tack the film onto the end of the newscast, the last forty-five seconds to two minutes: "And here's everything that happened on the police beat." That sort of treatment.

The second time CBS called, three months after our first talks ended,

Dick came around and said, "You're going to take that job if I have to hit you on the head, pack you in the trunk of my car, drive you to New York and dump you on the steps of CBS."

I told him that wouldn't be necessary. The network had come back with a better offer and I was thinking of accepting. A few days later he came back and said, "I want to go with you. You'll need me."

If he had not been quite so solemn, I might have laughed. "Dick," I said, "God knows I'll probably have a hard time holding a job myself. There's no way I can take anyone with me."

"Don't worry," he replied. "That time will come, and when it does, just know that I'll crawl on broken glass from here to Dallas to work for you."

The date was February 28, 1962, my first day in New York, and I spent it sitting outside the office of Ernie Leiser, my new boss, cooling my heels. I had held out for a correspondent's job, almost unheard of for a newcomer at the network, and I was there to find out where, what and how soon.

To my slight confusion, the first thing Leiser wanted me to do was an audition. He walked out of his office and stood over me. He had a gruff, Broderick Crawford manner. "Look," Leiser said, right to the point, "we want you to do an audition."

I tried to look cool but I was thinking, That's strange. Here I am ready to go to work and now they ask me to take a screen test.

Most people do auditions *before* they have a job, not after. And I already had been hired. Hurricane Carla had been my on-the-air tryout. Also, I knew CBS had sent to Houston for some of my newscasts.

But it developed that other people—who they were and how many I never knew—had questioned the wisdom of bringing in someone from outside and making him a correspondent immediately. Since the war, and Ed Murrow's original team, most correspondents had been brought aboard CBS as reporters and then inched their way into knighthood.

When I first raised the idea of starting out as one of the elite, I had been told it just wasn't done, certainly not at my age, twenty-nine. But Leiser, the chief of correspondents, and Blair Clark, a vice-president of CBS News, had gone to bat for me.

So I went along. Leiser led me to a studio where Charles Collingwood had just finished the midday news. I had listened to Collingwood during the war. He was, and is, one of my idols. I didn't stand in awe of him but I was pleased, in an abstract way, that he was there. I thought I might even get a chance to meet him. Almost immediately he left the news set and walked over to shake hands. He could not have been more gracious.

Before I had even reached junior high school, Collingwood had finished Oxford and had been hired by Ed Murrow. I also knew he had won the Overseas Press Club Award for his coverage of the North African campaign. When I was thirteen or so, and bedridden with rheumatic fever for weeks at a time, I listened to the radio constantly. It was a habit I acquired from my father, who besides being an avid reader was a listener of all newcasts. He cared nothing for music. I remember his yelling to my mother in the kitchen, "TURN OFF THAT FLOYD TILLMAN MUSIC AND GET SOME NEWS!"

When I went through that long period of bed rest I tuned into Collingwood and Sevareid and Murrow and Elmer Davis. I was a fan. The words, "This is Edward R. Murrow, in London . . ." Well, that was magic. So when Collingwood walked over, it made an impression on me.

In those few seconds I thought: I have just driven a fairly hard bargain with these people. I have held out to be a correspondent. I wonder how Collingwood feels about that.

There is a tradition around CBS, and tradition is a strange and powerful force. You can walk into Harvard or Notre Dame or, for that matter, Texas A&M, and the feeling of tradition is communicated to you somehow, some way. So it is at CBS.

A fellow like Collingwood I thought might be a little standoffish. But he wasn't. He said to the makeup lady, "Frannie, when this young man does his air work I want you to take good care of him." We had an adult conversation for about three or four minutes, and he wished me well.

Leiser had been kind enough not to tell Collingwood that I was doing an audition. He said, "Mr. Rather"—I couldn't remember the last time an older person had called me mister, maybe never—"is going to do some taping," and he let it go at that.

Frannie Arnold dabbed some pancake on me and someone handed me the script that Collingwood had used. Now, I had gotten my first television job, in Houston, partly by just sitting down and doing it. So that day in New York I didn't have much time between coming out of Leiser's office and meeting Collingwood, and I thought, Well, I'll do it that way.

For one thing, I was not accustomed to working with a TelePrompTer. In those days they were above the lens, they broke down, and I had no confidence in them. So I had a four-and-a-half-minute newscast to do and I would ad-lib it. For another thing, I wasn't about to read a script that Charles Collingwood had just read superbly.

I do not have a photographic memory. But I can look a script over—I am a believer in talking it through—put it away and catch the sense of what I have to say. The audition went well. We walked back to Leiser's office and he said, "Let's take a look at it." They ran the tape on a monitor and we watched. In other offices I knew other CBS executives were watching as well. It was a strange feeling.

Leiser said, "I think it would be a good idea if we started you in New York. Stay around here for, say, six months. If it takes longer, okay. But we'll know when you're ready and you'll know it. This gives you a chance to feel your way. I have the utmost confidence in your reportorial ability. I know you're good on the air. And you know that, or you wouldn't be here. But we'd like you to get the feel of our system, how we do things."

All that he said made sense to me. Until that day I had no idea what they had in mind. Later, when I telephoned Jean, she asked if I wanted her and the kids to move to New York. I said, for six months, there doesn't seem to be much point. If it takes longer, we'll see.

As it turned out, it took six weeks.

Until I came to New York I had not even talked contract. In fact, I had never worked under a contract. But Blair Clark, who ran that end of it, dealt with me with some patience. He had the kind of polish you identify with a certain background: prep school, Harvard, wealthy family (the Clark Thread Company).

He passed the papers across the desk and said, "This is the contract but I'm not going to negotiate with you. You ought to have an agent."

I laughed nervously. I thought he was joking. An agent? That was something for Hollywood people.

Clark corrected me. "No, you don't know you need one but I'm telling you, you should have an agent."

I said, "Whatever you say, Mr. Clark. But how do I go about getting one?"

He said, "I'll give you the names of three, but I won't recommend anybody."

I said, "As far as I'm concerned, we can put the names in a hat and draw one out."

He said, "Do it any way you want."

He wrote down three names and I picked the middle one, Nate Bienstock, now retired. By the time Nate got into the negotiations the only question was money. Nate said to me, "They're offering you seventeen-five, but in a day or two we'll have them up to twenty-two thousand."

I said, "Look, Mr. Bienstock, if it's all the same with you, I'd prefer to start at seventeen-five."

Nate's teeth clicked. "But that's crazy."

"Crazy it may be, but I'd rather start a little low than a little high." That was how I felt and that was how it was done.

The next morning was my first on the job, the first of March, 1962. I had been told to report at ten o'clock and I got there early. My instructions were to hang around the news desk and pick up the loose ends.

At 10:01 a jetliner went down in Jamaica Bay a few seconds after taking off from Idlewild (later Kennedy) Airport. The instant that news flashed, Dave Dugan, who is now on the faculty at the University of Missouri, started to race out the door with Herbie Schwartz, a cameraman. I turned to the man in charge of the desk and blurted, "I've covered plane crashes, maybe I can help." I had the feeling he wanted me out of his hair anyway. He said, "If you want to go and you can catch them, go."

I caught up with them at the elevator and drove out to the scene of the crash. As the reporter in charge, Dugan had his mind on the story. He wasn't in a mood to answer questions and on the way out I wasn't asking any. But he did say, "The best thing you can do is stay out of the way."

I said, "You can count on my doing that. I just want to help if I can." I meant to convey to him in no uncertain terms, Look, I'm not proud. Tell me what needs to be done and I'll do it. When we got there he turned to me and, in a decent way, said, "Do you think you could handle the radio end?"

He was saying, It would be a help to me but I know you don't even have your feet on the ground. And I was thinking, Man, are you kidding? Damned right I can.

Dugan did the television, and did it well. Frequently a reporter has to do both, and if something has to suffer, radio generally does. That is not the way it ought to be, but it is. Other help was coming, but we were the first to arrive.

When we started out, all we had was a report of a plane crash. Later it was established that the plane had carried ninety-five passengers and crew. There were no survivors.

There was no telephone in sight and Dugan said, "Gee, I don't know what you're going to do about a phone."

I said, "That's okay, don't sweat it. I'll figure something out." I walked to the highway and after a few minutes flagged a man in a telephone company van. As soon as I had explained the problem he climbed a pole, hooked up a phone and very quickly got it working. After that I did hourly reports on radio.

So within minutes of my first real workday at CBS I was covering a plane crash.

Within a few weeks I decided I did not intend to hang around New York for anywhere near six months. I went to Leiser and said, "Put me in the field somewhere. Anywhere. I just can't hang around here waiting for planes to crash. I'm not learning enough."

As it turned out, I was learning more than I was willing to admit. For example, there was the time I got a call in the middle of the night to rush deep into New York State and cover a depressing story, a number of babies having suffocated in a hospital. It was snowing, the kind of cold that makes your teeth ache, the crew was drunk and the car ran off the road five times.

My reporting on that story was, at best, undistinguished. And I could not say "Binghamton" correctly. I had never heard the name before and the word did not exactly roll off my tongue. The film story we did was barely airworthy. When I returned to the newsroom Leiser bolted angrily toward me. He ordered his secretary to leave the anteroom and hauled me back into his office. He knew he was going to shout at me and he didn't want her to hear through the door.

Leiser really dressed me down, as he should have. He said, fuming, "Here you are, I tell you how confident I am in your reportorial abilities, and you DON'T EVEN GET THE NAME OF THE TOWN RIGHT."

The fact was, I did have it right. I just couldn't pronounce it. But I didn't say that to Ernie. I just said, "Yes, sir."

But, luckily for me, Leiser was a strong believer in ordeal by fire. Shortly after that lecture CBS decided to set up two new domestic bureaus, with Hughes Rudd in Atlanta and myself in Dallas. I had been with the network not quite six weeks, and now I was returning to Texas as the chief of a new bureau.

I guess Leiser figured I could at least speak the language.

Out-Take

2

MORRIS

It may be too heavy a burden to lay on someone who is no longer around to defend himself, but a saint of a man named Morris Frank once "saved" me for a career in radio and television.

In 1954 I was earning sixty-two dollars and fifty cents a week working ten hours a day on radio, when, for openers, an insurance company in Houston offered to double my salary. They outlined a plan where, in no time, they said, I could be knocking down thirty thousand a year and vacationing in Acapulco.

My best friend at the radio station, Bill Zak, advised me to take it.

I was tempted. I went to my boss and asked what I could expect in the way of pay increases. He replied brightly, "A five-dollar weekly raise each year for the next three years, up to a top of eighty a week." That was local radio. The money went up in pennies.

I was still brooding about the future when I ran into Morris Frank, who wrote a daily column for the Houston *Chronicle*. Frank popped into the radio station each afternoon for a five-minute sportscast sponsored by a local brewery, Jax. His intro to the show was unforgettable. Morris would come on, half singing, "Hello, mellow Jax, little darlin'. In sports today . . ."

He observed that I seemed troubled. I admitted that I was thinking of changing jobs. Over coffee we talked about radio, the insurance business, career goals, money and the American dream. Finally he said to me, "Dan, you are one of those people who are doing what they were meant to do. You will never be happy doing anything else, least of all selling. You're like me. The first thing you would do is tell the client what was wrong with the policy. There is no room in the business world for a salesman who gives both sides of the product."

So I stayed in radio. Within a year the station had gone heavily into sports, and by broadcasting minor league baseball and college football games I was able to pick up extra fees. By 1959, those sportscasting fees had helped push my income to eleven thousand a year. I was not out looking for tax shelters, but we were comfortable. I enjoyed the work, and I got into all the games free.

When an offer came to move into local television my instinct was to stay put. The difference in money was hardly enough to convince me to cut away from a snug harbor. Besides, I liked doing sports.

When Morris heard about my indecision he sat me down for another chat. "Look," he said, "this is a feast-or-famine business. Another beer sponsor picks up the ball games next year and you're off the play-by-play and back to living on what the station pays you for reading the news. One of the rules is, never count as real money what you make moonlighting. But what you really have to know is this: television is where this business is going. That's the future. That's where you need to be, and that is why you can't say no to this offer."

And I didn't say no. I was intrigued by the idea that, even then, in 1959, Morris thought of television as an extension of the newspaper field, not a rival and not a replacement.

He had his own on-again, off-again exposure to TV. Once, his newspaper sponsored one of those "Meet the *Chronicle*" kind of shows, in which a bunch of nervous, giggly reporters would stand around looking uncomfortable and Morris would introduce them and develop a conversation of sorts. The day the show made its debut Morris was on a diet, as he often was. Halfway through the half hour his pants began to slip, and Morris had to hold a sheath of papers with one hand while he frantically fought a losing battle with the other to keep his trousers from dropping to his knees. During the rest of the program the cameras homed in on him from the neck up while everyone else guffawed. When his co-workers needled him later Morris replied, "Well, with the supporting cast I had, I figured I had to do something to save the show."

That was Morris Frank. He was literally the man who came to dinner, and to lunch, and to breakfast. He was acclaimed as a banquet speaker all over America. They loved him at the annual gridiron dinner in Washington. One year he admitted to the audience that he was uneasy in the company of so many politicians, judges and lawyers.

So saying, he made a point of walking down the length of the head table and handing his wallet to Tom Clark, the Supreme Court Justice and a fellow Texan. "Of course," he said, when he had returned to the microphone, "I've played poker with those ol' Dallas boys," and with that he fished into his pockets and brought out the contents of his billfold for the crowd to see.

With his halo of white hair, his double chin and gentle eyes, he looked like a cross between H. L. Hunt and Ben Franklin. There was just no meanness in him. He was a prolific writer of notes, the type of person who never seemed to overlook a special occasion, your joys or your losses. If your cat had kittens, you would get a scribbled note from Morris. I don't know of anyone who had more friends, and they included Presidents and busboys.

His father owned a dry-goods store in Lufkin, Texas. Morris worked for him up until the night he returned from a high school football game and ran into the local newspaper editor. He described the outcome to the editor in his own excitable, down-home way. The editor made him sit and write it, "Just like you told it."

Said Morris, "Maybe a newspaperman wasn't born that day, but I can guarantee you one thing, that's when a dry-goods merchant died."

How one comes into the business hardly matters. How one stays does. The Morris Franks helped make it a brotherhood. He once said, of his life in journalism, "I sometimes think that I've thrown out a crumb and got back a bakery."

I know that feeling. When I learned he was dying in the summer of 1975, at the age of seventy-three, I asked a friend in Houston to stop by his hospital room to tell him, one more time, that I hadn't forgotten what I owed him. The friend said Morris, too weak to talk, barely rose up from his pillow, smiled and nodded. I have no illusion that those words in any way helped him or eased his pain. But I know his words had helped me.

Chapter 3

NO NIGGERS
OR REPORTERS ALLOWED

A FEW of the boys were sitting around in the shank of an evening, when the talk turned to war stories. Old soldiers are not the only ones who tell them. Newsmen love to regale each other with such tales, when the drinks are cold and the mood mellow, usually under the general category of Head-Knockings I Have Known.

After others had offered several examples of raw-guts-and-whiskey courage, a CBS veteran named Laurens Pierce raised a hand. "You talk about guts," he snorted, in a voice filled with Alabama. "Hell, you don't know what guts is until you have to stand in front of a screaming race mob and put on your pancake makeup."

It may seem a curious note on which to begin a reminiscence dealing with so solemn a matter as civil rights, the hopes that were raised and the blood that was shed on behalf of this cause in the South in the 1960's. Pierce's observation, though, had the ring of many truths.

To begin with, his comment served as a reminder that even in the midst of the most urgent planetary issues, television must collect its debt. Everyone needs makeup in front of that camera. I mean everybody, whether he realizes it or not. Light-complexioned people with dark hair and dark eyes such as mine need it more than others. When I first broke into television in Houston I swore I would have nothing to do with face paint and powder. I felt to use makeup was phony and sissy and who needed it. Well, I caught one look at myself on a monitor and I could have doubled for a wanted poster in the nearest Post Office.

Applying your own makeup in the field is one of the small perils of the trade. It is one thing in a studio. Often there is a makeup person on hand to touch you up but if not, you do it yourself. At least, you have privacy.

It is an entirely different matter to have to carry around with you a compact of, say, Gay Whisper. Literally. In 1962 I was still getting used to carrying my own makeup when I boarded a Delta flight from Memphis to Birmingham. As I placed my coat on the overhead rack, the compact fell out and landed with a plop on the carpet.

The stewardess bent down, retrieved it and turned it in her hand. "Mah goodness," she said, in what I guessed was a Savannah, butter-wouldn't-melt accent, "who dropped this heah compact?"

She glanced around at each passenger and I just gave her an innocent, blank stare that said, Well, don't look at me. What would I be doing with *that*?

And the rest of the damned flight, I'm thinking, My God, I have to do a piece almost the minute I hit the ground and I really need that makeup. But I walked right off the plane without it.

So I always knew what Pierce meant, in a kidding-on-the-square kind of way. I am inclined to think that in terms of the civil rights story there is a bit of symbolism here.

The story of the South in the early 1960's turned out to be my proving period, my apprenticeship, with CBS. It was my first major assignment for the network and Ernie Leiser was watching me closely. Leiser, who had hired me, along with Blair Clark, had become my mentor. I could almost hear him saying around the office: "Putting this young man on this kind of story, day in and day out, coming from where he does, may be unfair to him. He will bear watching."

For a major part of my life I had too little race consciousness, virtually no feel for the special problems of the black person in America. Yet I can remember, as a boy, seeing my father stand up at a precinct meeting, the only white man there fighting to let the blacks vote.

This incident occurred right after the Second World War, when the veterans had started coming home. The Democratic primaries in Houston, as in many other places, were lily white and a nomination to any office was tantamount to election. The precinct meetings were held at a civic club on North Shepherd Drive, in that not so gracefully aging part of Houston known as The Heights. I was thirteen or fourteen, and I went along on my mother's orders. She sensed trouble and didn't want my father to go. When he insisted, she sent me with him, feeling, I think, that he was less likely to get into a scrape in front of his son.

Several black veterans showed up. Blacks had seldom, if ever, been allowed in the precinct meetings before and, for the most part, none bothered to attend. But these men had been to war, some had bled for their piece of America, and they had come to claim it. I have only a vague recollection of the scene, but there was a vote—on seating delegates, I believe—and the tension in the room was real.

A precinct meeting is a sort of mini-convention. They called for a vote and all the whites stood in favor. It was a classic case of the chairman trying to railroad a motion. But then, on the *no* side of the question, the blacks stood and my father rose with them.

It would be inaccurate to describe my father as a crusader for civil rights. He was not. But he had a personal sense of this situation. It was strictly a neighborhood issue. He knew these men. When my father stood, the chairman said, "Rags, you don't understand. It's not your time to vote. You're standing up at the wrong time."

"I understand all right," he snapped back. "These people have a right to be here. From now on whenever they stand up, you'll find me standing with them." The mood turned ugly. My father had been raised in that neighborhood. He knew everyone there by name and they knew him. He wasn't a man who picked fights, but he could handle himself. I expected a fist fight to break out. But there was just a raw flash of anger and, when we started to leave, some nasty words, and there was a little shoving.

Exactly what was going on, I didn't know, and I didn't ask, not then. I had grown up with blacks. Our neighborhoods were cheek to jowl. Our standards of living were not that different, and I had no real impression that they—or we—were deprived.

At college in Hunstville a sociology teacher named Rupert Koenninger further elevated my consciousness. Koenninger also served as a criminologist on the staff of the state prison there. Huntsville was rural Texas and the lines were more sharply drawn than in a city the size and mixture of Houston. Lawmen sometimes were tough, to the point of cruelty, on blacks. They routinely got a bad shake at the sheriff's office and at the courthouse.

At Professor Cunningham's insistence, I covered the trial of a black man accused of murder. I suspected he was being framed. There had been a fire and the bodies of a black man and woman had been discovered in the charred ruins. Later someone at the funeral home noticed bullet holes in the bodies.

The police reaction was typical. "Aw, they just burned to death. Bury 'em and forget it." After a great deal of talk had circulated around town a black man was arrested and charged with the fire and killings. It was not hard for me to imagine another scenario: The woman, it was whispered, had been entertaining some white men. Then things got a little tight on somebody in town and they just went out there, shot her and a companion, and burned the place down.

Some of that story came out at the trial. But the jury found the black man guilty and he went to prison. The trial was a sad but useful lesson. As a reporter, later and in larger contexts, you call on your experiences and apply them. Koenninger had raised these questions in class, which may not have been a prudent thing to do, given the times and the place. He would say, "Dan, as you move around town you see the police chief and the sheriff. Do you think they treat blacks the same as they treat whites?"

"Well, no, of course they don't."

"Have you thought whether acting that way is constitutional? Is it legal? Is it right?"

Then he would just drop the subject and let our own answers sink in.

As foul as the racial attitudes of East Texas had been, they were not as hateful as those of Mississippi, Georgia and Alabama, and it was a quantum difference if you were black. Some white people might have difficulty seeing the difference, but it finally became apparent to me.

In my new assignment I landed in Albany, Georgia, and what had occasionally happened in East Texas turned out to be routine. I could not believe what I was seeing. To the extent that racism and brutality had existed in Texas, I can only plead that my awareness was still developing. Ernie Leiser sensed my innocence.

The first time I met him he said with a smile, "I didn't know but what you'd come riding up here on a white horse, wearing a high hat and spurs and a six-shooter. The only question is whether you can overcome Texas." He said it in a light way, at the same time letting me know they had reserved judgment.

I found myself frequently on the defensive in those days. At one point I heard a voice in the background over the phone, in New York, make a comment that nettled me. Ernie Leiser in New York, Bill Crawford and I in Memphis, were on a conference call discussing a special broadcast we were preparing. I heard someone say, "Do you honestly think Rather can handle it?"

I was pained by this comment. Crawford, an experienced producer and friend with whom I had traveled many miles, said later that the question was reasonable. He argued that the doubt expressed may have concerned only the setting up of coverage, the writing and the supervision of the film. But I took the comment to mean, this is a southern race story and here we have this fellow from Texas covering it.

This is a cliché reaction, I know, but I had never thought of myself as a southerner. As people so often heard Lyndon Johnson say of himself, I thought of myself as a westerner, or southwesterner. Most Texans do. The voice in the background that night in Memphis had a strong New York texture, and I suppose I jumped to the conclusion based on regional prejudice, just as I thought he had. But I do know that Ernie's answer to him was an unqualified, "Damned right he can." And I knew then that I had long since passed whatever test Ernie Leiser had in mind.

In a way, perhaps my concern may have been related to the stark contrast between myself and Hughes Rudd. A superb writer, Rudd had a sensitivity that was constantly bruised by the events around him. We sat in a bar a few nights before he left Atlanta, and I listened as he talked about why he had asked to be relieved.

Rudd was an observant fellow. He formed quick impressions and at one point he said to me, "You're either the most insensitive son of a bitch I've ever known, or else you have an ability that can be helpful in this business. A facility, at the time something happens, not to get caught up in the emotion of it. My trouble with this story is that I get so wrought up with some of the things I see happening that it eats on me in a thousand ways."

As Rudd talked, he clenched and unclenched his fist. He was not saying I had something he envied or admired or resented. Instead he was saying he felt so strongly about this particular story that it made his job more difficult, more complicated. He was telling me, a younger, less experienced reporter, that I had a quality, a detachment, that might be valuable and I should try to refine it.

Either I was born with or had acquired this trait at such an early stage that it had already passed beyond my control. Good or bad, the trait was there, automatic, a reflex. With a certain kind of story something goes click and you lock into your work gear and just do it. At some point after the event, and I never know exactly when, the automatic reactions and the sense of distance give way to a flood of emotions. It has worked that way for me on every major or traumatic story I have known.

But I'm not one of those people who can watch an autopsy and turn to the next person and say, "I feel like Mexican food tonight." And I was totally unprepared, emotionally and intellectually, for the evils committed in the name of racial segregation. Who would have believed that a police chief would turn loose vicious dogs on children? Who would think that adults could turn over an elementary school bus and beat on its side with ax handles? You had to see some of that to believe it. Through the efforts of network television many people did see such terrifying events. And some still didn't believe.

As a reporter, I was prepared. I wanted to get the story. That in itself was seldom a routine matter. Often we were placed in conflict with even the people who worked with us, so emotionally charged were the issues. A station manager in one Mississippi city accused CBS and our crew of being Communists and told us, "Get your asses outta here." I gave him the old honest-men-may-disagree speech and calmed him down, but he never fully relented. He felt that either CBS had been infiltrated by Commies or, as he put it, "You are just so stupid you don't know any better." That seems laughable now. But you faced these situations on a semiregular basis. I made mistakes when I tried to finesse the problem rather than meet it head on.

There were situations you could not finesse. When a fellow standing in front of your nose rams a round into the chamber of an automatic shotgun and says, "You and all those people and all that camera gear, get it loaded in that car and get scarce," no slick moves there.

There were some occasions when I would feign an accent. I would get about as Texas as I knew how. Of course, there was a difference between just chatting somebody up and giving out good ole country-boy talk, hunkering down, as LBJ called it, and really posing as something you were not.

One of my mentors during this time was a cameraman named Wendell Hoffman, a lanky, stringbean, rawboned farmer. Wendell rose six three, wore glasses, had a high-pitched voice and the very long arms of a basketball player. He was in his fifties, indefatigable even then. The best advice I received came from him.

We went out to interview a leader of the so-called White Citizens Council in a disagreeable part of Louisiana. At this time the notion was fairly general that rural Mississippi was the meanest place for a black man or a reporter to be. But those who covered the story regularly knew better. It could be vicious and, in some cases, lethal in Mississippi. But I had been told about pockets in Louisiana that were even worse.

We went into one Louisiana town, shortly after I had arrived on the scene, to interview this spokesman for the cause of white supremacy. If he was a member of the Klan, we didn't know it. But he quickly expressed some really outrageous opinions. My idea was to coax along the interview, but consciously or not, as Wendell was to say later, I led him to believe that I agreed with his sentiments or at least sympathized with him.

As we drove off, Hoffman spoke right up. "That was a mistake. You're just starting and you're going to run into this sort of thing all the time. You've got to think through how to handle these situations."

His point was, before long I would appear to be on the side of the bigots. He didn't offer any advice. By raising the question, though, he forced me to come up with my own answer. I'll do my best to get along, I decided. I'll be courteous but not obsequious; if I'm going to err then I'll do so on the side of courtesy and gentility. I would, however, make it clear that there is a point beyond which I would not go.

Later we also settled on a rule—for me, for all of us—to dress well. That decision may sound frivolous. But the rule proved important, as a symbol, because this was the first indication to these people that we meant business. I could walk in wearing blue jeans and a plaid shirt—and some did—and fade into the crowd and work around the edges. But that way was not as effective as showing up with my shoes shined, pants pressed, coat on and tie straight. That said: I'm a professional. Here to do a job. I want to get along. But don't try to con or intimidate me.

That approach worked best with everyone but the fanatics. And nothing worked with them. It worked with the police chief, the sheriff, the mayor, the Chamber of Commerce and, yes, the station managers who so often had their foot on our oxygen line. I walked into many a station knowing that the manager felt, in his heart, we were at the least unfair and, at worst, Commies. Our goal was to establish a level of respect. Once we did, we could do business with them.

A case comes to mind concerning an old fellow, since passed on, southern to the core, who owned a television station in Memphis. If you were remaking *Gone With the Wind,* Memphis style, you would want him in it. He had long flowing white hair that curled back over his ears. He wore the Mississippi style, Colonel Sanders white hat. In his own mind he was the last of the southern gentlemen. He sipped nothing but straight

bourbon or mint juleps. His family line went back through the Con-
federacy. He was Dixie and damned proud of it. Nobody was going to
out-magnolia him.

He made that clear the day we walked in, and he said what he had to
say in front of his staff, which I admired. He said to me, "I don't like
what's going on, none of it. Matter of fact, I'm not too fond of you or
your people. Nothing personal, understand. I just don't like you.

"But I want you to know one thing. We may be country but we care
about what we're doing as much as you care about what you do. We're
professionals. I'm sizing you up to see if you are. And if you are, you'll
find that whatever you need from us, you're going to get."

He owned both the TV station and the hotel that housed it on the
ground floor. Actually, all he had done was enlarge his radio studios and
operate a TV station out of the same space. We practically lived there for
months. They didn't have the best facilities but, sure enough, they gave
us what they had. The first two days you could feel the tension. By the
third day it had begun to loosen. After a week we were living too close,
like residing with perpetual house guests.

During the violence at Oxford we had rushed a mobile unit from
New York. The crew drove day and night to get there, then plugged their
lines into the station in Memphis. No one could be certain that what happened next was caused by our mobile unit. But all the lights blew out.
Not just in the station, but all over the hotel. The station was off the air
momentarily; before power could be restored some water pipes burst and
the lower floors of the hotel were flooded. Technically, I didn't think the
mobile unit could have caused all that damage. I took that position and
it was going to be hell getting me to change my mind. When the old
gentleman came down to the station to survey the ruins, I thought, Man,
we've really ripped it now.

He looked around, yelled at his staff, "Get some buckets and start bail-
ing this place out. Get those lights turned back on and"—nodding at me—
"see that these people have whatever they need." And then he left.

Whenever I could I hired extra help from the local station to fill out
our coverage. Word would come that trouble was brewing in some small
delta town. We would want to protect ourselves, but our crews would be
tied up elsewhere, with Nelson Benton or Lew Wood, two of our reporters. So my assistant, Melba Fry, and I would follow the fairly common practice of trying to hire a local camera or sound man on his day off.
But I had to know the local people pretty well. First off, I wanted some-

one who could do the job. On that day he would be representing CBS News.

On a less technical level I was uncomfortable about sending people into potentially dangerous situations. I always felt strongly about that. Routinely, I would call a staff reporter—usually Benton or Wood—and say, okay, you have to go. And here is your crew. But, laying down the phone, I was damned conscious of putting him in a position where he could get hurt. Or worse.

For local people the job could be even stickier. Once, a home-grown cameraman covered a story for us and a gang of thugs came after him with sawed-off cue sticks. Believe me, that is a lethal weapon. He fled into a clothing store and hid in a back room, hanging by his arms from inside a rack of men's suits, while the posse hunted for him. He had a heart attack on the spot. It was a while before he recovered.

The story wasn't worth that kind of pain and anguish.

I never found it easy to send people on dangerous assignments. Doing so, I think, would have been nearly impossible if I had not covered such stories myself. That was one record Walter Cronkite always had going for him. We all knew when Walter got on the phone and asked a man to take a tough call, that Walter had been there. He knew the dangers and that made a difference. When the fellow at the other end hadn't paid his dues, I didn't like it. And still don't. I guess few do.

Insofar as we could predict events, I tried to take the riskier assignments myself. I don't say that to sound noble or self-serving. To be candid, it is quite true that these situations often figure to produce the best stories. Rather than showing leadership, you could argue that I was in a position to skim off the best stories for myself. And there is some truth in that argument.

Ambition is a part of the business too. I got my pick of the stories and I took my pick. I did feel strongly, however, that if there was going to be a tough one, I ought to draw it. But God knows, there were plenty to go around.

Not often, but sometimes, the phrase *"I can smell trouble"* is literally true. It is in the nostrils, as real as the odor of newsprint.

The night U. S. Marshals escorted James Meredith onto the Ole Miss campus—the first black student ever to enroll there—was certainly one of those times. General Edwin Walker had suddenly appeared on the scene, lecturing the students and the rednecks who poured in from other places on the American Way of Life. I found Walker's presence somewhat ridiculous at the time and laughed about it. I saw the first stirrings of the crowd as an open-air puppet show, Punch 'n' Judy stuff. It struck me as comic, a former army general standing under those hundred-year-old trees, rallying southern manhood against the threat of one lonely black freshman. But I quickly changed my mind. I could see what was coming like a storm at sea.

Meredith was to arrive on the night of September 30, 1962, and attend classes the next day. The entire town of Oxford, if not the entire state of Mississippi, seemed to be waiting that dark evening. We had our first sniff of trouble weeks before the confrontation when we tried to make motel reservations and were told we couldn't do so by phone. The response struck me as strange. It turned out the motel clerks were trying to avoid taking reservations for anyone who might be black.

We drove from Memphis to Oxford some days later and stopped at the first motel we saw. It had a sign in the window, hand-penciled on gray backing, a sheet of cardboard from a laundered shirt, that said: "NO DOGS, NIGGERS OR REPORTERS ALLOWED."

Wendell Hoffman, my cameraman, laughed in that cackle of his and said, "I think that tells us what we want to know. We'll just be moving right along."

But I insisted on going into the office and making the lady at the desk tell me to my face that we couldn't get rooms. Then we drove into town, landing at what turned out to be a better motel anyway. The Rebel Motel, I think was the name of it. The people there could not have been nicer. No mistake, they were Mississippi to the marrow, but they were courteous.

Unfortunately for us, the rooms had no dial phones. I told the manager we were reporters and might receive calls from New York at one or two o'clock in the morning. I asked if someone would be at the switchboard.

"No, sir, there wouldn't be."

I said, "What would happen to the telephone?"

"Your telephone?"

"Yes."

"Your telephone wouldn't ring."

I persisted, "What would happen to the one that rings?"

"It would just keep on ringing," the manager replied. "We live in the back and we just go to sleep."

Later, however, the motel geared up to handle the invasion of reporters and a clerk was assigned to handle the night switchboard. But we were in the vanguard, before the main herd of reporters arrived. And to show you the curious effects of television reporting on the central nervous system, we slept a little less soundly those first few nights, knowing the phone would not ring.

The night of the riots when Meredith arrived, a free-lance cameraman named Gordon Yoder had driven into Oxford from Dallas. A tall, red-headed, devil-may-care fellow, Gordon announced that he was going to drive his station wagon onto the campus. One of the rules of the road is that you don't force advice on anyone. Every man has to make his own judgments. Several of us, however, tried to caution him. "Gordon, under the circumstances that might not be too good an idea." But he ignored us.

Within minutes after he reached the campus the crowd turned over his station wagon and it burst into flames. It was a harrowing experience and a near miss for Gordon and his wife, who was with him. The Yoders managed to scramble out the front doors not a moment too soon. Gordon couldn't believe what was happening. The students, and many who were not students, were just running amok.

Studying the faces in the gangs around Yoder's car, I remarked at the time that some were young, but they didn't have the look of college kids. Some, in fact, had rolled in from out of state, from Alabama and Georgia and Arkansas, drawn to trouble as a magnet draws metal shavings.

Earlier Wendell and I had discussed whether we should station ourselves inside the Lyceum Building—the administration offices—or outside, in the crowd itself. For our purposes the building possessed some disadvantages. Our movements would be restricted, making it difficult to find out what was going on. We would have a limited view of only one small part of the scene. If we stayed with the crowd we would also have access to a telephone, and the Tenth Commandment of journalism is that no story is worth a damn unless you can get it out. The only thing the Lyceum Building offered was more security.

So we made the decision to keep to the grounds. I had sent to Atlanta for more staff. If we get enough people in Ole Miss in time, I thought, we could put someone in the Lyceum Building.

With nightfall the first grim sign of hard trouble was at hand. The body of Paul Guihard, a French reporter, shot to death, was found behind the Science Building. I had talked with him only a few minutes before he had been shot. He had been killed, I am certain, in cold blood, because he was a reporter, or foreign, or both. It was no stray shot that got him. The night was off to a chilling start. The riots would last fifteen hours and would require the presence of three thousand federal troops to end them.

At such times it helps to have people around whose character, and work, you know. One of these was Dick Perez, my old taxicab buddy from Channel 11 in Houston. Perez showed up late one night, on his own, a few weeks after I had started covering the civil rights story full time. With some exasperation, he said, "Rather, I'm amazed at you. You keep going into these clutch situations and you don't have me at your side. I don't know how you expect to do it."

I had to appreciate Dick's spirit. When the civil rights story turned dangerous to cover, there were news people I would call who told me, quite frankly, and I didn't blame them, "There isn't enough money around for me to go to Oxford or Meridian or Birmingham."

Perez was a welcome, if slightly comic, sight. But there were practical matters to consider. I said, "Among other things, Dick, we've got a union problem." He could not free-lance with CBS and work for a non-union shop, which the station in Houston was.

He said, "To hell with that. I'll quit my job." Now here was a family man with seven kids. He had just appeared, unannounced, on his own time. He did indeed quit his job. With no promises. I called on him, now and then, when he had a day off, for spot assignments that fell into the tough category. He was more than a guy who took pictures. He was a good newsman.

So that night at Oxford, Dick was at my side. I was, in fact, paying him out of my own pocket. He was not on the CBS staff or in the union, though in time we were able to help him join both. Dick was willing to take the dirtiest assignments. As an aside, one of the surer ways of breaking into journalism is to take the jobs that no one else wants. Perez would march into some cross-creek town and accept whatever guff was handed to him because he wanted to work for the network so badly.

At Oxford, Dick and Wendell Hoffman performed with great resourcefulness and without fear. It was night, remember, not the best time for television news. Whenever anyone turned on a light—which meant every time we needed to film—one or more bullets would attempt to knock it out. We had to film and move. Film and move. After a while we worked out a pattern: Turn on our battery-powered, portable light, film for fifteen seconds by actual count, turn off the light—if we didn't get hit—and then run, because we were bound to catch gunfire or bricks or both. We had no way of protecting ourselves, except to avoid the crowds, keep moving and stay low.

The phrase, "Get high and shoot bloody," started among television people with the civil rights coverage. The expression stemmed from the fact that those of us who covered civil rights on a regular basis had to learn survival techniques.

To get high and shoot bloody meant just that: If it appeared there was going to be violence, climb as high as you could. If we saw a nearby building, we would get on top of it or on an awning, porch, or just high ground. To shoot bloody meant to look for where the heads were being knocked or the shots fired because doing so would produce the most memorable film.

We couldn't use the first technique that night at Oxford. We couldn't get to the high ground.

Still, the entire operation had the feel and mood of combat. I had Perez, Hoffman and Laurens Pierce with me on the campus. We were in frequent touch with Hughes Rudd, who had flown down to Jackson, the state capital, to cover events there. We reported our movements and the temper around us to Rudd. Those were the two fronts, the two datelines on the story, Jackson and Oxford.

Our coverage was as good as we could make it, but no doubt those who saw our film on their sets the next morning may have been unable to get a full sense of the shock and peril that gripped the campus all night. The darkness, the terrain, and the confusion worked against us. Looking back, it might have been smarter if we had made the Lyceum Building our command post.

As it turned out, we spent most of our time crawling around on our bellies, circling the campus. We weren't playing war games. We just wanted to avoid being seen with all that equipment. I once crawled around the edges of the Lyceum Building, which was surrounded and in a state of siege, and managed to slip inside. There were no telephones available in the Lyceum, but if a cameraman had been with me he could have at least shot film of people being wounded and bullets bee-stinging the windows. But I didn't bring one, again, because at one point he would have had to make a naked dash of about thirty-five yards. To ask someone to do that while carrying a camera and other equipment would have made him too inviting a target.

The casualty toll that night included two dead, one of them Paul Guihard, the French reporter, and countless wounded, many of them just bystanders. The other man who had been killed had simply cruised out to the campus to see what was going on. Violence *is* a spectator sport. He was hit by a stray bullet right in the middle of his forehead.

The curious and vicious thing about the riots was the fact that they began as an Ole Miss pep rally, in the afternoon, with a football weekend atmosphere. But there were people on hand whose purpose was to incite trouble, to whip the students into a mob. The afternoon started out, literally, with Ole Miss football yells and the singing of "Dixie." The students and others were swept up in the moment, the contagion of music and martial speeches.

One could see the hysteria building. Some of the students saw what was happening, became frightened by it, tried to defuse the growing confrontation. Others wisely left. The Lyceum Building became the center of the drama. One sniper had positioned himself on top of the Science Building, across the way. Shots were coming from other rooftops, classroom windows and even trees. But the most dangerous area was on the periphery of the Lyceum, in the shadows, where the bushes and trees provided a natural cover between the buildings. There were groups of twos and threes, hiding in ambush, taking shots or whacking people in the head and knees with clubs.

For fifteen hours an American college campus turned into a virtual battlefield because white authorities did not want black students to sleep or study there. The lonely, embattled figure of James Meredith became the symbol of the black tide of the future. Ross Barnett, the Mississippi governor, had blocked the court-ordered registration of Meredith for ten days. But now the U. S. Marshal sent by Robert Kennedy, then the Attorney General, had escorted Meredith onto the campus and into the dawn. The next morning, while the sullen and frustrated rioters of the previous night were held back by troops and federal agents, Meredith attended class. By midday the sun had burned off a haze that hung over the campus like gunsmoke. As I walked around Ole Miss my feet kicked empty cartridges and gun clips that littered the paths like pebbles.

Two dead, many others wounded and mangled, the use of federal force: that had been the price to open the doors of a great state university to all its people. In December, Ross Barnett was charged with criminal contempt for defying the court order to admit Meredith.

I never got used to that part of the job, observing the capacity public officials had for turning mischief into violence. A year after the Ole Miss riots, the governor of Alabama, George Wallace, called out the National

Guard for the opening of a grade school in Birmingham. I had sympathy, and empathy, for the guardsmen. Most were young. Few, if any, had been fully trained. These were not combat-hardened veterans. Later, when the Kent State tragedy occurred, I thought about the lunacy of giving loaded weapons to summer soldiers and throwing them into an inflamed situation.

This Alabama unit was assigned to a school whose integration had become the focal point of white resistance. The crowds inevitably gathered. And an order came down from the company commander to "sweep the street. Move everyone out."

The young guardsmen raised their weapons in the cross-rifle position and marched, shoulder to shoulder, down the street. There was no use waving a press card and saying, "Hey, I'm a reporter." As a matter of fact, I did just that, and a guardsman cracked me with his rifle butt, knocking me down. One thing I learned quickly: the worst place to be is on the ground. That is where you get trampled.

The guardsman had tried to clip me on the chin, missed, and caught me on the side of the head. He did it viciously. But the young private marching next to him was indignant and snapped at him, "You shouldn't have done that." The private reached down to assist me but I was already scrambling, trying to get out of the column's way.

Wherever a reporter traveled in the South in the sixties he was likely to feel forebodings. Often they turned out to be justified. It was hard not to be in a state of perpetual gloom, seeing so much hate, wondering how schools and campuses had become the trenches of a free society.

Some newsmen weighed the risks and packed a gun. I discouraged carrying arms among my own staff. I would like to say that I didn't allow it, period, and in theory I did not. I had laid down the rule that no CBS crewmen could carry a weapon of any kind, including a pocketknife. That prohibition had less to do with any aversion I might have felt toward handguns than with my professional judgment that it would be best for us not to be armed.

A journalist's best position at any time is: Look, I'm a reporter. I'm doing a job. I don't take sides. If someone in the vicinity had been shot and a hostile cop or a vigilante had stopped and searched us, it would be regrettable to say the least if the first guy they found carrying a gun turned out to be a reporter.

A couple of people who worked for us were very straightforward. They said, I don't mind going into this kind of trouble. But I know the area and I'm not going there without a weapon. Dick Perez, on the other hand, reacted to danger by decking out in a short-sleeved shirt and tight-fitting pants. I chided him one day about his dress because he was chunky and his clothes made him look like a sausage. He said, not disagreeably, "I try to wear clothes that make it clear I'm *not* carrying a weapon."

Which brings me back to Laurens Pierce, and his reference to the civil rights beat as a kind of domestic war story. Once, on the outskirts of Birmingham, a black church had been bombed in a night-rider raid. This time, no one was killed. Pierce, two other crewmen and I arrived in a hurry, at dusk. The lawmen were already there and looking for clues. They began to make things difficult as soon as we unloaded our cameras. I also became aware that four or five nasty-looking characters had collected near us. Soon they were bombarding Pierce and me, trying to agitate us with profane comments.

A word about Pierce. He was from Montgomery, Alabama, and his voice and manner reflected his origins like a neon sign. He was short and wiry, with what they call in the fight game quick hands. There were a lot of fellows like Pierce on the Confederate side in the Civil War, which is to say, men with a high sense of honor, duty and a gift for Scripture quoting.

Laurens Pierce had lived on a farm. It was there, I always believed, that he had developed his talent for improvising. You could hand him a piece of machinery and he not only could figure out how it worked, he could improve on it. He constantly tinkered with our cameras. They were larger in those days, and heavier by ten to fifteen pounds, and a cameraman had to carry the camera on his shoulder with a battery pack, attached to a sound man by a kind of electric umbilical cord. After a while Pierce invented something called the balsa wood door to replace the metal one where the cameraman slid in his film. This reduced the weight of the camera by a pound or so, which was good. The problem was that Pierce kept experimenting, so that a reporter would do an interview and the next day New York would call and say the film was okay, but it had a sunlight leak. The reporter would mutter, "Pierce and that damned balsa wood door."

He was also good with radios, and we developed our own radio contact system. His mechanical abilities and other talents made him a valuable man. We made it a practice to recruit film cameramen who were also good reporters. They are, in fact, photojournalists and vastly underrated, easily the key people in our whole industry. A TV station can cover a story without a correspondent, but it's much tougher without a cameraman.

So Pierce was the cameraman this day when the toughs began surrounding us. The police had motioned that we were to avoid contact, had actually marked off a point beyond which we could not go. The cops had a case to investigate and were not really interested in our problem. At that moment I was not yet sure we had a problem.

At first there were only three men, then seven, and finally a dozen rather menacing figures crowding around us. The light had begun to fade and the police had already moved farther away. One of the men stepped out and began walking alongside, stalking us as we filmed, trying to provoke a fight. We had been through this scene before, and part of the drill was that the sound man would be responsible for the cameraman's head. It was a rule of the road that we developed out of necessity. In order to film, the cameraman has to keep one eye to the eyepiece of the camera and squint the other shut. The camera stands high enough to protect one side of his head, but the other side is exposed. So the sound man had to stay as close to the cameraman's head as possible. He had to protect the blind side.

We walked along in a kind of formation. Soon three others had joined the first agitator and we got into a pushing scene. We didn't push back. We knew from experience that the troublemakers wanted to goad us into fighting.

One of the toughs toted a closely sawed-off shotgun. In fact, the gun was sawed off so low there was some question in my mind that if he ever fired it the thing might just explode in his face. He had pointed the shotgun down his pants leg and then he suddenly brought it up against my ribs. He said, "You take another step, mother-fucker, and I'm going to blow you apart."

I was off to Pierce's other side. His so-called non-hit side. Well, tough talk is cheap, but I knew the man wasn't kidding when I felt the pressure of the sawed-off shotgun.

All of this happened in seconds. In the next instant, suddenly reaching around from the other side of the camera, there appeared a .38 on a .44 base revolver. One of our crew, the sound man, had jammed the pistol against the redneck's temple. He was an Alabaman, a friend of Pierce's, who worked for the local station and hired out to us on his days off. He was country, and had the habit of calling other people "sonny." He said to the man with the shotgun, "Sonny, I think you want to stroll."

Quickly the shotgun dropped to Sonny's side and he backed away. This tough was wide-eyed and scared. He had good reason to be. (I wasn't exactly without concern myself.) The others retreated with him. There was more profanity, but they gave us room and we left. If you had been sitting in a tree looking down, it might have resembled something out of a John Wayne movie, though a little overacted. But I remember the sound man holding the gun steady and saying, as we backed toward the car, "If you think I'm bluffing, gents, just try me."

That scene could have turned into a bloody mess. I have to admit I lectured our gun-wielding hero and told him I'd rather not see him carry a gun again. But he knew I was thinking how thankful I was that he had violated the rule.

I suppose this is not the sort of problem you can cover in a journalism class. I am certain that none of my superiors at the network ever learned about the incident, at least until now. They would have been aghast. I am also sure that if you talked to any television crew, among those that were in and out of the South during those days, you would find they had similar stories to tell. War stories, if you please.

The police? They were fifty yards away and out of earshot. In fairness, I don't believe this was a case where they were looking the other way. I think they were simply involved in their own work and paying little or no attention to us.

Yes, some reporters carried guns; on assignments where violence is probable some still do. When correspondents land in a war zone a time comes when each has to make a conscious decision about how, or if, he is going to protect himself.

But this happened in America, in a part of the country once famed for its grace and leisure and civility. Ironies aside, there is no doubt in my mind that the farther a reporter stays from a weapon the better off he is.

I know, as the gun lobbyists keep reminding us, guns do not kill people. People kill people. But with a gun it is a whole lot quicker.

Out-Take

3

EXPENSE ACCOUNTS

Newsmen in the field and the accountants at home fight an endless war of nerves. Part of the problem is that, by temperament, good reporters are seldom very organized. Accountants are good, decent, and orderly, and they never understand how anyone's expense account can be three months late.

And you tell them, wearily, "Gawdamighty, I've been facing down people in tank towns from here to Dry Rot, Georgia, dodging cue sticks and sawed-off shotguns, and you're asking me why I can't get my expense accounts in on time?"

And the accountant says, "Well, gee, you ride the plane from Birmingham to New Orleans. You could do them then."

All newsmen have their favorite expense-account stories, none of them alike. Print reporters have one set, the TV types another. Foreign correspondents tell their own, and those differ from the yarns spun by the chaps on the domestic beat.

I can testify to what may be the Mona Lisa of expense-account stories. This one took place in Jackson, Mississippi, in September, 1962.

The night started out, as those nights often did, with a few of us sitting around in a bar after a long day's work, comparing notes and gigging each other. Claude Sitton of *The New York Times* and Hughes Rudd of CBS had gotten into one of those friendly, foolish, no-one-can-win arguments about the corruption of money.

"You're spoiled," Sitton was saying, "and money does it. Television's endless money—"

"Now, dammit," Rudd broke in, "we don't have all that much money."

"Sure you do," Sitton said. "I see you. You people spend money like it was going out of style. You stay at the best hotels. You got rent cars coming out your ass. Meanwhile we newspaper fellows have to slug along with a little notebook and a ballpoint pen, run our hand over the brim of our hat and stay at somebody's boardinghouse."

That conversation went on for many nights. Sitton was a meticulous reporter and I learned from him. Curiously, he liked television, had made his peace with it, but enjoyed kidding TV people who were then, and to a lesser extent still are today, defensive about the better ride it offers. He was slight of build, gray hair going to white, an amiable sort. Sitton and Rudd would have a fine time, neither one budging an inch. My role at these sessions was generally to sit quietly and listen. As Sam Rayburn used to say, "Just sit there and study at the feet."

As the night wore on, Sitton took the position that television would never reach its potential, as journalism, because its answer to every problem was, when in doubt, spend money.

Rudd grew indignant. "You're just stuck in the past," he said. "Don't tell me *The New York Times* doesn't have plenty of money. You talk about using your wits. Sitton, your real problem is that you don't know *how* to get expense money out of people. I've worked for newspapers, magazines, wire services. Never had a problem getting money. It's all in knowing how to do it. Why, I could get three thousand dollars in here before daylight if I had to."

Instinctively, Sitton and I both checked our watches. It was already 1:30 A.M.

Claude said, "Now wait a minute. You're letting your mouth overload your ass a little here. Nobody is going to send any broken-down reporter such as you three thousand dollars at one thirty in the morning."

Rudd said, "Well, how much do you want to bet?"

They wagered a fifth of Wild Turkey that Rudd could not get three thousand dollars in expense money before daybreak. Not the least of his problem was the fact that Western Union doesn't remain open twenty-four hours in most small southern towns. But Rudd was undaunted. Weaving slightly, he made his way to the nearest pay telephone and dialed the news desk at CBS in New York.

Of course, that is the network's nerve center. Every CBS correspondent is indoctrinated with the idea that, wherever he is, in Pakistan or Pomona, he must stay in touch with the desk. And as long as he does, he can get help. It happened that we were in Jackson at the height of the search for Ross Barnett, the governor of Mississippi, who was trying to duck a court order to integrate the university.

As a rule, the younger people catch the overnight shift on the news desk. When Hughes got his man he said, in his most professional voice, with only an occasional slurred word, "This is Rudd in Jackson, Mississippi. I want three thousand dollars in expense money and I want it sent within the hour to the Western Union office here."

Sitton was listening in on the extension and he heard the young deskman say, "Yes, sir, Mr. Rudd. You bet, Mr. Rudd. [Pause] But as you know, Mr. Rudd, I'm only authorized to send out fifty dollars. I'll have to call somebody at home to okay this."

Rudd said, "You do whatever is necessary, lad. You know your job. My job is to get to you and I'm telling you I need three thousand dollars before dawn."

So the kid called a middle-level executive and roused him out of bed. The executive said, "What the hell does Rudd mean, three thousand dollars? What could he possibly need with it?"

Next this man called Rudd and demanded to know what was going on. "Here's the situation," said Hughes. "You know about Governor Barnett. Well, in order to avoid having a warrant served on him, Barnett jumped on a boat and tried to flee down the Mississippi from Jackson to New Orleans. We learned of this exclusively, and I chartered a boat to follow him. Unfortunately, the boat ran aground on a sandbar and we have to get her pulled off. Now, I have a bid from a salvage operator down here who says if we can do it before morning—he has another job to do after that—he can do it for three thousand dollars."

Naturally, Rudd was concocting this entire wild story off the top of his head and Sitton was doubled over. It was too much for the still-drowsy executive and he bucked it to the business office. In a few minutes Rudd repeated his story. "The boat has run aground. It's our responsibility. I have a salvage bid and, as you know, the people who do the job charge according to bottomage. [Meaning they measure the bottom of the boat. How Rudd knew this esoterica I haven't the faintest idea.] You can call any salvage outfit in New York, if you want, and they'll tell you three thousand dollars is a bargain price for this boat. [He had described it as being sixty-one feet, another figure he pulled out of the air.]

"You call somebody in New York," he went on, "and if you can beat that price I'll kiss your ass on the state capitol steps. And if you don't get the three grand here by daybreak it will cost us twelve thousand dollars tomorrow to get it off the sandbar."

Lo and behold, a salvage company in New York was asked what it would cost to pull a sixty-one-foot boat off a sandbar, just give us a round figure. They said, "Well, that's a pretty big job. It could run eight to ten thousand dollars."

The newsroom called Rudd right back and said, "The money is on the way."

Rudd, of course, returned the three thousand and by the time the story circulated around CBS it was rated one of the more inventive practical jokes. However, Ralph Paskman, the gruff city editor type who ran the newsroom, refused to be seen or heard laughing about it. "Bad example for our younger reporters," he told me, adding, "If you ever try such crap, Rather, I'll break your knees."

Chapter 4

A QUIET
AT THE CENTER

THERE WAS ONLY ONE white face in the room and it was mine. The time, the summer of 1962. I had walked into a private home in Albany, Georgia, determined to meet the man who had shaken America's concept of itself as a fair and benevolent society: the Reverend Martin Luther King, Jr.

The civil rights movement had begun in Alabama in the late 1950's. King had angered many whites, and disconcerted others, with his talk of *equality now* and *passive resistance.* But they did not mark him as dangerous until he led his followers into the streets. This country will tolerate almost anything as long as you don't block traffic.

That day in Albany the scene was chaotic, telephones ringing, someone trying to arrange bail for an undetermined number of people, someone else attempting to work out a statement with a spokesman for the police chief about what would happen the next day. I couldn't see Dr. King through the layers of people around him.

Finally I recognized Andrew Young, talking with a baby-faced young black whose name, I learned later, was Julian Bond. I tried to introduce myself to Young. He didn't even turn his head. I was just another reporter. I finally reached out and grabbed his shirt sleeve and said, "Hey, I want you to listen to me for fifteen seconds." That got his attention.

"I want to meet Dr. King," I said. "My name is Rather. With CBS. I'm going to be here for however long it takes to cover this story and I'm not about to begin my work without knowing one of the principal figures. And I'd like your help."

He studied me. "Okay," Young said, "I heard you out. Right? And I can tell you, it isn't going to happen."

I waited a moment, then said, "Now let me tell you. I don't want to be disrespectful. I don't want any trouble. But I am going to meet him. What I'd really like to do is meet him under the best circumstances. But if you insist, I'll make my own arrangements."

Young cocked his head. He walked away from me, and in a moment he was back with Dr. King. To my surprise King seemed genuinely interested when we were introduced. It was more than, hello, how are you, glad to see you here. He said, "Let's sit down and talk for a moment."

Sure, it might have been the mere fact that I was from CBS, someone who could be helpful to him. Those who claimed that Dr. King tried to manipulate the media were correct. So did the police chief. And the mayor. It went with the territory. But at the time my sense of it went deeper. He leaned toward me, and I think he had heard the trace of a Texas accent. He knew that it wasn't Georgia or Mississippi. For whatever reason, he seemed curious about me. Perhaps I struck him as young—I was thirty then—to be doing what I was.

We found a couch and sat down. My first impression was that in the midst of all the disorder Dr. King was secure within himself, under control. He had his own thoughts together, knew what he was doing. He often talked, as I got to know him, about a quality he called "peace at the center." He had it. If you had walked into that room, that day, and looked at him, you would have thought this was the only man in that house, maybe in the entire country, who had a sense of peace. I later came to feel that this image was studied on his part. I think he knew the value of projecting an aura of calm.

He had another capacity that impressed me. He listened. Later, I would see him in a crowd with a hundred or more people milling around, tugging, trying to shake his hand, get his ear, all talking at once. If he and I were talking even for only a few seconds, I knew I had his full attention.

It is possible, of course, that I am making his courtesy seem more than it was. Maybe he just wanted to get out of the middle of the maelstrom. But I found Dr. King asking three questions to every one of mine. He asked where I was from, how long I had been in television, how I happened to be assigned to Albany.

I told him I was relieving someone else. Then the next question seemed to pop out of nowhere. He asked me what denomination I was. Not what religion. He took it for granted I was a Christian. I said, "Lutheran. I was raised a Baptist but my wife converted me."

He chuckled a little and said, "That's the usual way. Women convert men, rather than the other way around."

All the while Dr. King paid attention. His eyes were not flitting around the room. His mind, as far as I could tell, was not on something else. He wasn't just going through the motions. Soon one of his aides appeared and Dr. King stood and said, very formally, "I'm sorry, but I have to go now, Mr. Rather."

Our contacts would become less ceremonious over the years. But though I interviewed him several times that summer, in Albany, I was never able to talk to Dr. King alone. It was usually in what we in the trade call a gang bang, with the subject standing amid a gaggle of reporters and microphones licking out at him like snakes.

Up to now there had been a pattern to his appearances. Dr. King or his lieutenants would arrive in a town, and there would be a confrontation between them and the local law enforcement agency and/or the mayor or the city council. Often the reporter would not know if this encounter would last an hour, a day, a week, a month or indefinitely. At times, Dr. King and his own staff wouldn't know. On occasion they would go into a city in response to some local appeal. But Albany was not of that design. King had hand-picked Albany as a place to make symbolic points. And he had said so, openly.

It was an intriguing test. A book could be written on that summer in Albany, the people, the emotions, the currents that ran through the town. The police chief was a man named Clyde Pritchett. He was not a typical small-town police chief. Albany, in fact, did not have a small-town mentality. It was a small metropolis.

Pritchett was more intelligent than most police chiefs I had encountered, more sophisticated, in the best sense of the word. He was dedicated to enforcing the law and didn't give a damn who was involved.

But I came to Albany with no such knowledge, to relieve Hughes Rudd, who had been there for weeks and was weary of what now shaped up as a long-running story. I rolled into this Georgia community and, literally, walked around gape-mouthed for several days. What quickly became obvious were the under-the-surface storms that were putting pressure on Pritchett as the town's symbol of law and order. A stranger like myself had to perceive and understand the tides of feeling that split the town. Every time a black stuck his head up, there were those who wanted Pritchett to "zap the nigger." Others said, well, if "they" don't come into the churches or press for an integrated swimming pool, don't zap them. At least, not in public.

I was most unprepared for the church issue. I suppose I should have been. But to hear even ministers say, "The one thing that really grates on me is to have to sit in church with them." That was inconceivable to me. I didn't want to believe what I heard, tried not to, but there it was.

Yet another group in Albany said, look, we know how most of you feel, but it's bad for business and it's bad for the town's image. And, finally, there were people who had been born and reared in Georgia, who felt that times and conditions had changed, and that grievances truly existed that needed to be redressed.

In Albany we found a cross-section of humanity, even down to the 10 percent who simply didn't want to be bothered. Pritchett was just the right police chief to make the equation complete, because he, unlike some others, did want to do the right thing. Like most of us, he sometimes had trouble deciding what was right. As the pressures increased it became visibly more difficult for him to answer the questions he asked of himself: what was right and what ought to be done.

Reporters found him fair and polite and generally good to work with, up to a point. Pritchett, in the beginning, was in many ways sensitive to all the sounds and furies. As the pressures grew and began to work on him he became more aloof. He wanted to do the right things, for the city and for his own ambition. I imagine he could say, if I handle this well, who knows? Maybe they'll need a new chief someday in Atlanta or Mobile.

Literally thousands of arrests were made in Albany that summer. The King strategy was to make them arrest so many blacks the jails just would not hold them all. The defensive strategy was equally clear: if you think we don't have enough jails to hold all your people, Dr. King, we'll prove to you we do.

Day after day Pritchett worked very hard—and successfully—at not putting himself in the position of going one-on-one with Dr. King. He worked hard at saying, I'm not a protagonist or an antagonist and I'm not here to get into a showdown. I'm here to enforce the law. Whether the law is right or wrong is someone else's argument.

If one wanted to put the outcome this way—and I suspect it would be too shallow a judgment—one could say that Albany was among the places where Dr. King "lost." That is, his strategy of filling the jails didn't work. And, for the short run, he did not get his way in Albany. For his purposes, Albany turned out to have been a bad choice.

He did fill up a lot of newspapers with pictures of blacks being arrested every day, which had a certain value. But what he wanted were pictures of blacks in church and in the swimming pool. The statutes might not have been rewritten overnight, but the facts of life would have changed. His people would have been in places previously closed to them.

But the jails held them.

The police simply staked out the areas Dr. King wanted to integrate, and if a black got within a block of the church or the pool they would arrest him for unlawful assembly. Or failure to obey a police officer. The cops had an endless array of city ordinances and state laws they could, and did, use. All over the South, the civil rights movement met this kind of resistance, the only measurable difference being in the amount of blood that was shed. Albany produced no heroes, and no martyrs.

Birmingham was another story, the city of Bull Connor and vicious police dogs and water hoses and hatred as ugly as an open sore.

CBS scheduled a special, ninety-minute broadcast on Birmingham and we wanted, needed, an interview with Martin Luther King, Jr., who was there, pitted against Bull Connor.

Bernie Birnbaum flew in to Birmingham to produce the program. Bernie is a short, cuddly, round-faced cherub of a man with glasses and a constant cigar. One always had the impression that he slept with that cigar. To my knowledge, he was the first man in America to wear what are now known as Earth Shoes. Even before that, he wore what his associates called little spaceman shoes, round-toed things with laces on the side, sold in New York at a store known only to Bernie, as far as anyone could tell. He is, in short, an individual.

In a descriptive way, he would be the stereotype of the New York, or New Jersey, eastern seaboard, Jewish liberal. Fast moving, fast talking, with an accent that was out of the garment district. I had to be alert to understand Bernie.

Birmingham was no tourist retreat in those days. I met Bernie at the airport. We had worked together on the Billie Sol Estes case in Texas months earlier and I knew him to be direct. He stepped off the plane and his first words to me were, "How tough is this, kid?"

I said, "Plenty tough."

He said, "Good. Let's go see Dr. King."

Bernie sees things in terms of pictures. His training was in film making, not journalism. But in his own way he is a superb journalist.

We piled into my car and as we drove away from the airport I warned him that this was not going to be as easy as he thought. Connor had vowed to cut off Dr. King from the news media. There already had been too much

publicity to suit Bull. He felt the press was either being "used," or playing
Dr. King's game.

As the Birmingham police chief, Connor was a prototype of the character
who played the sheriff in the Dodge commercials. But this was not play
acting. Connor had surrounded the motel where Dr. King was staying. He
used a mobile trailer, parked in the street, as a command post.

Cops ringed the hotel, allowing no one in or out without credentials
issued by the Birmingham police. It was like a siege, or a blockade.

I tried to explain the situation to Bernie. "Yeah, yeah," he said. "But
do you have an interview arranged?"

I said, "No, we haven't even been able to see King since he got back
into town."

Bernie said, "Well, that's crazy."

I said, "Bernie, a lot of crazy things are going on here. And let me tell
you straight out, this is no place to muck around. Unlike some places you've
been where you can say, well, I can talk my way through it, these people
will get violent with you in a hurry. You're going to have to be careful.
To get through the police lines you need a pass. I've already made an
application for ours and it was refused."

"On what grounds?" he asked, with indignation.

"They don't need any grounds," I said. "They can do it on the grounds
they don't like my looks." I stole a quick glance at Bernie's profile. "And
I can tell you that by the time we get there, if you think they don't like
my looks, friend, you have no chance at all."

While he was silent I added, "But here's what I'd like to do. I've asked
to see Connor himself. They're stalling us but I think I can bluff my way
in. You're not going to like this but, frankly, I don't care if you don't, it
has to be done this way. I'm telling you that if we're even going to get
inside the hotel, this is the only way we can do it."

I still had an old, slightly frayed press card issued by the Houston police
when I was in radio. The card was outdated, but I had clipped off that
corner. My employer was listed as the *Houston Chronicle,* which owned
KTRH radio.

I said to Bernie, "When we get there, first off, I want you to stay in the
shadows. The less seen of you the better. You've got to be there to get
your credentials. But I do not want you to open your mouth. Not a word.
Because the second you say a word, it's going to be all over, and Bull
Connor is going to refer to you as a *nigger-loving Yankee son of a bitch,*
with great sincerity, and the luckiest thing that could happen to you then

would be if he puts you on the next plane out of Birmingham. Also, that cigar has to go."

Birnbaum didn't understand any of my machinations. But I intended to pass us off as two reporters from Houston. Connor was very conscious of regionalism. I planned to tell him I was here with a photographer, we had just arrived, and wanted to get through the police lines. I was going to do a whole routine.

I explained again to Bernie. I warned him that if Bull got a close look at him, if he heard him say anything, he would know instantly he was not from Houston, or Texas, or that part of the planet. We even talked about buying him a hat to cover part of his face. Instead, we waited until night and when I walked up to the trailer Bernie eased over to a nearby tree and stood there, out of the light, while I talked to Connor.

Bull Connor was in his glory. On television every night. Pushing around blacks and reporters and anyone who got in his way. He put me through his own little version of the litmus test. "What the hell you ovah here for, wantin' to give all these niggers mo' publicity?"

I said, "Well, you know, it has become a national story and the position of our paper is that we try to see for ourselves."

He said, "Well, all you'll see heah is a bunch of smart-ass niggers."

I said, keeping my voice flat, "That may be, Chief. But we do need the credentials."

Just when it appeared I had Connor cajoled into clearing us, Bernie, who had done everything I asked to that point, to my absolute consternation could not stand the self-denial any longer. He reached into his coat pocket and pulled out a long, green cigar. I thought to myself, "Omigawd, if Bull sees that, it's all over." But by then Connor was deep into another harangue, didn't even notice and finally stamped the passes.

Let me say that Bernie was uncomfortable with the whole procedure. Later he complained to me, "Look, your strategy worked, and I guess you did the right thing because it got us in, but don't ever put me in that position again. What really needs to be said to people like Bull Connor is, 'If you don't sign that press card we'll have the troops in here in the morning.' "

Bernie's idea of freedom of the press was rather broad. He was also hurt because I jumped on him about the cigar. "Well, dammit," he said, "people from Texas smoke cigars."

"Not that kind," I said. "They don't smoke green cigars. They smoke Loveras, or El Productos, and they're brown." I told him his cigar, wrapped with greenish leaves, looked like a turd and no one in Texas would be caught dead smoking one. We were just lucky Connor didn't spot his stogie.

We slipped inside the motel and found Dr. King's room. This was 1963 and he knew the FBI was watching him closely. He may have known he was being recorded. He had grown visibly suspicious. Between the police trying to keep us out and his own people being protective, we had a problem making contact with him. We waited hours.

I had seen Dr. King a few times since Albany, but once inside the room I observed a change in him that startled me. He looked haggard. He had put on weight. He was short with his people, not abusive, but impatient. When he was angry he showed it by talking even more deliberately than he normally did. I remember him turning to someone and saying icily, "I asked you, twice, kindly, to do it." The effect was almost lethal.

Dr. King's conversation was guarded. His answers that night tended to lean toward yes and no and I see. He still listened carefully, and he gave you that eye contact. But there was tension. He asked where we wanted to do the interview and how many people would be involved.

I told him we wanted to use two camera crews. He pointed out that to bring in television lights and that many people would be to create a potentially dangerous situation. There had been bombings, he said, several of them, in and around Birmingham. He wanted us to be aware of the risks if we set up an interview in a heavily lighted room. (Some weeks later a bomb went off in the room next to Dr. King's. He wasn't there at the time and no one was injured.)

We said we could accept the risk if he could, and he agreed. Once the details were settled the conversation took an odd turn. He began to speak of his suspicions of the FBI. Most reporters there at the time knew that FBI agents were swarming all over Birmingham. I recognized some of them from other places, other stories. I thought then that King overreacted to the Bureau's presence. He gave the agency its due in many ways, but that night he pointed out something new to me. He said most people had the impression that J. Edgar Hoover never made any political speeches at any time, anywhere. But Dr. King went on to quote chapter and verse from a speech Hoover had made in Mississippi, in the late 1950's, in which he talked with passion about states' rights. Given his experiences, states' rights to Dr. King meant only one thing: code words for segregation.

The Bureau was J. Edgar Hoover, and Hoover had put himself on record as favoring states' rights. So, Dr. King had concluded, Mr. Hoover in many ways runs a great agency, but he is not somebody WE can depend on. He did not look to the FBI for protection or justice, he said. He was particularly rough on the agents in Mississippi. At that time he considered them, at best, an extension of the kind of Mississippi troopers Dr. King and other blacks knew too well, the lawmen who made night rides and belonged to the Klan and took part in violence outside the law themselves.

That night in Birmingham he made clear to me that he feared the FBI was acting as a pipeline to Connor and the Birmingham police. I didn't think so. My impression was that the word had filtered from Hoover himself for the agents on the scene to observe, and to record whatever they saw and heard.

But this surveillance was what really galled Dr. King and his men. That the FBI stood around, as they put it, and took notes while a local lawman, for no cause, reached out and grabbed a black man by the nape of the neck in an alley and beat the living hell out of him. Dr. King asked how that could be allowed. The FBI side was: Yes, that is an offense, but not a federal offense. The civil rights laws were later changed to cover some such acts, but back then the FBI contended that it had no jurisdiction. The FBI insisted it was not a national police force.

In theory, the basis for an argument existed. But emotionally King and his people were having none of such reasoning.

It was certainly true that FBI agents were crawling all over Birmingham, and they were taking copious notes. At breakfast one morning I spotted a fellow circling the tables. I knew him to be an agent and I learned later that he was posing as a magazine writer. One morning he sat down at my table and I thought to myself, well, here's the FBI man and he's doing his job.

He began to make conversation and I cut him off. "I don't intend to give you any information," I said. "None at all. No offense. I understand what you're doing, but I know it's better for me and probably better for you if I just tell you that I'm a reporter. I don't pass on information about Dr. King and what his people are doing to the law, and I don't pass on to Dr. King what the law is doing."

More often than not, Dr. King was counseling restraint to the younger members of his group. He felt strongly that there was a certain pace, a certain rhythm, to the movement. If you pushed too hard, too fast, the effort could be counterproductive. This was not a speech he gave in public. But he said it privately many times.

Hosea Williams, who had spent a lot of bad time in jail in Savannah, was one who made clear that he wanted to push harder and faster than Dr. King was willing to go. With others, such as Andy Young and Julian Bond, the feeling was less strong, but even they sometimes grew impatient.

Dr. King was, of course, a powerful orator. Nothing new or original in that statement. But given his reputation as a public speaker, I still question whether his ability to reach really deep down inside people was fully understood. That is a reporter's assessment; not what he did to me but what I saw him do to a crowd. Okay, you might say, sure, the blacks, what did you expect? But people are people. I know a first-rate orator when I see and hear one. And Dr. King was among the best of our time, beyond question. For among other reasons, he could weave his spell with groups both small and large. And he was no demagogue, pandering to the differences in people.

I have observed speakers who were marvelous in front of large groups. But the smaller the crowd, the more naked they stood. King's nationwide reputation as an orator was made during the march on Washington, where he delivered his "I Have a Dream" speech. I never felt that was his best oration. I had heard King when I thought he was in higher form. Anyone who covered him had.

But that speech, carried in full on television, made him. Before that most of the country had heard Dr. King, if at all, only in fifteen- or thirty-second film clips on the evening news. He sometimes came across in that form as shrill, just another black revivalist.

Like many orators, Dr. King needed time to warm up. It was not unusual for him to speak for one, even two hours at a stretch. He wasn't Castro-esque nor like Khrushchev, speaking for seven hours or more at a whack. But you only had to hear him once or twice to know that this was a man of special gifts. If you could set aside his cause, set aside your own attitudes, and just listen, you realized his power.

He was, at bottom, a great preacher. I have in my time sat through a good many sermons, some in the line of duty. When Dr. King came in to deliver the sermon on a Sunday morning he was superb. Not as good as his father, mind you, but superb.

He had all the techniques, the whole repertoire, the thunder, the hush, the lilt. He knew when to let the voice build to a crescendo, when to let it fall and build again. He had a well-honed ability to size up an audience, to know what message he could get across and how. He could incite people, if he chose, and his enemies often accused him of whipping crowds into a frenzy. But much more often, Dr. King was cooling things off. He was a force for restraint.

In view of the disclosures that pelted the news throughout 1975-1976, many of Dr. King's suspicions of the FBI evidently were justified. It would be difficult, I think, to overstate his suspicions. As for the now infamous "bedroom" tapes that purport to expose Dr. King in a series of —in the Victorian term—compromising positions, I heard the first of them in 1964. I doubted their authenticity then and still do.

The fact is, I know nothing of Dr. King's sex life, didn't want to know then and don't want to know now. The subject is not one I have any taste for, and I consider the tapes largely the product of Hoover's warped feelings about Dr. King.

I happened to hear another reporter talking one day about "the tape." I said that I had never heard of its existence and that nothing in my experience, my contacts with King, would lead me to believe that such activities could have happened. This reporter, safe to say, was not an admirer of King. He was pleased to accept anything about him that was derogatory.

I was not exactly rising to the defense of King. I simply said, "Let's not talk from emotion. Let's talk about facts." I said flatly that I did not believe the tape existed.

The next day he brought a copy around and with some gleefulness played it. I asked where the tape came from, and he said from another reporter, and that reporter had gotten it from another. About a third of the way through I just said, "Shut it off."

The tape was so completely repulsive that I could tolerate no more, and I'm not being pious. I will say this. I fault myself for not following up on what was a valid story—true or not. The source should have been tracked. It developed, at the least, that the FBI distributed and may even have manufactured the tape.

I don't know that the tape was a fake. But it would have been easy enough to do; certainly, if you wanted to discredit someone as badly as Hoover did Dr. King. The sad fact is that, although J. Edgar Hoover was a religious and a moral man, he had a racist strain in his character. As Ramsey Clark once put it, "He was very emotional about communism and sex and King." From the outset Dr. King believed himself to be a target of the FBI. But he did not have a deep-rooted distrust of all whites, as some of those around him did. He certainly did not feel hatred. More than that, his basic philosophy was to see each individual as a human being.

He could give you a very nice little sermonette about that idea, and he practiced it. He attempted not to generalize about whites, not even southern whites. But he would talk about specific people. He would talk about Bull Connor. He saw him as "just a big, ill-tempered pit bulldog, attacking whatever came into his pit. We knew what he was. We simply had to decide whether to stay out of his pit."

Dr. King had a talent for character exposure. A new reporter would come onto the beat, say, with the look and sound of a rural southern redneck. I found myself saying, Boy, I don't know about this one and, lo and behold, I would see Dr. King take to him right away. I would wonder if the Reverend might not be letting himself get taken. But, always, the fellow would turn out to be straight as a flagpole.

I remember a specific case. Sims Fentress, a reporter now with *Time* magazine, had a style and an approach that was down-home country, and he never apologized for it. Dr. King recognized instantly that beneath that drawl was a complete professional.

The reverse of that was a sound man for another network, who at night would start working on a six-pack of beer. Before long he would trot out his standard speech about what dupes the rest of us were, how Martin Luther King was a hypocrite and possibly a Communist, who didn't believe in what he was doing. "And, if I wasn't making twenty-five grand a year, I'd blow the whistle on the black s.o.b."

Even before I met this fellow or the rest of us knew what his inner feelings were, Dr. King, whose radar seemed to be scanning all the time, had picked up a blip. He avoided that crew whenever he could and, in their presence, never took his eye off that individual.

About national figures Dr. King's opinions were not always predictable. During those months in the South we talked often about President Kennedy. His basic feeling was that John Kennedy had intelligence, and he admired that quality. "But about the subject at hand," he would say, meaning desegregation, "he is still in the learning process." He thought JFK wanted to do the right thing, but did not have a good feel for how difficult it would be. He was critical of the President for making deals with southern politicians. Dr. King knew what was happening. He knew that Kennedy needed to get certain bills through Congress, and many of those bills depended on a chairman who was southern, though not necessarily a segregationist. Still, tradeoffs could be made, and were, shortly after Kennedy came to office.

I marked well one night in 1962 when Dr. King said to me that, in purely political terms, President Kennedy had "almost missed the boat." And he explained: The time for reform in civil rights had long since come and gone. But reform was going to happen, one way or another. Politically, President Kennedy was either going to attach himself to the rightness of the cause or he was not. He did, but just barely in time to take credit for any progress. In 1963 King thought the President went to greater lengths than he should have in trying to deal with Ross Barnett, then the governor of Mississippi. He thought that was a shameful thing to do, that Kennedy's position should have been: where human dignity was concerned, *no deals*.

At the same time, Dr. King did not admire, and was suspicious of, the Vice-President, Lyndon Johnson. In our conversations he kept coming back to Johnson's votes in the Senate. He understood a lot of them, he said, but the poll-tax vote disconcerted him. Johnson had voted to continue the poll tax; later he developed a long, tortuous explanation of how that vote was not really in favor of the poll tax. But Dr. King was having none of that disavowal.

But even before Johnson became President, Dr. King said that he believed racial harmony had a better chance of being achieved first in the South. And that conviction was the one thing Dr. Martin Luther King and George Wallace shared in common. He, Dr. King, would dispassionately analyze the problems in places like Boston and Detroit, and he could see peaceful integration in the South long before it came to those places.

The fact was, in most southern towns and small cities, the people knew each other as people. They might not always see each other as equals, but they recognized each other, their families, the land, where they lived. In the North they did not.

He did tell me once that Johnson might be on the wrong side of the problem but he at least understood the issue. Dr. King did not feel comfortable with Johnson as the person to solve that problem, or to give Kennedy advice on how to resolve it. I might add he had an exaggerated idea of Johnson's influence on Kennedy. He was also suspicious of Johnson's ties with Congress, where Johnson had dealt so long with those same committee chairmen Dr. King distrusted.

But after Johnson became President, Dr. King was pleased, and mildly surprised, that he made civil rights legislation his top priority. He praised Johnson for his action and also acknowledged that he had misjudged him in some ways. At the same time Dr. King was wise to the fact that Johnson, in view of where he was from and given his record on social legislation in the past, indeed had a chance to be a President of all the people.

I don't believe Dr. King had heroes or that he felt obligations. But he never underestimated an enemy. He considered George Wallace a very dangerous man. He said once, "Wallaceism is bigger than Wallace. But in a way we're fortunate." He feared Wallace, but in a grudging way respected him, because Wallace was on a platform shouting his beliefs.

He also recognized before almost anyone else that Wallace touched an emotion in people in a lot of places outside the South. In national political circles Wallace as late as 1962 was still perceived as a corn-pone, redneck big-man-in-Alabama but nowhere else. Dr. King realized even then that Wallace had the potential to touch a chord in people in Montana and California and Oregon and Pennsylvania. While others underestimated both Wallace and his sphere of influence, Dr. King saw that he had the tools of an effective orator. He said, "Wallace is smart enough so that he only gives three, maybe four speeches, but he polishes them. He doesn't have twenty-five or fifty. He just has four, but he works on them and hones them, so that they are little minor classics." Some of this has been said since then, but King was saying it in 1962.

At least Wallace was out in the open. The people who really worried King were those you never saw, who could pick up a telephone and talk to someone like Police Chief Pritchett, and no one would ever know. And they were not out there shouting at the rallies, shouting at Dr. King, "Nigger, go home." You never heard them or saw them, but they could manipulate the strings of power in a divided community.

One of those people Dr. King genuinely feared was Leander Perez, of Plaquemine Parish, in Louisiana. Perez controlled much more money than anyone realized, and his tentacles reached into a lot of places. Perez ran the parish, which was rich in oil and gas reserves. His title, I think, was County Commissioner, but he was the boss in the old, traditional fashion. A memorable photograph of Perez appeared on the front page of a New Orleans newspaper one day. Dr. King picked up the paper, but said nothing. He just put his finger on the picture, leaving me to wonder what he was thinking. Shown together were George Wallace, after his election victory as governor of Alabama, Ross Barnett and Perez. The three of them were attending some Mississippi function, possibly the swearing-in ceremony for Barnett. At the time they were three of the best known names among segregationists in the South. They were the "Never!" group. Only Bull Connor was missing and, in truth, he had the legend but never the power of the others.

I came to feel that I knew Martin Luther King, Jr., on personal terms. I did not consider myself, nor did I seek to be, one of his intimate friends. I felt about him as I do anyone I cover—a reporter needs that bit of air space. But after a time he tended to put you on a first-name basis.

He called me in Jackson the morning Medgar Evers was murdered. Evers, the field representative for the NAACP in Mississippi, was shot to death in front of his wife and children by a person who lay in the grass across the street from his home, picking him off with a high-powered rifle.

Through a set of circumstances I was the first reporter on the scene. One of the things Nelson Benton and Lew Wood and I had worked very hard to do was to build up a network of sources all over the South so we could anticipate events. We wanted people to call us and say, "It looks like real trouble is brewing here." This applied not only to civil rights stories. When you have a bureau in New Orleans (where we later consolidated two bureaus), with thirteen or fourteen states to cover, such a network was the only reasonable way to do business.

So I received a call within minutes after Medgar Evers had been shot. I may have known about the murder before the police, certainly not much later. At the time, we were in Tuscaloosa, Alabama, where George Wallace had been standing in the schoolhouse door. We chartered an airplane and in the wee hours of the morning flew into Jackson. We got there about dawn.

I met Charles Evers that morning in front of the home of his dead brother. No other reporters had arrived by the time I did my first radio report from a pay phone down the street from the Evers house. Most of the national news people were still in Tuscaloosa. When the word spread, they hustled down en masse.

Dr. King heard my radio broadcast. He had been in touch with other people by then and knew what the situation was. But he placed a call to me at the Sun and Sand Motel in Jackson, where the CBS crew sometimes stayed. We had driven directly from the airfield to the Evers home. It was late in the morning when I checked in. A message was waiting at the desk: "Volunteer called," and a number.

I had told King once how he could reach me if we ever needed to talk. Then I smiled, realizing how silly it was for Dan Rather to think that Dr. King would call him at all, but if he did so, to a motel in, say, Birmingham, how would it look if he left word: please have him return Martin Luther King's call. That wouldn't be too smart on anyone's part. So I said, "If you prefer, leave a message that Mr. Volunteer called."

The choice of code name was mine, I'm sure. I had reason to remember it later because after I had gone to the White House to cover LBJ I heard that same name on a White House squawk box. At the time Volunteer was the Secret Service code for Johnson, a device that could be used in, say, a motorcade route, over a low-band citizens radio, to let the press secretary know where the President was: "Volunteer is at Tenth and K." It was a way of not telling the whole world. Later it may have been the code name for Bill Moyers. But the first time I heard "Volunteer" paged at the White House my head spun around.

Dr. King wanted to know if there was any possibility that the police had been involved in the shooting. Not just the Jackson police, but any of the law agencies. I had to tell him that I surely didn't think so, but there was no way of knowing.

I had been to Jackson one other time, in 1958, when my brother, Don, a junior college All-American at Del Mar, appeared in an all-star football game. I drove my parents and my sister, Patricia, there to see Don play. Until the civil rights story brought me back, I hadn't been to Mississippi again, but I came to know the state well and to like it. Among other things I understood William Faulkner for the first time. I had tried many times to read him. I had a high school English teacher who tried to encourage me, but about three pages was as far as I could go at one gulp. I just couldn't fathom him. I thought to myself, these sentences are interminable.

In college, even with the urging of Hugh Cunningham, I had only been able to get through some of his short stories. But after spending some time in Oxford I went back to Faulkner, and I began to understand.

There were a substantial number of good people in Mississippi who knew what was right, but just had a very hard time, for a long while, speaking up and doing it.

Against that background, I did not often get angry. I like to think it is not in my nature. Also, like all reporters, I got close to an awful lot of tears and pain and injustice. If a reporter reacts to all he sees, he will stay angry most of the time. But the Medgar Evers case hit me harder than most things I had seen. For one thing, I was spending so much time away from home I was becoming increasingly concerned about my own children. I knew my absence wasn't good for them, for me, or for us as a family. It was straining my marriage.

Brutality and violence were not new to me. But this was different. Evers had been murdered on his doorstep. His children were desolated by what had happened. Here someone had lain in the grass, snakelike, across from a man's home, had waited for him to climb the steps to his porch and in front of his family had shot him in the back and then had slithered away. I felt great waves of anger. I also thought about how this despicable act must make the country look.

A man named Byron de la Beckwith was arrested, and later tried, twice, for the murder of Medgar Evers. Both trials resulted in hung juries so, in the eyes of the law, he was and is an innocent man, although there have been persistent reports that Beckwith went around the state boasting that he had killed Evers.

The day of his arrest the *Clarion Daily Ledger,* in Jackson, Mississippi, ran a headline that by any journalistic standard would have to be rated a classic. This was the same paper whose editors had said to me many times that the network coverage was unfair and unbalanced. I had acknowledged that no doubt it sometimes was.

Their headline that day read: "CALIFORNIA MAN ARRESTED IN EVERS KILLING."

Byron de la Beckwith, who was Mississippi to the core, had through an accident of his parents' travels been born in California. Understandably, the people at the *Ledger* had been hoping that the act had not been committed by a Mississippian. They resemble Texans; every state is prideful, but they are more so. In Mississippi tradition, they wanted to believe that decent men didn't go around shooting unarmed people in the back. You might shoot him in the front, but not in the back.

So when someone discovered that de la Beckwith's birth certificate listed California, the *Ledger* could not resist leaping on this geographic fluke.

There were other, less serious occasions when Dr. King called. At least once, he took issue with a story I had done. He wondered if pressure had been applied by one of our affiliate (southern) stations. He had appeared at a rally in Memphis, I believe, and his speech failed to make the Evening News. The call was not unlike those I would receive later from Lyndon Johnson, saying, "That was a helluva speech I gave tonight, had my wife and daughters watching to see it on the air and it didn't show up. Where was it? You trying to tell me something?"

The tone wasn't quite so strident with Dr. King. He was genuinely fearful that the southern affiliates could conspire to limit the coverage of the civil rights movement. He didn't say so in a heavy-handed way, but the message was there.

I told him, with conviction, "Dr. King, that is something you'll never have to worry about." The number of station managers who would attempt to exert that kind of pressure was small. More to the point, it was counterproductive. In that instance, though, I was able to explain to him the very reason the film didn't make the news. His speech was in the lineup early and got bumped by something that developed later.

Dr. King was a sociable man, his manner soft and easy. As a person, as a subject, as an influence on my career, I rate him in a very special category. I had never been forced to think much about civil rights and the black experience. At the time of Little Rock, in 1957, I was working in radio in Houston. I can recall having discussions with Bob Hart, then my boss, about the stories that were moving on the wire each day. I did not understand what was happening. The violence in Little Rock was inexplicable to me, other than in the context of high school kids getting into postgame football riots. I understood that kind of compulsive mayhem. But the bestiality, the depths to which some were willing to sink, I didn't know existed.

I was in the CBS studios in New York on April 4, 1968, the night the bulletin from Memphis hit the wire that Martin Luther King had been shot. I had long since left the civil rights beat, had served a turn at the White House, gone overseas, and covered the war in Vietnam.

But I remembered Memphis.

The instant someone tore the copy off the wire and read the paragraph out loud, I picked up the phone and dialed from memory the police station in Memphis. There wasn't time to look up the number or go through an operator. I harkened back to Dallas and Kennedy. The switchboard would be jammed almost immediately. I had to get and keep an open line, if I could.

A reporter half ran through the newsroom asking if anyone had any sources. I shouted back, "I'm on the line to the Memphis police now." The cop on the switchboard knew nothing. When I said, "This is Dan Rather, with CBS News, in New York," he almost hung up on me. He didn't want to be involved. New York. CBS. Red flags everywhere.

Finally he said, "I can't keep this line open. If you want to talk to someone, tell me now."

I said, "Give me the police chief."

"He's not here."

"Then give me homicide."

What went through my mind was this: If I could talk to someone who knew what had happened, I thought I could judge whether he was telling me the truth and how serious the situation was. The questions were like a stepladder. Was Dr. King seriously wounded? If so, was he critical? If critical, was he now dead? You ran it up just that way. The police-beat experience came into play automatically, like a computer tape activating.

I was switched to homicide. I identified myself. The cop at the other end said, "There is not a thing I can tell you."

I said, "I know that. But I only want to know one thing. Is he dead?"

He repeated, "There's not a thing I can tell you."

The second time he said that, I knew King was dead. I asked him to transfer me to the chief's office. A spokesman assigned to handle calls from the press got on the line. I told him, "I know Martin Luther King is dead and I simply need to verify that fact."

He said, "I'm not the one to verify it."

I said, "In that case I must ask you to deny it."

He said, very quickly, "I'm not denying it."

"Then it is true, I take it."

"You take it any way you want."

In the meantime I had obtained the name of the hospital from the officer in homicide, and I had another reporter contact the doctors. We soon verified that King was dead.

I walked over to Casey Davidson, who was helping supervise the newsroom. I said, "Casey, here's the situation: King is dead, but I don't think we ought to go with that as step one. You better prepare a bulletin though, because I'm telling you he's dead."

He asked me how I knew. I told him I had talked with two people at the police station, no denials. Another reporter had received the same response from the hospital. Casey started to turn to someone to ask them to prepare a standby bulletin—we had writers on duty for that sort of thing—but I said, "No, I'll write one." And I did, very straight:

> Dr. Martin Luther King, Jr., is dead.
> Dr. King was shot by an assailant, or assailants, at approximately 7:15 P.M. Eastern time tonight at a motel in Memphis.

We were the first to confirm on the air the death of the man who had led the battle to win the rights promised his people one hundred years before. He had died as many, including Dr. King, had expected he would.

Within hours we had swung into special coverage. Four of us teamed up to put the material together: Perry Wolff, later the executive producer of "CBS Reports"; Andy Rooney, a writer then, now known for his documentaries, and Charles Kuralt. We had interviews with Roy Wilkins and Whitney Young. We followed that portion with a long conversation about where the country seemed to be headed.

We had been through the civil rights movement, had seen the passage of an entire package of laws in 1965. Here it was three years later and seemingly nothing had changed. There were few answers that night. But it was one of those times when television gave you a sense that something has happened in the village. If you're alone at home, with your thoughts, you can turn on the TV, where you will hear and see other people discussing the crisis. Someone on that panel may put into words a thought close to what your own feelings are or may raise a question you need to weigh. You won't feel quite so alone. There is a sense of community.

When we came off the air at midnight I went straight to my room at the Tuscany Hotel. I did not fall asleep quickly. I went to bed thinking, here is the loss of a great leader, but more than that, here is the loss of a great resource for this country. Dr. King wanted to, could and did, communicate with whites. He could touch the white conscience without always, immediately, generating fear.

If one were to make a list of the important Americans of the twentieth century, not only would Martin Luther King, Jr., be on it, his name might lead it. Certainly, if the test of a man's greatness is in the changes he brought about, King would rank ahead of all the politicians of his time. Yet I am aware that among many young blacks, especially outside the South, Malcolm X might rate above him as a hero.

I met Malcolm X twice, did not know him, did not really cover him. But I never thought he was as radical, or as violent, as he was made out to be. He had a more cynical view of reality than Dr. King did. He was militant in his approach to the problems. There was acid in his language. In those ways, he was what many whites mistakenly thought they saw in Martin Luther King, Jr. The two men came out of starkly different environments. Malcolm X was a product of the ghetto, Dr. King the child of a church family.

But both died at the end of a gun.

By the fall of 1963, the education I had been getting, in human terms, Hughes Rudd had already been through. The civil rights story had become the whole thrust of what we were doing in the South. Rudd had moved to Chicago to get away from an assignment that had grown in pain and drudgery. But I woke up every morning in a new world.

When Hughes left Atlanta, CBS decided to consolidate that bureau and the one in Dallas. I was to head the new bureau and I decided to relocate it in New Orleans. At the time our Atlanta affiliate, strange as it seems now, did not carry the CBS Evening News. That omission could make a difference when we had to process and feed film to New York. I ruled out Dallas, at least in part, because it was beyond the range of where the real news was breaking. The story traveled, but mostly it followed Martin Luther King, and Dr. King was making his stand in Dixie.

Those were my thoughts as we began to reestablish our bureau in New Orleans, in November, 1963. I was still getting settled when the word came down from CBS that President Kennedy was planning a trip to Dallas.

Out-Take
4

FLASHBACK

On the morning after John Kennedy was nominated for President in 1960 I found myself in the basement of the Biltmore Hotel, in Los Angeles, nursing the only cup of coffee I would have for the next six hours.

I was there to cover the convention for Corinthian Broadcasting, and I had with me a cameraman named Bob Wolf, later the best police reporter I ever knew. All the news directors in the Corinthian chain were in Los Angeles that week, competing against one another and against every other reporter in the country. That competition, in microcosm, is how the business works.

Corinthian had brooded a while about whether to spend the money to send anyone from as far away as Houston. But they had, and Wolf was a good, workhorse guy to have along. At most local stations in those days you ran a one-man band. I had learned how to take a sound camera, set it up, turn it on, come around in front of it, do the interview myself, then turn the camera off, take it back to the station, process the film and edit it. I was never very good, but I had to do it. At the Democratic Convention I had the luxury of having Wolf with me. It was us against the world.

From the start our goal was to film an interview with the Democratic nominee. A local news director's getting any kind of an interview with a presidential candidate had to be considered a coup. Our man was John Fitzgerald Kennedy, forty-two, the young Massachusetts war hero who had upset the party pols.

Now, Wolf and I had no credentials other than the standard press tags, and try as we might, we could not get within a country mile of Jack Kennedy. It was Wolf who said, "You know, we can chase him all day but we're never going to catch him. What we're going to have to do is get in one place, just stay there like a duck blind, and hope he passes by."

I said, "That's good, very good. I believe you're right."

Corinthian had set up a booth in the basement of our hotel. Most of the larger news outfits did the same. Wolf said, "Our best bet is the basement. They've already held some news conferences down there. They might come through again. We'll just have to take a chance."

We were up at five the morning after the nomination. And we waited. And waited. Through lunch and into midafternoon. We didn't leave for Cokes or coffee or anything. We had positioned ourselves right at the corner where, if Kennedy was to appear, he would have to pass to get to the elevators. We mapped it out and there we made our stand.

The head of Corinthian Broadcasting in those days was Wrede Petersmyer, and he had walked in while we were setting up. He could observe us from the company booth across the way.

Sure enough, as luck would have it, the press office announced that the nominee was heading down to the basement for a news conference. So Wolf and I were winking at each other and dry washing our hands and thinking that it might really work, and that this might be our day.

Senator Kennedy swept into the room with a flotilla of security people surrounding him. It was just one great wave that simply washed past us. I stuck the microphone out and saw it knocked from my hand. Wolf turned on his camera and all he got was ceiling, arms and haircuts. Wolf, not a man of gentle tongue, cursed loudly. He actually took a swipe at two or three people and said, "You got in the way of my camera. You do that again and you'll be crippled for life."

Petersmyer was off to one side with a bemused look on his face. And Wolf said, "Boy, it would really be sweet if we could get this with Petersmyer standing there." It would be saying, yeah, it was well worth the money to send these two jokers out here. So Bob was determined that we hold our position and we did.

The press conference ended and back came the flotilla. What Wolf did was climb up on a high table and hand me a long microphone cord. This time we decided that we would make one move and go straight to Kennedy, rather than wait for him to turn the corner. And the plan worked. I just cut through the traffic and squeezed in front of him with a mike. The security people tried to brush us out of the way but Kennedy stopped.

We had our interview, one on one, with the Democratic nominee for President. Wolf was grinding away. You could hear Wrede Petersmyer a few feet away, saying, "Jeezus, great, great."

Just then the table collapsed under Wolf. He tumbled down, but he never stopped rolling the film and he motioned for me to go on as he regained his feet. It was not one of your classic, smooth interviews. The candidate stayed just long enough for me to ask if he planned to campaign in Texas. That was not as dumb a question as it may sound now, because the early thought was that Lyndon Johnson, as part of the ticket, would cover him there.

But Kennedy said indeed, he would. He thought the election would be close and he considered Texas a key state. And then the wave washed on.

Well, we were ecstatic. Wolf just jumped up and down with glee, and Petersmyer walked over and shook hands, saying, "Boy, there was a piece of work if I ever saw one."

No, it doesn't sound like great shakes now. But we were a couple of greenhorns, from a local station, beating the rest of the herd to an interview, on a hard news day, with the man who was going to be President. I can tell you how the other Corinthian news directors felt. They were saying to themselves, We've been had.

Years later I wished I had kept a clip of that film. What I wanted, of course, was the picture of myself with John Kennedy. But it was erased and reused, probably the next time the station covered a fire.

Chapter 5

DALLAS: ALL THE DOCTORS WERE BUSY

SOME JOURNALISTS tend to approach a major news story in the manner of an insurance adjustor after a fire. Winning, losing, tragedy, grief, courage, all become incidental to the job, ashes to be sifted later. This may not be an attractive quality, I suppose, but it is that way with some of us—perhaps stronger in my own case than most. Often it can be useful and to plead otherwise would be a deception.

This is why, in the midst of mourners, a reporter can feel his pulse race; why he will sometimes walk closer to the flames, so he may use the light; why he can look back on an instant of unmeasurable shock and think, Yes, I was lucky to have been in that place at that time. Emotions simply take up too much room and that point needs to be made now.

Until nearly the last moment I had not planned to be in Dallas at the break of noon on November 22, 1963. I had been asked only to set up the coverage—as chief of the new CBS bureau in New Orleans—for President Kennedy's pre-campaign swing through Texas. My first reaction was one of irritation. I was still struggling to get the bureau organized. The civil rights movement was exploding all around us. Now this. And it was mostly desk work: deciding how much coverage was needed, what resources to commit, arranging the lines and wires and labs that would enable the stories to move.

We had less than three weeks' notice when Ralph Paskman, the editor of CBS News, called from New York. Ralph was an early mentor of mine. Whatever protest I had hoped to make he brushed aside quickly. "I know," he said, "but you'll just have to do all that and this as well. We need your recommendations as fast as we can get them."

I quickly put my report together. The President's swing would take him through San Antonio, Houston, Fort Worth, Dallas and Austin. "This is not a routine trip," I said. "Not routine politically. Not routine in terms of security."

Paskman said, "You'll have to explain that to me, about the security." Ralph had been a reporter. He was aware that Dallas had been the scene of angry political incidents. His question was intended to draw me out. Whatever manpower CBS assigned to Texas would be based on his judgment.

So I reviewed the recent trouble signs: Adlai Stevenson had been spat upon in Dallas in October; even Lyndon Johnson had been brushed by a picket's sign. The John Birch Society flourished there. IMPEACH EARL WARREN bumper stickers were a big seller. And General Edwin Walker had recently moved to town and was a popular speaker at Right-wing rallies.

The President's advisors were known to be nervous about his visit to Texas. Some Dallas businessmen had urged him to postpone the trip until the temper of the city had cooled. But the 1964 election was less than a year away. Texas figured to be important, and Kennedy had fences to mend among the state's Democrats, notably among the supporters of Governor John Connally and those of Senator Ralph Yarborough, that rare species, an elected Texas liberal.

Dallas had been a tough town for the Kennedy-Johnson ticket. A strange town. A mixture of Texas crude and satin evening gloves. A Lincoln Continental town, with a raccoon tail flying from the antenna. A modern, handsome, yet angry and righteous town with a layered society—layers of politics, oil, banks and merchant princes. I had lived and worked there and you had to be blind not to know that Dallas had a character entirely its own.

Paskman agreed that we should lay on double coverage all over Texas and quadruple it in Dallas. He went to the top and fought for more people. When the President's party left Washington, CBS was staffed for the road as fully as a network can be without planning an invasion. Still, I do not mean to invest in this any mystic implications. We were preparing for the unexpected. An incident. A reaction. A story. We were not having visions.

But whatever was to happen in Dallas, I knew we would be in an un-usually good position to cover it. One factor was our connection with KRLD, one of our better affiliate stations, whose newsroom and film labs we would be using. I had worked out of there in 1962 when we established a Dallas office (later replaced, along with the one in Atlanta, by the central bureau in New Orleans).

After an uneasy start I had developed a good relationship with Eddie Barker, the news director at KRLD. Eddie's position was clear and, I thought, understandable. "Look," he said, "if CBS had to hire someone to run a Dallas bureau, I'm not saying I wanted the job, but I would have liked a howdy-do. And I didn't get it. I'm not going to cut you up or anything of that sort. But on the other hand, I'm not going to bust my butt for you or CBS."

To overcome that coolness required some effort, but we came to know each other, and by the time of the Kennedy trip those feelings were well behind us. That background needs to be explained here only because of what would come later, when everyone's patience snapped.

Once the coverage was organized, my time was my own. The camera crews had been assigned to certain points, the film drops had been set up along the motorcade route and the feed from the station (KRLD) to the network was arranged. Barker's people had handled those chores for CBS literally dozens of times and I knew there would be no problems. At that point I was not to be involved directly in the coverage of President Kennedy's arrival. My hope was to coast through a relatively low pressure day.

Someone, however, discovered that Friday—November 22, 1963—was the ninety-eighth birthday of John Nance Garner, the irascible Texan who won enduring fame by comparing the vice-presidency—which he held during FDR's first term—to "a pitcher of warm spit." So it was decided that I would fly that morning to the Garner ranch at Uvalde, Texas, and film an interview, then return to Dallas and feed the piece, with the rest of our coverage, to New York. We saw it as a light sidebar on what might otherwise be a day of heavy politics, the kind of story that might not even get on the air.

Miss Texas Wool was waiting on the veranda when Garner made his appearance shortly after breakfast. He had a shot of bourbon in one hand and he tried to pat Miss Texas Wool on the fanny with the other, as only Cactus Jack could do. And that was how I happened to be in Dallas at midmorning, delivering an interview we had filmed on the occasion of a former Vice-President's ninety-eighth birthday, the morning of the day that John F. Kennedy would be murdered.

Everything seemed under control when I walked into the newsroom at KRLD. Reporters Nelson Benton and Lew Wood had flown from the New Orleans office and we were all geared to go. Then at the final moment I discovered that one of our film drops was still uncovered: the last one on the parade route. The President's motorcade would end at a railroad overpass just beyond an old brick building with a name no one knew—the Texas School Book Depository. The caravan would then turn onto the Stemmons Freeway, pick up speed and continue to the Trade Mart for a luncheon speech.

So our last film drop was to be staked out just on the other side of the overpass, and we were short a man to staff it. And I said, well, what the hell, I'm not doing anything, I'll go over. I made sure the Garner film was in the processor, then checked the phone lines: the open one to New York and another to the Trade Mart, where Eddie Barker was standing by to cover the President's speech. Our plan was to feed the picture to New York, where the decision would be made to transmit live to the country or edit the speech for use later.

While that was going on, others would be bringing in the film that had been dropped off along the motorcade route. From that point on, my job, basically, would be to edit film, which would be processed at KRLD, where another editor and I would put together the piece that Bob Pierpoint, then the White House correspondent, would narrate. Bob and I might never see each other, but it would be my responsibility to feed his work to New York.

Everything was ready. It was only a four-block walk to my post, so I picked up a yellow grapefruit bag and started out the door. I suppose I should explain about the grapefruit bag. It had two uses: one, to identify whoever held it as a CBS person, and two, to carry the bulky film cans when the cameraman tossed them off the truck as the motorcade rolled past. Grapefruit bags have the advantage of being both strong and colorful.

Now, this is not the type of assignment a correspondent usually craves, but at least it was outdoors. The day had turned out well, sunny and balmy. Morning winds had driven away the clouds and the threat of rain. They wouldn't need the bubble top on the President's limousine.

I picked out my spot on the other side of the railroad tracks, beyond the triple underpass, thirty yards from a grassy knoll that would later figure in so many conspiracy theories. I stood and waited, clutching my yellow grapefruit bag, feeling a little silly. I checked my watch. It was nearly

12:30 P.M., the time the President was due at the Trade Mart. The motorcade was running late.

Time is always the enemy in this business. We had a slight margin under the original plan, but now the deadline was going to be tight. We were an hour behind New York and there would be the usual pressure to feed early, allowing more time to edit and write lead-ins at their end. I would be looking for Tom Craven, Jr., a cameraman I barely knew.

Suddenly I was aware that a police car had passed me, taking the wrong turnoff, going like hell. Then I thought I saw the presidential limousine pass, a 1961 Lincoln, a blur. But I did not see the President. I thought I picked out Mrs. Kennedy. And Governor Connally. Or had I? The motorcade, or what was left of it, continued toward the Trade Mart.

I had not heard a shot. I was only vaguely aware of the hustle and bustle and noise and confusion taking place somewhere behind me. None of the scene came with any precision. All I had was this sense, an impression, of what I had observed—a police car, a limousine, then another limousine. One of them, I thought, was the President's. The rest of the motorcade was already in disarray. Something had happened. But what?

Among the first lessons I learned in journalism, as taught by Hugh Cunningham, at Sam Houston State, had been: No story is worth a damn unless you can get it out. In that moment when the universe was about to be rearranged, I had a flashback to freshman journalism. It is, of course, an axiom of the trade. And that thought flashed through my mind: This is a bad place for me to be.

I had to hotfoot it back to the station. Whatever had happened, if anything, I was doing no one any good standing there with my yellow grapefruit bag. The five blocks back to KRLD seemed longer now, but I started off at a full run. I knew the neighborhood, and I could be there in a matter of minutes.

I topped the railroad grading a few yards away and paused long enough to shade my eyes and look for the camera truck. It was nowhere in sight. (In those days the truck often traveled well back in the motorcade; because of Dallas, it now usually travels in front.) The moment I cleared the railroad tracks I saw a scene I will never forget. Some people were lying on the grass, some screaming, some running, some pointing. Policemen swarmed everywhere and distinctly, above the din, I heard one shout, "DON'T ANYBODY PANIC." And, of course, there was nothing but panic wherever you looked.

Perhaps I should have stopped and taken out my notebook, grabbing people and asking questions. But I needed only five seconds to make up my mind to hustle back to the station. I ran every step. When I literally blew into the newsroom the place was still calm, the office force unaware that anything had gone wrong.

I headed straight for the open line to the Trade Mart. As I did I yelled out, "Turn up the volume on every radio you got, all of them, state police, local police, sheriff's department. Get 'em up, high." Nothing had flashed yet but all of the police bands were becoming busy. I could hear Eddie Barker from the Trade Mart, asking, "Where's the motorcade? They're running late. What's happened?"

"Eddie, this is Dan," I said. "I think something happened out there. And I think it's bad."

He said, "So do I. We're picking up a lot of funny talk on the radio. The cops are all asking each other what the hell is going on."

Bill Cevarha, the station's assistant news director, immediately began moving all of his reporters to the shooting scene.

By now it was total confusion on every radio. I kept hearing numbers and codes. I knew enough of them from my days as a police reporter to pick out pieces of what they were saying. One officer told another to "cool it" and switch to a nonpublic channel. Then I caught a reference to Parkland Hospital. Instantly, I looked up the number and dialed it. The switchboard jammed almost immediately. I sensed at the time that I was lucky to get through. The operator wasn't hysterical, or panicky, but she was clearly busy.

I found myself blurting out that I was a reporter and *don't hang up on me.* I got that out right away. She cut me off and said, "The President has been shot. I don't know anything else." I repeated myself. "Please, don't hang up. You say the President has been shot. Are you certain of that?"

She said, "That's what I've been told. I don't know anything else."

I said, "Is there anyone around, anyone else who can talk to me? Is a doctor around?"

She said, yes, hold on, and the next thing I knew a male voice was on the line.

"Sir, are you a physician?" I asked.

"Yes, I am."

"The lady on the switchboard says that the President has been shot and I'd like to verify that with you."

"Yes," he replied, "the President has been brought in and it is my understanding that he's dead. But I'm not the person to talk to about it."

I said, "Would you repeat your name for me, Doctor?"

He said, "I'm not the person you need to talk with," and there was a click on the line.

I dialed right back, and as I did I shouted to the people in the newsroom, "He's been shot." I didn't add that a doctor at Parkland Hospital had told me he was dead. If you have covered enough police beats and emergency rooms, you tread very gently with that kind of information. At the moment the fact that the President of the United States had been shot was compelling enough. A reporter learns not to jump too fast.

Two dials and I was able to get through the switchboard a second time, and again I blurted out the words, "Please, don't hang up on me. I'm a reporter with CBS and this is very important. I have been told that the President has been shot. I must verify that. Is there anyone there who can?"

She said, "All the doctors are busy. There is great confusion here. But what you heard, yes, I believe that is correct."

I said, "Is there anyone in authority who will talk to me?"

She was losing her patience. "Don't you understand? All the doctors are busy!" There was a pause, then she lowered her voice and said, "Two Catholic fathers are standing here in the hall."

I said, "Would you ask one of the priests if I might speak to him?" There was a mumbled conversation in the background, then a man's voice came on the phone.

I said, "Father, the operator tells me you just happened to be there. I'm Dan Rather, with CBS News, and I'm trying to confirm whether the President has been shot."

With a matter-of-factness that stunned me he said, "Yes, the President has been shot and he is dead."

I said, "Are you certain of that?"

He said, "Yes, unfortunately, I am," and he left the phone.

I cannot tell you what I thought at that moment. Certainly, this was no time to measure the magnitude of what had happened or to reflect on the insane chance that had caused it to happen at that time, and in that place. I only knew that a tumultuous few minutes had passed since I began my four-block run from behind the grassy knoll. On the United Press International news wire the first words of a bulletin dictated by Merriman Smith had clattered out to the rest of the world:

DALLAS, NOV. 22 (UPI)—THREE SHOTS WERE FIRED AT PRESIDENT KENNEDY'S MOTORCADE TODAY IN DOWNTOWN DALLAS.

The time was 12:34 P.M. Exactly five minutes later another flash interrupted the flow of teletype copy.

KENNEDY SERIOUSLY WOUNDED PERHAPS FATALLY BY ASSASSIN'S BULLET

Meanwhile I was on the phone to Eddie Barker at the Trade Mart, comparing notes. Quickly, I told him what I had. What did he think? "Look," he said, "I'm here with the chief of staff of Parkland Hospital. He tells me the President has been shot and he is dead."

At 12:41 P.M., the UPI updated its original bulletin:

DALLAS, NOV. 22 (UPI)—PRESIDENT KENNEDY AND GOV. JOHN B. CONNALLY OF TEXAS WERE CUT DOWN BY AN ASSASSIN'S BULLETS AS THEY TOURED DOWNTOWN DALLAS IN AN OPEN AUTOMOBILE TODAY.

At the other end of the telephone line in New York at least three people, maybe more, were listening in. They were waiting for the words that would be reported over CBS radio to whatever audience was out there, already petrified with disbelief. These seconds were critical. Television was already on the air, live, with Walter Cronkite talking in cautious, deliberate, qualified, hopeful terms.

I was plugged into three or four lines at once. Eddie Barker was talking into one ear. A few feet away I could see Cronkite on the television screen, his face just beginning to show anguish. Then, very sharply, someone on the New York radio desk said, "Dan, quickly, tell me exactly what has happened."

I thought I recognized three other voices in the background—Hal Terkel, Marian Glick and Mort Dank. All three were veteran editors. Each had been on the other end of telephone conversations with me dozens of times before in difficult story situations: riots in Birmingham, Meredith at Ole Miss, the murder of Medgar Evers. They knew my day-to-day work as well as anyone in the company. Perhaps better.

In one of my ears, Barker was repeating what the Parkland Hospital official had told him at the Trade Mart.

I was trying to watch and listen to many things at once. My mind was racing, trying to clear, trying to hold steady, trying to think ahead.

When Barker said again that he had been told the President was dead, I said, "Yes, yes. That's what I hear, too. That he's dead."

A voice came back, "What was that?" I thought it was Barker again.

It wasn't. The "What was that?" had come from a radio editor in New York. I responded to what I thought was Barker with "I said that's my information, too. That he's dead."

The radio editor shot back, "Did you say 'dead'? Are you sure, Dan?"

"Right, dead. The President definitely has been shot and I think he is dead," I said, still believing I was talking all the while to Barker. "That's the word I get from two people at the hospital."

I said it unemotionally. Thinking back, I could have, *should* have, exercised more care. I am, to this day, sensitive and questioning of myself about what followed.

It was now just past 12:16 P.M. by the clock. The first wire service details, suggesting strongly that the President had not survived, wouldn't move for another few minutes. At that point I heard what my mind then recognized clearly as someone in New York announce around the radio desk, "Rather says the President is dead."

I don't believe I gasped when it was said. There wasn't time.

The next sound I remember hearing was the silence of CBS radio, then the voice of Alan Jackson saying, "The President of the United States is dead," and the playing of "The Star Spangled Banner." CBS had an entire standby procedure for such emergencies. Radio had gone to it.

I began shouting into the phone to New York, shouting that I had not authorized any bulletin or any other kind of report.

Confusion burst anew. I was told that I had said not once but twice that Kennedy was dead. Now it came through to me: those weren't Barker's questions I had been answering.

I felt a chill. It dawned on me that it was possible I had committed a blunder beyond comprehension, beyond forgiving. I raced through my own mental checklist. What did I have? Well, I had a doctor at the hospital who said the President was dead. A priest who said, definitely, he was dead. And the hospital's chief of staff, who had told Eddie Barker he was dead.

If you were working the cop shop in Houston, Texas, at Number 61 Riesner Street, what you had was a dead man. But this was the President of the United States. It was a story no one wanted to believe, and you couldn't take it back. If I had been given, say, two seconds to think about it, if someone had asked, "Do you want us to announce that the President is dead and play the national anthem?" I would have said, whoa, better run that past someone else.

It has never been clear exactly how, and by whom, the signal was given to announce the bulletin and play the anthem. Months later, Mort Dank told me, "None of us were ever sure ourselves."

But if there was any blame to fix, it was mine. The anthem was playing and now the executive editors, Ernie Leiser and Don Hewitt, came on the line, wanting to clear the air for television. "Have they announced it?" Leiser asked.

"No," I said. "Let me make that clear. They have not announced it."

"But is it true?"

"Yes, I believe it to be true."

"How do you know?"

I went through the numbers for Leiser and Hewitt. By this time Barker was back on the other line from the Trade Mart, urging New York to break the story on TV. He was steadfast about it. "I know it's the President," he said. "I know what reservations you have. But I tell you, sadly, it's true. And waiting won't change it." But New York wouldn't go. Not on television. Not immediately.

Even if you are right (and, parenthetically, God help you if you are wrong) you are not going to go with a story of that proportion as confidently on television as you would on radio. It is just the different intensity of the two mediums, the size of the audience, the weight of the news.

On radio we had a beat of seventeen minutes on the other networks. Under the circumstances whether that mattered, whether that was important, whether it was worth the pangs of later conscience, is a valid point to argue. Certainly, being first is at the heart of how news is gathered and reported. But I couldn't answer the question completely then and can't now.

A little after 1 P.M., a surgeon named Malcolm Perry walked helplessly away from an aluminum table and another doctor drew a clean white sheet over the body that was on it. The official announcement was made to the press at 1:33 P.M., Dallas time, by Malcolm Kilduff, the assistant press secretary. More than half an hour had passed since CBS radio reported the death of the President. It does not take much imagination to know what was going through my head most of that time. I knew if the story was wrong I would be seeking another line of work. Rightfully so. I also knew that I wasn't wrong.

Over the years I have batted around the moral and professional conflicts we encountered that day with many people. One friend, CBS vice-president Bill Leonard, has said to me a number of times, "I thought so then, I have thought so since and I think so now, we were too quick to go."

One large part of my journalistic heart says he is right. The other side says, "Yes, he is right—in theory." But this wasn't theory. It was real. All of us did the best we could during those pressurized minutes. And we proved to be accurate and first on one of the biggest stories of our time.

A reporter trains himself, works a lifetime and prays to be on-the-line when a story of that magnitude breaks. If such an event *has* to happen, one hopes to be there, and to handle it well.

All of us at CBS have had years to second-guess ourselves. Many of us emerged with a special pride in how we worked as a team that day. There were, of course, lessons to be learned. The imperfection of the telephone as an instrument of communication, for example. The importance of repeating and emphasizing key words, even in so-called "back channel" communications between reporters and editors. But the most important lesson may have been this:

There is something that kicks over inside you—like the omni on an airplane where you switch on the remote control—on a certain kind of story that causes the adrenalin to pump so strong you are acting almost purely by instinct, by training. Whatever your field, whether a surgeon or a plumber or a steeplejack, when the moment comes you do those things you are trained to do automatically.

I was struck later by the fact that even as his hands first probed the awful wounds of the body of John Kennedy, Dr. Perry said he was thinking, He's bigger than I thought he was. A personal observation? Or medical? Or both? We think, we work, on more than one level.

At no time did we stop and tell ourselves, in some smaller way what we said and what we did would become a part of the history of that week. The button is pressed: you hotfoot it back, you open the phone lines, make the calls, ask the questions, trace and retrace, and someone is in your ear saying, "The President has been shot and is dead." A desk assistant turns to an editor and before you know it, the news has gone out. You can't call the story back but you think about it.

I would like to be able to say this with some delicacy, without sounding callous or unmoved. I am not attempting to write another account of the death of a President. I am not trying to touch again those emotions that have been so squeezed and massaged and stroked and fanned so many times since. I only want to give, as fairly as I can, my reaction to the events around me; in this case the story of how that story was observed and reported and retold.

What I kept thinking was this: We are ahead on the story. I wasn't yet considering the human and national tragedy behind it. Right or wrong, I was thinking about the story.

One after another, more developments were pouring in; bulletins were literally going off like flashbulbs.

Governor John Connally, who had been sitting in a jump seat opposite the President, was wounded. A bullet had penetrated his chest and wrist and lodged in his thigh. He was in surgery. The wound was serious, but not fatal.

An early report that Lyndon Johnson had suffered a heart attack was quickly established as false. The Vice-President had walked into Parkland Hospital behind the aluminum litters carrying Connally and the already dead John Kennedy. He held his right arm over his chest. Some reporters recalled that a massive heart attack had felled Johnson in 1955. But not this time. The gesture was an involuntary one. The pain he felt wasn't physical.

Within minutes after the shooting the Dallas police had sealed off the Texas School Book Depository. At 1:15 P.M., fifteen minutes after the President had been pronounced dead, a patrolman named J. D. Tippit spotted a man whose description had been broadcast, an employee missing from the warehouse. They were two miles from the scene of the assassination. The man was on foot, walking along Tenth Street, between Denver and Patton. He had on a thin, light-colored jacket.

Tippit stepped out of his squad car to question him. The man pulled a gun and fired three shots. The officer was dying as he hit the ground.

Six blocks away, inside the Texas Theater, alerted by a salesman who worked at a shoe store across the street, the police swept in, looking for the gunman. He was sitting in a section halfway down, in the middle of an aisle, when they found him. He jumped up and drew, but his gun misfired and five policemen swarmed all over him.

The manager of the theater had brought up the houselights and stopped the movie. It was entitled, *War Is Hell.*

The time was 1:45 P.M. By two o'clock reporters were told that a suspect in the murders of John F. Kennedy and patrolman J. D. Tippit had been taken into custody. His name was Lee Harvey Oswald, twenty-four, born in New Orleans, a high school dropout and ex-marine who had been court-martialed twice.

Investigators soon discovered that Oswald had a Russian wife, had lived in Moscow and was a professed Marxist. Fear and suspicion in Dallas had centered on the Right wing and would continue to haunt the city. But Lee Harvey Oswald, a chronic failure all his life, five foot six, with a small, petulant face and the charm of a ferret, was at the other end of the political spectrum.

Within an hour of the arrest the police disclosed that a paraffin test of Oswald's hands and face showed that he had fired a gun. Back at the school book building a rifle had been found. They were piecing together, they felt, an airtight case. The press wanted to know everything about Lee Harvey Oswald, and the Dallas police were eager to oblige.

Of course, there is no way to overstate this: there had not been a bigger story in the history of American television. And, really, wasn't this when all the craziness started? Dallas, Oswald, Ruby, Watts, Manson, Ray, Sirhan, Bremer, Vietnam, Watergate, FBI, CIA, Squeaky Fromme, Sara Moore . . . the endless lunatic newsreel.

And here it was happening in front of our eyes. Beginning at 1 P.M. that Friday, CBS went to continuous live coverage, around the clock. It would go on until Tuesday. All over the country people were sitting in their living rooms, stoned on tragedy, watching us do our work as reporters in a way they never had before, or since, or probably ever would again.

If you are a TV newsman, almost your first thought, your first instinct is: *film*. Was there film? Within the first three hours after the shots were fired, it was obvious that CBS had no usable film from the motorcade. From what we could establish quickly, neither did anyone else, partly because of the shadows and the hook turn right at the scene. So we started a search for anybody and everybody who might have been there carrying an eight-millimeter camera.

Eddie Barker's people began calling all over Dallas. And slowly we picked up a trail. Someone had seen a man standing at a certain spot. Someone else thought he was in the retail clothing business (wholesale, it turned out). We ran our leads through the FBI and the Dallas police. Finally we had a name: Abraham Zapruder. This heavyset man, in his fifties, kind face with skin the color of oatmeal, was to become one of history's great accidents.

When we reached him Zapruder did not know what he had. We

didn't either, but we helped arrange for Eastman Kodak to process the film. This job had to be done by the best equipment. It had to be done fast. And it had to be kept confidential.

By Saturday morning Zapruder had put himself in the hands of a lawyer. This, I thought, could be trouble. But I was keeping New York advised and I kept insisting, "Look, it's his film, and if he has anything at all, we have got to have it."

No one disagreed. My instructions were, one, to get a preview of the film, and two, bring it back to the station if I could. All sorts of crude ideas rushed through my mind. What if he gave it to NBC? What if he sold it to someone else? Our office—that mixture of CBS and KRLD crews —had done the legwork that turned up Zapruder. We had helped get the film processed. I felt we had at least a claim to it. For a moment I thought, if I have to, I'll just knock him down and grab the film, run back to the station, show it one time and then let him sue us.

Later someone at the network suggested half jokingly, but only by half, that I should have done just that. But I walked over to the lawyer's office to hear the ground rules, and the first person I saw there was Dick Stolley, then with *Life* magazine (now the managing editor of *People*). My heart sank. My hope had been that no one else had yet run across Zapruder. But here was Stolley, a tough and experienced competitor as I knew from past contacts on the civil rights story. What was more, *Life* had a reputation for paying big.

The lawyer laid out the ground rules for us: He had set up a projector in a private room. You went in, looked at the film one time, took no notes, came out and gave him your bid. I was already saying to myself, the bid comes second. The first thing I am going to do is look at the film, then knock the hinges off the door getting back to the station and describe what I had just seen. Then, and only then, would we get into the bidding.

Which is exactly what I did. I stepped into the room, did not even sit down, looked at the film one time, hooked it out of there and fled back to the station. Of course, I had told the lawyer as I left that I had no authority to make an offer. I would have to consult with CBS News executives in New York. And I extracted a promise, I thought, to withhold any decision until I could get back to him.

Keep in mind that no other newsman, at that point, had seen the film. My television competitors were not even there. Meanwhile, on all three networks, the coverage was nonstop.

Within seconds after I walked into the studio I was on the air, describing what I had just observed. To this day it is one of the chores of that day I remember most.

Having seen the film once, I had to describe it in detail, live, on television, while millions watched. Given the circumstances I would like to think my description was good. Regrettably, it was not without error, in terms of what was unsaid about the movement of the President's head. A few who have tried to sell themselves as assassination experts misused that account to build a false premise.

It is gruesome even now, and always will be, to talk about this scene, but the single most dramatic piece of the film is the part where the President's head lurches slightly forward, then explodes backward. I described the forward motion of his head. I failed to mention the violent, backward reaction. This was, as some assassination buffs now argue, a major omission. But certainly not deliberate.

At the risk of sounding too defensive, I challenge anyone to watch for the first time a twenty-two-second film of devastating impact, run several blocks, then describe what they had seen in its entirety, without notes. Perhaps someone can do so better than I did that day. I only know that I did it as well and as honestly as I could under the conditions.

But here is where the case gets tricky. Years later, a group of assassination buffs took an audio tape of my description of what I saw in the office of Zapruder's lawyer and laid it over the film *as a narration*. So the impression was given that Dan Rather was part of the conspiracy. Either that or he was a Communist dupe, or something, how else could he have seen the film, etc., etc.

There remain, of course, many questions about the death of John Kennedy. With responsible people asking serious questions, I have little argument. Certainly, some of the assassination buffs are responsible people. Some got into the chase for their own ego trips, others for publicity or money, some for a combination of both.

Even now I would not object to anyone's saying, this is the way Dan Rather described the Zapruder film after seeing it once, *that* weekend, without notes, in Dallas. And here is what the film actually shows. Conclusion: Dan blew a piece of it.

For the record, at the time that was not the omission that concerned me. I had described the film once when an editor in New York asked me to do another take. They were just not comfortable with a reference I had made to Mrs. Kennedy's getting out of the car. I said, it was unclear, no one could tell from that distance and in the brief amount of time that elapsed why she had climbed onto the trunk of the car. I laid out three possibilities. One could only guess whether she was trying to go for help, whether she was fleeing and trying to get out, or attempting to help the Secret Service agent get in.

At the other end of the phone in New York the editor, a friend of mine, said, "Dan, we think you need to do it again."

I said, "No, I don't have time. I want to get back over to the lawyer's office and see the film again. We still have to make a bid."

"This once," he said, "do yourself a favor. We're going to do it again and we'll make it quick. But leave out the part about her trying to flee."

I said, "You've got to be kidding." And I started to argue, "It doesn't reflect badly—"

He cut me off. "Look, I don't want to argue about it. You do what you want. But we're going to go again in ten seconds and my suggestion to you is that you leave it out this time."

I left out that reference. And I wished I had not.

But the story was gone. I paused just long enough to call the lawyer and tell him I was on my way, then rang New York back. I am not certain how many people were involved by now. Cronkite, Leiser, Blair Clark, possibly others. I told them, "It's up for bids and we have to bid now."

Someone asked me what I thought.

"Hell, I have no experience for this sort of thing," I said. "I've never bid on anything in my life."

It was decided that I should start at $10,000, for a one-time showing only. I would buy the whole rights if I could get them, but I was to go after a deal to show the film once, exclusively. Even before we finished talking, I was told that Don Hamilton from the business office was on his way to the airport to help me. I was to hold on, stall for time if I could.

When I returned to the lawyer's office I was in for another shock. The film, he said, had been sold to *Life.*

"What do you mean?" I shouted at him. "It was supposed to be up for bids. We haven't even put in our bid yet."

"*Life*'s bid was preemptive," he said.

"Now what the hell is that supposed to mean?"

"It was just a preemptive bid," he said, and he walked away.

I stood there, in the middle of his office, stunned.

Zapruder was sitting in a corner, confused but happy. He made a point of coming over to me. He didn't say he was sorry. Obviously, he was not. But he indicated to me that *Life* might have paid as much as $500,000 for the rights. I don't vouch for that figure, but it was certainly a great leap from the $50,000 the magazine later tried to suggest had been the final price.

I tried in an act of desperation to talk tough, which meant I raised my voice and paced back and forth and kept saying things to imply no deal existed since our bid wasn't heard. I remember, clearly, crying out there was an ethical problem here. Both Zapruder and his lawyer ignored me. *Life* had the film.

Later CBS offered to rent the film from its new owners for $100,000 for one showing that weekend, and were refused. They would not even entertain the idea. (In November, 1973, in a story for *Esquire* Magazine, Stolley wrote that *Life* had agreed at the Saturday meeting to pay Zapruder $50,000 for print rights only. The film was flown to New York and shown privately to the company's top executives. Upset by the head wound scene, they decided the film had to be kept off the air until emotions cooled. *Life* raised the figure on Monday by an additional $100,000 in return for *all* rights to history's most famous amateur movie.)

What was to happen in the years to come, none of us could have imagined. To begin with, in editing the film for use as still pictures, *Life* lost one frame. It was invaluable, of course. The bungle also fueled the assassination buffs, who asked, how could they have lost a frame? There were a thousand ways, actually. But what happened, I believe, was either through carelessness or bad luck.

The fact was, however, a frame *had* been lost, and when I first heard the news I was heartsick. I thought, my God, they have the only footage in existence and *this* is how they treat it. I knew how precious the film was. We had searched everywhere, in the days that followed, for anyone else who might have carried a camera. We ran down every clue. We had people assigned to it full time, for weeks. Nothing of real value turned up except a few snapshots.

What I did not know at the time was that *Life* no longer had the only copy in existence. Their security was so lax as to be almost comical. Any major executive in the Time-Life Building who wished to look at the Zapruder film could call down and order a print sent to his office.

For years it was not shown on television or in theaters. But, frequently, whenever a *Time-Life* wheel ordered up a print for himself, offhandedly or otherwise, several bootleg copies would be produced. An underground industry soon developed.

By 1972 bootleg copies of the film were appearing everywhere, under all kinds of weird circumstances. That year, while I was covering the Republican Convention in Miami Beach, the film was shown in a kind of carnival setting that became known as People's Park. One of our own staffers said to me one day, "How in the world could you have done 'The CBS Warren Commission Report' after seeing that film?"

This is jumping ahead of the story, of course, but this story has never moved in a straight line. CBS had spent roughly a half million dollars of their money and a year of my time on a show that set out to disprove the Warren Commission findings. And we could not do so. In fact, we came up with better evidence than the Commission that Oswald acted alone.

Some people said it was a whitewash. And some people are just not interested in the facts, one of which is this: What bigger story could I ever break than to show that a conspiracy did exist, and to disprove the Warren report?

But the challenge in my colleague's voice startled me and I said, "What the hell are you talking about?"

He said, "I've just seen a presentation of the film across the street, and so ought you. It'll change your mind, for damned sure."

We were so involved with working on the convention, I couldn't get away. So I sent someone who had worked with me on the investigation we had done. I was really concerned that evidence had turned up we had missed. But the film and voice narration had been edited, distorted, cut and reversed so that it amounted to an outright fiction to prove that eleven Cubans jumped out of a manhole cover to kill Kennedy. Or some other strangely concocted theory.

The point is, all those bootleg copies had gotten into circulation and were adding to the problem. Creating new ones, in fact. A good deal of that cynicism could have been eliminated, I always felt, if the public had been allowed to see the film soon after John Kennedy's death and in a clearer context. Sure, there will always be doubt, even among those who have tried to be reasonable about the conspiracy theories. The human mind loves a mystery even more than it craves a solution. But public disbelief was fed by not allowing the film to be shown on television, while it circulated on the fringe in a kind of dark, undercover spirit.

Perhaps no one could have shown the film, in decency, that weekend.

But it was kept off television for more than twelve years on the ground that the pictures were too gruesome for home viewing. The film *was* gruesome but, like war, it was reality.

There was a final irony to the Zapruder film. Henry Luce's lieutenants were so convinced they had bought and captured a piece of history—an investment that would pay and pay and keep on paying—they refused every offer to sell off any secondary rights.

And in 1975, Time, Incorporated, gave *back* to the Zapruder family the film and all claims to it, just to get out from under the burden ownership had become. They said, in effect, here, we don't want it anymore. It was as if, like the Hope diamond, some curse had attached to the film. And, in some ways, it had.

Out-Take

5

CHECKBOOK JOURNALISM

Such as they were, the negotiations for the Zapruder film represented my second major brush with what is now called Checkbook Journalism. I simply had not been exposed to this issue in the past, partly because none of the companies I had worked for had any money to pay anyone for what they knew.

But rare is the news organization or reporter that hasn't paid for a story at one time, in some way, somehow, over or under the table.

There are degrees of Checkbook Journalism. Whenever newsmen argue about the morality of this practice, as we sometimes do, the conversation usually ends up sounding like the old joke about the fellow who asked the young lady, "Would you go to bed with me for a thousand dollars?" "Yes." "How about for ten dollars?" "Of course not. What do you think I am?" "We've already established that. Now we're haggling about the price."

When I was starting out in radio, I tried to persuade the management at KTRH to provide me with an allowance for buying coffee for people on the police beat. Sounds minor, I know. But when you are making sixty-two dollars and fifty cents a week, you discover that coffee, donuts and a tip will add up. Night after night, my instincts struggled with my budget.

At the station expense money did not exist. When I proposed that they reimburse me, my suggestion got nowhere. Tom Jacobs, the program manager and keeper of the purse, thought the idea was subversive. He hinted that, for my own good, I should not let others hear such talk.

As a last resort I tried to deduct the money I had spent from my income taxes. Then my return was audited and the IRS agent accused me of attempting to bribe members of the Houston police force. He insisted that if I wanted to keep the deduction I would have to sign an affidavit. I finally gave up. The money was gone.

Once in my career I wanted an interview so badly, the story seemed so important, that I paid a person out of my own pocket. The sum was not small and, in fact, I had to borrow it. I was careful that the money was my own, and not the company's, and I never tried in any shape or form to get it back.

The lesson I learned was an important one for any journalist. I thought the fellow I planned to interview could solve a criminal case. For many reasons, I can't be specific about when this happened, or who and what was involved. I do believe he told me the truth, insofar as he knew it. But the pieces didn't fit and I didn't break the case.

Even if the result had been all I wanted, I would never try that method again. To this day I have been unable to shake the idea, the sure knowledge, that I did the wrong thing.

My first actual test of conscience over Checkbook Journalism occurred on a story and a dateline long gone: the enrollment of James Meredith as the first black student at Ole Miss. This was in the autumn of 1962, a full year before Zapruder.

Meredith was not the ordinary news subject. Among other things, he was one of the most courageous people I have known. It was a triumph of sorts for a reporter, in that time and place, just to see James Meredith.

CBS had a program then called "Eyewitness," a weekly broadcast that tried to deal with people and events who were, or figured to be, a piece of history. The producer of the show wanted Meredith as a guest.

I went through a miniature version of *The Perils of Pauline* just to get through to him. I tracked him down to a small apartment in Jackson some distance from the campus. Meredith was not at all receptive to doing the interview. Understandably. His position was, "Look, I've got enough trouble already."

He was suspicious of my presence, my motives, my identity. There were others in the room. We went through a kind of quiz. How did they know I was who I said I was? They thought I might be an agent from the CIA, the FBI, the Klan, the White Citizens' Council. They had seen television, but I wasn't exactly a household face.

But Meredith finally warmed up enough to start talking. And what he talked about was keeping himself alive. There was none of that what's-in-it-for-me line. He wasn't concerned about money. But the question did arise. Someone else said, "Look, if you do this at all, and I don't think it's a good idea, they ought to pay you." I swallowed hard because I knew our policy wouldn't allow it. I explained our position to him.

Meredith said, "No, that's right. If I do it, I don't want money." I was struck by the fact that he was sharp enough to see the downside for him, the newspapers saying, well, Meredith is out peddling his story. He did the show and without payment.

CBS held the line against so-called Checkbook Journalism for a very long time. In fairness, so did the other networks. The practice did not begin with the H. R. Haldeman television interviews in 1975. Magazines had been doing it for years.

But the subject is indeed complicated. When I moved to England in 1965 I found that paying for news was a way of life over there. I never quite got over my surprise at receiving a bill for fifteen pounds from a member of Parliament, the day after I had filmed an interview with him. Patricia Bernie, my assistant and a British subject, informed me, "Everybody, but *everybody,* is paid for interviews."

True enough, everyone from the man on the street to the House of Lords expects to be paid. And is insulted if he isn't.

At home, at least for me, the Meredith and Zapruder cases were exceptions. Most of the time the subject doesn't even come up. There was a period when all of us at CBS felt strongly that we should never pay for interviews other than, say, presidential memoirs. It is easier all around if TV maintains a no-pay policy. But the issue is not so clear if we are doing a magazine of the air, as opposed to a daily news show. Different outfits for different reasons have different policies.

I frankly don't know the answer. But I do know this. Once we make a habit of buying stories, as one would a painting, we run the risk of turning every major news event into an auction. For myself, I am much more comfortable with a policy that says, we do not pay for anything. News should not be for sale. Period.

Chapter 6

WATCH THE MAN
IN THE HAT

UNDER THE PRESSURES of a clock you take as much for granted the things that happen by accident as those that happen by design. I remember, on Saturday of *that* weekend in 1963, wheeling around and singing out, "I need a body to stake out Mrs. Paine's house."

Ruth Paine was a young mother, a Quaker, separated from her husband, in whose home Lee Harvey Oswald had boarded his wife and two daughters, one a baby. And at that moment a stranger walked into the KRLD newsroom, stepped up and said, "Hello, Dan. I'm Don Hamilton. I'll go."

This was the young accountant CBS had dispatched from New York to help me negotiate the purchase of the Zapruder film. By the time his plane touched down in Dallas and he could get to a phone he knew he was already too late. No matter. He wasn't too late to pitch in on a story that would consume us all.

Hamilton is slim, prematurely gray, Princetonian in appearance. His entire experience had been legal and financial. Later he would become a CBS vice-president, on the business side. But that day he went into the pits with the rest of us. I could not have asked more of a trained reporter. He didn't stop to ask, where is it, how do I get there or what do you want me to do. When I looked up again he was gone. He found the address, staked out the house, took up a position and a few minutes later phoned in. "This is Hamilton. I'm across the street from the Paine place and here is what's happening. . . ."

Events went like that for four days, tapping our energies and our imaginations and our resources. We all but raised a citizens' army of cameramen and sound technicians and passengers fresh off the plane from New York.

People were seeing on the air what the FBI would call "raw data." And the pace was going to get even more frantic and certainly more bizarre. We were still flying on instruments, pushing ourselves past the shock of the Kennedy murder, trying just to stay on top of the news, thinking that, at least, the worst was over.

We had a sense of filling a public need, pompous though that may sound. One of the tests of society is how leadership changes hands, particularly in a time of stress. And this was part of our job: to say to the country, all right, these are the facts. This is where we are and this is what has been happening. This is what you need to know to decide, in your own mind, how you and we and the country will come through this period.

By late Saturday night the coverage had leveled out; "calmed down" would be putting it a little off center, I think. For the first time since the story broke I had a chance to telephone my wife Jean in Houston. People had a compulsion that weekend to reach out by phone and talk to someone. They desperately needed the voice contact, the reassurance that, no, he or she can't believe it, either. Besides being my lover, my consoler and encourager, Jean has always been my conscience. She said to me that night, very deliberately, "This has been one of the better things you've done and you ought to know that." Then she paused. "But it's one thing to hear you on the air with no emotion coming through. I thought I'd hear it from you now, Dan, on the phone. And I don't. It isn't there. And I don't know how to react to that."

I said, "I don't have time for it, Jean. For one thing, if I ever let myself go, I won't be able to do what has to be done."

Quickly, she said, "I know. We'll talk about it another time."

But she was puzzled, I could tell, and a little irritated with me. In human terms. She was at home, in front of her television set, seeing and hearing the events of that weekend as other people saw and heard them. She knew that if I was going to err in any way, it would be on the side of keeping myself under control. It is possible, I am sure, to be too professional at a time when some sign of feeling, of grief, can touch a chord. There was a wetness in Walter Cronkite's eyes, and his voice was husky, though still firm, when he announced that the President was dead. And people were moved.

So there it was again, the detachment that has been, for better or worse, a part of my public face. This is not the kind of attitude you think out. Hughes Rudd had told me, not too many months before, that it could be a strength. To many of the Nixon people, and to some others, I know it came across as coldness, arrogance.

I understood how Jean felt. On the phone, exchanging husband-and-wife talk, she expected to hear some expression, some thought, some word that would reveal what was inside me. The release wouldn't come. No matter what the pressures may have been elsewhere, a reporter could not take off fifteen minutes to weep, not then, not in Dallas. At least, I could not.

The next morning, Sunday, figured to be tense and wearing. In Washington the body of John Kennedy was to be buried at Arlington National Cemetery after a long, solemn procession up Pennsylvania Avenue. In Dallas we were working on the transfer of Lee Harvey Oswald from the city jail to the county jail. The move meant we had three points to coordinate, including the central command post in New York.

I was wrestling that morning with assignments. I felt Nelson Benton should have more air time and put him down for the Oswald transfer. A major portion of the on-camera work had fallen on me, all of which was unexpected and unplanned, and Nelson had some hours coming.

This was more a case of CBS training at work, I should explain, than a generous spirit. We had drilled into us—it is still true, but more so then than now—that sometimes you carried the ball and sometimes you blocked. When it was your turn to block, you didn't bitch about it. As CBS News expanded, as the celebrity-attention side of the business gained more weight, we lost a little of that unselfishness.

Nelson Benton did a lot of blocking and, looking back, the situation could not have been easy for him. As a reporter, he was just as experienced as I was. I had always prided myself on one thing: There are people smarter than I am, but nobody is going to outwork me. In a kind of mental parentheses I would add, but if anybody can, Nelson *might*. He worked his heart out every day. But he was at a disadvantage. He did not run the bureau. I did. He did not always draw deuces, of course. Much of the time he drew jacks and queens. But that weekend he had done an awful lot of legwork and on Sunday morning I made a note to myself to even the scales if I could.

A reporter does catch himself keeping score at such times, I suppose. The fact that I was in Dallas in what had been intended as a backup role had not been lost on me. But when the story exploded, CBS was suddenly on the air, live; what is helpful, almost critical, in that kind of circumstance is the ability to ad-lib. This is one of the gifts that has made Cronkite so effective. It is a talent that has to be developed.

I sharpened mine over the years, on those days and nights describing University of Houston football games, recreating minor league baseball games, and doing play-by-play four nights a week over KSAM and climbing a light pole to see the action. That was where you learned to ad-lib.

If I were to compile a list of the weaknesses of the young people moving into the networks now, writing would be first on the list and the ability to ad-lib a close second. Of course, in the conditions that existed in Dallas that weekend there was no time to write copy. No time to think, much less to sit down at a typewriter. I was shuttling back and forth between the television and radio studios, feeding reports to New York, describing, interviewing, editing film. When it was air time you just had to walk in and talk.

I had carried much of the load with considerable help from people like Nelson Benton and Bob Pierpoint. As the White House correspondent, Pierpoint had one responsibility: to get as close to the President as he could and stay there. When the bullets rang out, he had a choice to make: Lyndon Johnson was, within two hours, the new President. Bob left Parkland Hospital and the body of the man he had traveled across the country to cover and flew back to Washington with Johnson. Before and after, he filed some masterful pieces of journalism, reports he dictated over the phone.

This is where broadcast journalism differs so from print. At times Pierpoint would call while we were on the air. Cronkite and I would actually be talking back and forth between New York and Dallas. And in the middle of our conversation I would whisper into the nonbroadcast line and tell Walter to keep talking. While Walter filled, Bob would dictate his story; that is, he might repeat whatever Mrs. Connally had just said after leaving her husband's hospital room. I am not a note taker in the classic pose of a reporter who whips out his notepad and scribbles furiously. I do carry a notebook and pencil. No reporter worthy of the name can walk out of the house without those articles on his person. But for broadcasting, for my own style, what has worked best for me is to watch and listen as closely as I possibly can, trying to *burn* it into my head, so that if I have to describe a scene again and again I can. I do take down direct quotes. That is one thing I try to get exactly.

So Benton, Pierpoint and Lew Wood had been filing a flow of reports by phone. Lew was another reporter I had overlooked in terms of sharing the air time. He certainly understood, but at one point he came to me and said, "Hey, Dan, I'm unassigned and I'd like to do something. I know you have a thousand things to think about, but this *is* a piece of history and I'd like to be in on it." I was grateful he put it on that basis, but I was embarrassed for not having thought of him. That was the feeling. No one knew exactly where to step, or how softly. No one wanted an advantage, but everyone wanted to be involved. No one wanted to push, but you didn't want to be a piece of furniture, either.

I penciled in Lew Wood to take the other end of the transfer of Lee Harvey Oswald.

There was a memorial service for President Kennedy Sunday morning in Washington. CBS carried the service live as the rest of us settled into our assignments: Rather in the studio at KRLD; Benton at the point of transfer in the now-famous basement of the Dallas city jail; Wood on the steps of the county jail; and Harry Reasoner on the anchor, in New York. Our information was that the service would end at ten o'clock, Dallas time, and the network would come directly to us.

The schedule for Oswald's transfer already had been made public, and the Dallas police were getting very skittish. So were we. Jesse Curry, the police chief, had promised his friends in the press corps that the move would be made at 10 A.M.—just as the church service would be ending.

The transfer ran late. And so did the service. Captain Will Fritz of the Dallas police department had decided to question Oswald one more time before letting the county and federal agents have him. Well after 10 A.M., Jack Ruby dressed and drove to the Western Union office to send a money order to Fort Worth, to one of the girls who stripped in his nightclub. If the transfer had gone off on time, Jack Ruby still would have been at home.

In the meantime a crowd had gathered outside the jail, on both sides of it, on Commerce and on Elm. The cops were tight as ticks. Nelson Benton, cautious as any good reporter would be, kept insisting for at least an hour that "we have to come here early. They may take him out a side door . . . they could go at any time." That word was passed along to New York and there was a good deal of talk about when the switch to the Dallas jail should be made. Benton was about to come unglued, he was so fearful we would miss the moment. As the clock moved past 11 A.M. he was saying, "We've got to take it *now.*"

I repeated that to whoever was on the other end of the phone in New

York. "Let us have it. We have to have it now. They can't keep him in there much longer."

"Yeah, we know," the word came back. "But we can't. We're locked in to staying with the memorial services. And then Harry has about a one-minute essay."

Part of the problem was simply programming. The transition would be smoother if we didn't go directly from an altar behind the coffin in Washington, to the President's suspected killer in a Dallas basement. So the thinking was part technical and part taste. Another factor was that Reasoner had written a piece, the kind he did so well, and this seemed an appropriate place to fit it in, as a bridge between the two scenes.

As the service was ending and the parade formed for the march to the Capitol, with six gray horses pulling the black-draped caisson and a seventh, riderless, leading the way, Roger Mudd began a report from the Capitol. By this time Nelson Benton was, I hesitate to say *screaming* but he was making a din. With great passion, he kept shouting, "Take it, take it, take it. They're at the door."

I said to New York, "You've *got* to come to us now!"

And they were saying, "Hold on just a minute. We have to get through this Mudd piece, then Reasoner."

We were ranting away over the phone when suddenly the man in the tan cowboy hat, Detective J. R. Leavelle, stepped out with Oswald handcuffed at his side. Leavelle held onto his right arm. Officer L. C. Graves was on the other side, his hand cupped around Oswald's left biceps. Oswald was wearing a black sweater and slacks and above both eyes were the bruises he had acquired during his arrest.

They were just like that, walking quickly behind Captain Will Fritz, when Jack Ruby lunged out of the crowd and fired one shot from a .38 caliber, snub-nosed revolver. The bullet struck Oswald one inch below the heart. It was the scene everyone saw, everyone remembers, a freeze-frame for the mind. The time was 11:20 A.M. Jack Ruby, a balding, fifty-two-year-old Dallas nightclub owner—the Carousel Club—had just gunned down the man accused of killing the President.

And CBS missed it. Mudd was within ten seconds of finishing his piece. We had waited ten seconds too long. I felt physically sick. For the first time that entire nightmare of a weekend I just about threw up. They could see the shooting in New York. They had the picture. Benton was describing what he was seeing, knowing that at least the scene would be taped and played back. But between breaths he was still pleading into the nonbroadcast line, "Come to us. My God, come to us."

All of this, of course, was crammed into a few seconds. First of all the pandemonium, the enormity of what was happening, the bedlam in the basement of the Dallas city jail. And secondly our own competitive situation, which was ghastly. (NBC was on the air, live. ABC was caught on tape, as we were, but went to the scene instantly.) Nelson was still yelling into the private line, I was babbling, but no one in New York needed to be told we had a problem. You could hear them in the control room, everyone from the janitor up, shouting that "something happened."

Someone said to me, "Have they shot Oswald?"

I said, "Damned right."

With that they threw the tape on the air, and seconds later we went to Nelson at the jail. But we had not been broadcasting live from the jail the instant Oswald was shot. For the first time that weekend, I thought, we have been "beaten." In the context of what was happening that must sound awfully picayune. I may overemphasize the competitive aspects of television, the joy of being on the air first. I know my wife thinks so. But this is one test of the trade, one of the rewards, and there is no point in trying to justify it. I suppose it would sound indelicate, listening to a surgeon talk about the perfect incision.

But to me, this *was* television. Not only do you have to be in the right place at the right time, you have to be doing the right thing. You not only have to be good, you have to be lucky. For the next hour and a half I brooded over the fact that we had lost a race against our competition. All week long, until then, we had our competition hands down. This was one of those stories when the pieces had fallen into place. We had the right planning, the right people and, if a tragedy of this proportion had to happen any place, it happened in a city where we had the right facilities.

I know, the country was coming apart and I sound as if I were out there playing a violin. But at some point I began to wonder if we could run the scene—of Ruby lunging toward Oswald—in slow motion. The technique had not been used in hard news before, and not very often even in sports, though today it is an everyday occurrence. This was 1963 and it required newly developed equipment. But KRLD, which telecast a lot of football, had it. There was a technician at the station who had worked with slow motion and I stopped him in the hall. We practically blurted out the same thought at the same time. And unknown to both of us, Don Hewitt in New York was on the phone trying to reach me to suggest the same idea.

So about an hour and a half after Jack Ruby's back flashed in front of the cameras we reran the film at slow speed and even froze the key frames, which in addition to being very high drama allowed people to relive that scene almost as it happened. That may not be your idea of a public service, but I believe it was worth doing. This time the answers were on the screen.

Bear in mind that the world of videotape was not then what it is now. We had the film rushed back and we had to use a jerry-rig to do the job. We used three technicians, one at the top of the reel, one at the bottom and one actually threading the film through this crude setup. The rig worked. The result was a first for hard news: slow motion and freeze-frame.

Of course, anyone outside of the business would say, what the hell is this about? What difference did it make? But if you were there that morning and you were a broadcast journalist, there were questions that had to be asked. The killing had happened so fast that some witnesses said the man with the gun was just a "blur." In regular motion he loomed onto the screen, the .38 at arm's length, pointed at Oswald's belly.

I remember taking a pointer and saying as the film rolled, "Okay, watch the man in the hat." That was Ruby. In slow motion, you could follow with your eye as the hat moved out of the crowd, out of the fringe, and follow the arm that ran to the hat. Was he shot once or several times? In slow motion, over and over, you could see that there was one shot. And, strange as it may sound now, at the time there was a question: Did the doctors let Oswald die on the operating table or was he too far gone by the time they got to him? By running the film in slow motion we could eliminate any doubt. The range was pointblank. He was virtually a dead man when Ruby fired.

Officially, Oswald died at Parkland Hospital. One of the doctors who worked on him was Malcolm Perry, who two days before had massaged the stilled heart of John Kennedy. Oswald's spleen, pancreas, liver and one kidney had been hit.

At 1:07 P.M., Dallas time, Oswald was pronounced dead. What now? The sensation was not unlike falling down a bottomless flight of stairs in your dreams. We had been without sleep, most of us, since Friday at dawn. In the space of two days and seven minutes, we had covered the death of a President and the man who murdered him. I wondered if things would ever be normal again.

Jack Ruby.

What did anyone really know about him? Had there been anything worth knowing? Out of Chicago. Didn't smoke or drink. Tough, vain, thick through the chest, but only five nine. The kind of man who talked a great deal about *class,* but defined it largely through a life he had never led. A local police character, the Dallas press described him. Did any murderer, caught in the act, ever utter a more pathetic line than Ruby, when the cops pounced on him in the Dallas jail? *"You all know me . . . I'm Jack Ruby."*

For the rest of that day and on through Monday people were again seeing television in the raw. Our studio was like some kind of bizarre telethon, with people wandering on and off the stage, phones ringing, voices carrying, one act tripping over the next.

Someone had heard that a stripper working in Tyler had told someone else she had once seen Ruby and Oswald together.

Get her.

We found her telephone number, called, had her driven to Dallas. Suddenly she was walking into the studio and the director, frantic, gave me a signal to throw it back to New York. *On camera* I said, "Walter, do you mind taking it back for a few seconds? I have something to check on here."

I walked off the set. "We've got the stripper from Tyler," the director said, "the one who claims to have seen Ruby and Oswald together."

"Well, has she?"

"She just got here. No one has had time to ask."

I shrugged. I may have even lifted an eyebrow. But I said, "Okay, then, let's bring her on."

She settled into the chair next to mine, slowly, smoothing her dress, turning the simple act of sitting down into a performance. I cleared my throat and said something like, "Walter, we have Miss Honeysuckle Galore [or whatever] in the studio with us . . . [*turning*] . . . Miss Honeysuckle, I understand you have said to someone . . ."

Now, if you could have chosen the ideal way to conduct an interview, that probably would not have been it. But, in effect, we were calling most of our plays at the line of scrimmage. As a result some of what we put on the air later proved to be nonsense. But much of it was superb.

If that weekend, beyond the trauma, became a shared experience in journalism, it was because without exception those called on responded so well to the pressure. It is not true that people usually do. At least, I know

I have been in situations where I did not. As a group, however, this was not one of those times. In many instances the cameramen and the lighting and sound men, who too often are unfairly thought of as strictly technicians, as the welders and the welders' helpers, were being sent out to do reporting jobs and, as in the case of Don Hamilton, they were splendid.

Wendell Hoffman, who had been one of my early tutors at CBS, volunteered to check out Ruby's club, to learn what else he could about the reports that Ruby and Oswald knew each other. Off he went, with a notepad and a pencil and his own pure nerve. We even put Hoffman on the air, in that twangy Kansas voice of his, from a phone outside the Carousel, a dingy walkup in the 1300 block of Commerce, near the Adolphus and Baker hotels. He reported that the place was closed, boarded up, but some of the regulars were milling around and he had talked to them. None of the old customers, he said, had ever seen anyone who resembled Oswald inside the club. That was not a bad story right there.

What we were doing was part radio and part improvisational theater, and I suppose if you are looking for an off-the-wall definition of live television, when it works, that would serve.

By late Monday the numbness was setting in again. There were still so many questions to be answered, now so many new ones, we felt we were losing ground. I slugged down coffee, looked at the same faces for hours without seeing them, had conversations and didn't remember them.

All the while there was an atmosphere building that I can only describe as creeping paranoia. The city of Dallas, the people who lived there and loved it, who had never heard of Oswald or Ruby, were being bombarded and humiliated. Most of the criticism was simply irrational. But it kept growing.

I could see Eddie Barker, the news director at KRLD, grimace whenever something was said on the air about Dallas, whether by a network commentator or someone just being interviewed. There were repeated references to the political climate, the far Right fringe. Over and over you heard the same lament: It could have happened anywhere, *but it happened in Dallas.* Why us?

A wire service had moved a story earlier that the youngsters at a Dallas grade school had cheered when the news of the assassination was announced over the public address system. The story was written in such a way as to leave the impression that Dallas was so Right wing, so filled with meanness, that little children could celebrate the death of a liberal President.

Well, school kids applaud almost anything that comes through a loud-speaker: a fire drill, the lunch menu, notice of a lost library book. But this was a story that received heavy play around the country. So on Tuesday morning Hughes Rudd and a CBS camera crew went to the school where the incident occurred and interviewed some of the teachers and students. Later we had an in-house council on whether to even use the piece. The discussion was private, but some of the KRLD staff, through Barker, made clear their belief that the original story was unfair to Dallas and ought to be shelved, quickly.

Frankly, I agreed with them. To my recollection, Rudd was lukewarm and insisted, "Don't let whatever time we spent on it be a factor. As far as I'm concerned we can drop it." At any rate the piece did run. The call was close, but from our point of view the story was balanced. And fair. They are not always one and the same. But the KRLD people, to a soul, thought it was a gratuitous story that kept alive an impression of Dallas that was cheap and damaging.

The film appeared that night, Tuesday, on the CBS Evening News. Within minutes Barker flew into the newsroom and braced himself. His face was flushed. He was visibly irritated. Keep in mind that he had been working like a deckhand himself, had kept the same blinding hours, had been under the same and more complicated pressures.

He glared across the room and said, "Out. All of you. Out."

I had no idea what was on his mind. Obviously he wasn't kidding, but I thought, well, maybe one of our crew had broken into the Coke machine. Why that occurred to me I cannot say, but I did not think it was serious and I certainly did not connect it with any festering problem.

No one moved or spoke and Eddie repeated, "I am ordering you out. You are no longer to operate out of here and you are to leave now. This minute."

I said, "Eddie, if you're not joking—"

He said, "Let me assure you that I am not."

I stood up. "Well, this is damned serious," I said, "and you're going to regret it. I don't believe you've thought it out. You have to know if you go through with this, you're through and the station is through."

That threat was meant as a bluff. I was groping. But there was no question that KRLD would be breaking the spirit, if not the letter, of a contract with CBS. Barker and I had words back and forth. I tried to talk him out of it, but my own anger was close to the surface now. I was in no mood to be diplomatic. Here were two guys whose veins were sticking out so that you could flick them with your fingernails like harp strings, who had been through a period that was beyond belief. Eddie cut me off. "Go," he said. "All of you. Out."

He had already indicated that it was not just Eddie Barker acting on his own whim. The station, the management of KRLD, was throwing us out. I turned to my people and pointing to each one said, "You, you, you and you, pack up now. Everything. Let's get out of here." Then I looked at Bernie Birnbaum, hard in the eyes, drilling him, because I needed to get a message across that I couldn't say out loud. The message was, grab what-ever you can get your hands on in the way of film. It goes with us.

Bernie gave me a nod. There was no intent to steal what belonged to KRLD. But some of that film we had taken, some of it was theirs, and some of it we had developed as a team. I did not want to get out of there with less than what was ours or with less than we needed to do our job. Much of the film was historic. We would sort it out later and give them a copy of whatever we had.

The confrontation was tense and implausible. One minute you are on the same side. The next minute you're the Russians.

Even as we packed our gear I realized we had another card to play. I knew that KHOU, the station in Houston where I had started in television, had bought a new mobile unit. We had enough film to carry us. All we needed was to move the mobile unit to Dallas, plug it into the telephone company lines and, in effect, we would have our own miniature TV sta-tion. We could feed over the phone lines to New York and go ahead with our broadcasts. Certainly not the best of circumstances. And we might lose our advantage over our competition. But I knew we would not be out of business.

Before we left the newsroom I called Cal Jones at KHOU in Houston. I wanted Barker to hear the conversation, to know that if they ran us off we would still be on the air. I asked Cal how long he would need to get their mobile unit loaded and on the road. He said he could have it in Dallas, for sure, by morning. I told him to get ready. I would get back to him with word on when to roll.

As I headed for the door Barker stopped me. On the one hand, he was hot and didn't care if the world knew it. On the other, we had overcome some early strain to develop a friendship, and he was trying to say, look, nothing personal. I couldn't accept that.

I said, "Nope, you can't do it that way, Eddie. This *is* personal. Whether you intend it that way or not, I'm taking it damned personal. On this story, in these circumstances, whatever it is that's going through your mind is wrong."

On that note I led the CBS crew into the street. Up to then I don't think anyone at KRLD had given any thought to how we would react or what we would do or where we would go. Once outside, I walked to the nearest pay phone and called Blair Clark in New York. I was steaming. I gave him a shorthand account of how I came to be standing on the sidewalk.

"They've what?"

"That's it. They've thrown us out. I don't have time to go into all the details now, but I wanted you to know about it right off."

Blair said, "I don't understand what the hell is going on there, but whatever you say and whatever you need, let us know."

I called Cal Jones back and told him to bring on the mobile unit. Then I calmed my crew, suggested they go back to their rooms and catch a few hours' rest and not say a word to anyone. There was nothing else that could be done that night. I stood on the corner, alone, for a few minutes after everyone else had left. I had been gone from my hotel for so long I had almost forgotten where I was staying. But I waited a few minutes more on the chance that someone might run out of the building and say, hey, we really didn't mean it, come on back, it was all a mistake.

No one did. So I hailed a cab and returned to my hotel, and for the first time in five days I put my head on a pillow. I thought, this has been one hellish time and isn't going to get any better very soon. I ought to grab some sleep while I can. I had dozed, off and on, at my desk. Maybe the line was going to come up in New York in five minutes and I would just nod off, waiting for a cue. Someone would walk in and shake me. When the adrenalin is going, you don't think you need to sleep.

I was out cold by 11:30 P.M. An hour later the phone rang. Jim Chambers, the station manager at KRLD, was calling. Jim was a good one. He might not agree with your politics, or what he perceived your politics to be, and he would be quick to tell you. But his own views were never a factor in the treatment, or service, he wanted his station to deliver.

"Dan, it looks like we have a little problem here," he said. "I'd like to have you come back to the station so we can talk about it." He said his car was already outside the hotel waiting for me. I was dressed and downstairs in a matter of minutes.

I remember two things about the ride: The car had electric windows—this was 1963 and that impressed me—and the driver took us in the back way. I should have known then that they were worried.

I walked into the conference room and found the board of directors already assembled. KRLD was then owned by the Dallas Times-Herald Corporation. Eddie Barker was there, looking pale and tired. Given what all of us had been through, that was not surprising.

Even beneath the strain I felt a kinship with Eddie. Everyone else in that room looked as though he was right out of the executive suite, expensively tailored, middle-aged or older. I was haggard and unshaven and I am not sure my shirt was clean. I looked as though I had ridden a freight train from Oklahoma City.

Jim Chambers was running the meeting. The station manager was cool and self-assured and he tried to downplay the blowup. "There has been a misunderstanding here, Dan," he said. "Two reporters are at the front door. They have a story that we've ejected you and the CBS staff from our newsroom and will no longer allow you to operate here. As you know, that isn't true."

I said, quickly, "Mr. Chambers, there is no misunderstanding about that. It *is* true. I know that and so do you."

There was some buzzing then, a lot of whispering into the next ear around the table. I knew one of the reporters waiting outside, Gladwin Hill of *The New York Times.* Chambers had prepared a statement. He assured me we could settle the problem, but first he felt it would be helpful if I read the statement to the reporters. I declined. I said, "I guess we need to call someone in New York. It has happened and I'm not about to tell whoever is out there an untruth. But I don't want to cause trouble and I do understand the situation here."

Among those at the table was Felix McKnight, the editor of the *Times-Herald.* My sense was that McKnight, an experienced journalist of tremendous integrity, had sent out the alert. He was a mover. The minute he got wind of what had happened, he knew this was trouble. Now he nodded and said, "All right, there's the phone."

I suggested that Chambers place the call and I gave him Blair Clark's home number. And Blair said, "Look, Rather speaks for us there." He was civil, but he expressed his displeasure with a force that surprised me and, fair to say, stunned Chambers. We walked it up the ladder to Dick Salant, the president of CBS News, and he gave the same tough response.

They were standing on a principle, a quality many critics feel is in short supply in television. The point needs to be made because it flies in the face of what people want to believe, especially today. I have often been told, after a speech or a lecture, by someone meeting me for the first time, "Okay, Rather, I came here not knowing what kind of fellow you were. And after looking you over in the flesh, hearing what you have to say, I'm prepared to admit I could trust you. But let me tell you who I don't trust, and that's those bastards in New York who tell you what to say."

Well, widely believed the legend may be, but true it is not. If anything, the power is weighted too much the other way. If you want to worry about something, the worry ought to be in the other direction. The responsibility and the latitude given to a line correspondent—to make decisions on your own—are much greater than anyone recognizes.

Chambers put down the phone and I knew he was unsettled, to say the least. Finally he looked straight at me. "Well," he said, "what are we going to do about the people waiting out front?"

I said, "I'm not going to do anything about it." I added that I was quite sure none of our people were responsible for other reporters knowing about the incident. And, indeed, we were not.

"If there is still any doubt in your mind," he said, "you have my assurance that you are welcome here." That was not what we had been told a few hours before, in terms that were hardly ambiguous, but there was no need to rub that in.

Chambers was still trying to draft a statement that would allow everyone to go home with honor. One or two of the other directors offered a word, or a phrase. Finally I told him I would make no statement or join in one but I had no objection if he issued his own. So Chambers sent someone to the door, and the writers were told there had been a disagreement and it had been resolved.

My friend Eddie Barker, whose reporting talents I so admired, remained my friend.

Then a wave of relief filled the room and the meeting began to break up. Chambers asked me to stay behind and we talked for a while, quite candidly. A decision had been made in a mix of emotion and frustration. Then it occurred to someone what the result would be: the loss of their affiliation with CBS. Millions of dollars were involved.

If the four days that had gone before were a crazy quilt of events, this was a small patch. Our eviction said something, I think, about the nature of the business, the money that rides on it, the tempers that surface.

As a parcel of time the nightmare did end, and Dallas began the long task of coming to terms with how much guilt, if any, the city had to bear because John Kennedy died there. And those of us who had only meant to pass through finally moved on. But in a way that is not hard to understand, it did not really end for any of us. We still carry that week with us, a wound that aches when it rains.

All the years that have followed—thirteen as this is written, or twenty or thirty—may not answer all the questions or erase those freeze-frames from our minds. The head lurching forward in the limousine. The man in the hat lunging at the handcuffed prisoner.

No, I did not feel then the emotions that swept up most other people. Maybe if I were better at my job, if it didn't require all the concentration I can summon, I could have done my work and suffered at the same time. But, frankly, that's too deep for me. The feeling of depression, the lost feeling that was so universal that weekend, I did not experience until weeks later.

When most other people were coming out of the fog, certainly through the worst of it, the impact hit me. I found myself dwelling on the events, reliving them, what they meant, what I felt about them as a person, not as a reporter.

I lost track of time, of days. I decided that the death of John Kennedy touched and unsettled our lives, but the death of Lee Harvey Oswald changed our character. With Oswald went our best chance to get at the truth and to exorcise the demons. I finally accepted the fact that no one would soon make sense of all that had happened in Dallas, if anyone ever could. Only then did I begin to pull out of a depression that had me by the throat.

Kennedy and Oswald were buried. Jack Ruby would die in jail. The autopsy would reveal that he had brain tumors, a spreading cancer and a blood clot in his leg.

I stayed in Dallas for two weeks, through the rest of November. By then I knew what my next assignment would be. The decision had been made not long after Lyndon Johnson flew back to Washington aboard *Air Force One.* The country had a new President, from Texas. And I was going to the White House to cover him.

Out-Take

6

LEAVING TEXAS

The rumor was around that CBS had promoted Dan Rather because of the Texas Connection. Those who believed it were convinced CBS was bringing up someone wired to Lyndon Johnson. If they had only known. Oh, if they had only known.

It was a strange time and a strange mixture. Washington was not only in transition but in turmoil. The shift of power is a visible and not very subtle process. The trauma after John Kennedy's death was real and the pain lingered. Johnson was sensitive to it, in the higher sense but in a defensive way as well. Austin wasn't Boston. He encountered that attitude everywhere.

The fact was, I felt lost among all the shifting tides and jockeying for position. I knew almost no one, in a city where who you knew was, or seemed to be, the one essential for survival. I didn't know Lyndon Johnson. He didn't know me. I didn't know one damned soul around him.

To top off my confusion, the new President had a secretary named Mary Rather. We had never met. But one day there was this offhand question from Blair Clark: "Oh, by the way, are you related in any way to Mary Rather?"

I quickly said, "No, I'm not," but I caught myself thinking, maybe it would help if I were.

Chapter 7

HALFWAY WITH LBJ

MY ONLY CONTACT with Lyndon Johnson had been of the most piercing kind, in 1955, when I was still a cub reporter in radio, in Houston. He was recovering from his heart attack and had returned to the LBJ Ranch to plan his political comeback.

At the time I was trying hard to convince my bosses at KTRH that we needed to expand our statewide coverage. Then a note moved on the wire one day that said Lyndon Johnson, the majority leader of the Senate, would hold a news conference at his ranch the next morning. I went to my boss and said, "We ought to be there. This guy might run for President someday."

After some wrangling, he gave me ten dollars for expenses and the day off and said, in effect, if you can get there, do something for the noon news.

I didn't even know my way to the ranch. But I hitchhiked to Austin and found the press office at the State Capitol and bummed a ride with Stuart Long, a veteran reporter. When we arrived, we found perhaps two dozen people milling around the pool in the morning sunlight, already drinking. The conference was set for ten o'clock. It was almost time, but Johnson hadn't appeared and was nowhere to be seen.

I had the distinct feeling of being an outsider at some kind of private hunt club. My main objective at that point was to sort of slide by, keep my ears open and not be noticed. I carried one of those bulky, wet-cell tape recorders, slung over my shoulder like a knapsack.

By 11 A.M. I was getting antsy. The Man was still nowhere in sight. I asked where I might find a telephone and was told that the nearest one was just inside the door to the ranch house. For all I knew, it was the only phone.

I called Houston—in itself no small task from Johnson City in those days—and told the news director that nothing had happened. A trifle irritated, he reminded me that the wires had indicated the press conference had been set for ten o'clock, and what the hell was going on there, anyway?

I told him I didn't know—I was shouting to be heard over a bad line—but I thought that maybe Johnson had decided that 10 A.M. was the wrong time for a news break, that not all of the afternoon papers, possibly only the street edition, would carry what he intended to say. That might take the edge off what otherwise could mean heavy play by the morning papers. So maybe, I reasoned, he had decided to wait until after lunch, to make sure the story was fresh for the morning papers and still had some headline potential.

I was sitting on a daybed. At that point the phone was yanked from my hand and this towering figure loomed up behind me and roared into the mouthpiece, "*This is Lyndon Johnson.* I don't know who the hell you are, and I damned well don't know who this rude *pissant* is. But I can tell you this: He doesn't belong here, I'm throwing his ass out, what he just told you is bullshit and if you use it, I'll sue you."

By the time he banged down the receiver I was already fleeing out the door, my tape recorder flapping against my back, mike and cord dragging behind me. I hurried across the driveway, past the running waterfall that spans the Pedernales, as the river snaked almost to his doorstep. I tried to use the old Boy Scout pace: you know, trot fifty, walk fifty, across the river bridge and into the trees and onto the blacktop beyond, heading in the direction of Stonewall, Texas.

A few minutes later a white Lincoln Continental eased alongside me, and Mrs. Lady Bird Johnson rolled down the driver's window. Paul Bolton, the news director at the Johnson radio station in Austin, was in the front seat with her. He had seen my tape recorder in flight and made a quick deduction. Lady Bird apologized. She wasn't certain why I'd left, or who I was, or what had happened. But she said, "I sure wish you'd come back. Whatever he said, he didn't mean anything by it, honey. It's just his way. He's had this heart attack and he's just touchy. Why don't you get in and ride on back with us and maybe kinda stay out of his way for a while and everything will be all right."

I rode back with them. And for the rest of the afternoon I tried to keep the biggest live oak tree in the yard between my line of sight and his. From time to time, Mrs. Johnson made a point of smiling and nodding at me. She was attentive and almost motherly.

It was simply a very Johnsonesque experience. He had invited a bunch of his newspaper cronies out for a day at the ranch, for background talks, his way of reestablishing his health and his political vitality. He had things to do and places to go and no mere coronary could stop him.

I did not so much as get another glimpse of Lyndon Johnson until 1960, then briefly, at the Democratic Convention. And then not again until, at a distance, in the motorcade at Dallas on November 22, 1963.

When I reported to Washington in January of 1964 I was, fair to say, a stranger to the President. Months later, when I finally worked up the nerve to ask him about that day at the ranch, he stared at me, his face blank, and said he had absolutely no recollection of it. I believe that was true. So far as I know, neither did Mrs. Johnson.

What I realized later was that she had gone through a lifetime of that kind of human gardening. She was constantly cleaning up his messes. She did so beautifully. It was a large part of her life, her role, and no small part of what she was about as a person.

As for LBJ, a good deal of psycho-historic, almost mystical higher b.s. has been written and spoken about him in the years immediately after his death. I never felt he was nearly so complicated as some have tried to portray him.

True, Lyndon Johnson had a powerful sense of the land that produced him. He quite literally smacked of it. I don't appraise that condition in terms of virtue or weakness. It was simply a reality well understood by many of us who came out of that blend of land and attitude.

I have been asked before about the curious clan of Texans who seem to form a kind of subculture wherever they are. I know the question has been put to Bill Moyers and Willie Morris. I only know that I am a Texan by birth and by choice—Texas is home to the heart and I don't want it any other way. If you grew up in Seguin or Wharton or Smithville, or in the wrong end of Houston, if you were not born to privilege or place, if you wanted to see some of the world, journalism and politics were two of the ways to do so.

The mood runs deep, that sense of place, of choices to make. Some may snicker at the Fourth of July picnic on the American Legion grounds. In some small towns a narrowness of outlook exists that is not very attractive. But it also plants a seed of patriotism in the best spirit. An *old-fashioned* Fourth of July simply means that you can believe as much of the speeches as you want. You can believe that, in this country, you can go wherever your spunk and talent will take you, however cornball that may sound.

But that conviction was part of Lyndon Johnson and I understood because it was, is, a part of me. In my own mind I am a southwesterner, a concept I define as a combination of old southern courtesy and rough western finish. That was LBJ's line. He was adamant about not being typed as a southerner, because that meant political handicaps. But it was also the truth. There is a distinction between being southern and being southwestern, and if you have never been to El Paso, there is no point in my trying to explain.

Yet it is also true that, for most of the years of his life, Lyndon Johnson was a man of the Potomac. He never lost his Texas instincts, never stopped cultivating or using those instincts he felt served him best, but he moved to the rhythms of Washington as well as any man who ever lived.

As slightly as I knew him then, I knew the nation's capital less. I had been there three times in my life, the first time for one day in the summer of 1956. I was hitchhiking to New York, got as far as Atlanta and decided to take the bus the rest of the way. It was what we called the Grey Dog, as opposed to a Yellow Dog, that being the kind of bus junior high football teams rode to their games. A rainstorm caught me on the outskirts of Atlanta. Tired and soaked, I stood by the side of the road until a driver saw my semaphores and stopped.

I picked up a newspaper left in the seat next to mine and read that the all-star baseball game was to be played that week in Washington. It developed that the bus would pass through Washington on the way to New York, so I made up my mind to get off and take in the game. It was one of those things I had always wanted to do.

Now, I advise my own kids—in fact, I forbid them—to hitchhike. But that was a different kind of hitchhiking. At least, it seems so in retrospect. I suppose that attitude gets into the psychology of being a father. But I was accustomed to thumbing rides. That was about the only way I traveled during my college years. My roommate, Cecil Tuck, the Weeper, and I had started out several times to hitchhike to the West Coast. Once, we got as far as Alvin, Texas.

But those were the 1950's. We were the on-the-road generation, celebrated in the writings of Jack Kerouac. The Beatniks were all our brothers.

So I got off in Washington to see the all-star game and, of course, in my innocence and stupidity had never considered that the game would be a sellout. But indeed it was. Then one of those unexpected, good samaritan gestures happened. I had gone straight from the Greyhound bus station to old Griffith Stadium, found a ticket window, walked up and said brightly, "I'd like to buy a ticket."

I had to wait for the guy behind the window to stop laughing. Finally he said, "Sonny, the game has been sold out for months."

A middle-aged man standing a few feet away heard that exchange. He walked over and said, "I have an extra ticket to the game and it would please me to give it to you."

I was thrilled. I offered to buy the ticket from him and was even more overjoyed when he wouldn't hear of it. I sat behind a post the entire game, but gloried in every minute, every pitch. The Cardinal third baseman, Ken Boyer, made a couple of spectacular plays and the National League won, 7-3. Thanks to a kind stranger, I had seen the all-star game. Then I went straight back to the bus station and on to New York.

In 1960 I returned to Washington for a week to film a series of interviews for Channel 11. That was as much a part of the Houston station's effort to lobby our congressmen as it was a journalistic enterprise, although I didn't know about such things at the time, which was just as well. I interviewed Bob Casey and Albert Thomas at their homes and received my first exposure, remote as it was, to how Washington worked.

Late in January, 1961, still with Channel 11, I covered the inauguration of President Kennedy (and Vice-President Lyndon Johnson). A hard snow fell that day and it took me, literally, seven hours to get from my motel on the outskirts of town to the armory where the great gala took place, where Frank Sinatra sang and Marilyn Monroe, well, entertained. I walked through the snow the last two miles to reach the armory, after the taxi driver gave up, and I never regretted it. I had a clear view of the President in his box and Sinatra in command on the stage. For me that was high cotton. I didn't realize then, of course, that it was high cotton for anybody.

That was all I had seen of Washington. When I was assigned to the White House my first orders were to stop off in the capital to meet Bill Small, the new bureau manager, and then go on to New York and make the assignment official. What the trip boiled down to was that Small and his assistant, Don Richardson, needed to approve of me.

But I knew so little about the city that I flew into Dulles Airport and decided, well, I don't want to walk in and meet my new boss with my grip in my hand, so I checked my baggage. The only problem was, I learned hours later, that my flight to New York left out of National Airport, on the other side of town.

I believe I can honestly say I was less prepared for Washington than I was for Lyndon Johnson. In a way I had been preparing for Lyndon Johnson all my life.

In fact, if you were asked to invent the classic Texan, in size and style and ambition, the way he sounded, the way he talked and looked, what you surely would end up with was someone very close to Lyndon Baines Johnson.

David Halberstam once wrote of him: "He was a politician the like of which we shall not see again in this country, a man who bridged very different Americas, his early days and attitudes forged by earthy, frontier attitudes, and whose final acts as President took us to the moon. He was a man of stunning force, drive and intelligence, and of equally stunning insecurity. His enormous accomplishments never dimmed the hidden fears which had propelled him in the first place; he was, in that sense, the most human of politicians."

I buy that assessment. All of it. He had come to office under the most wrenching conditions of any President since another Johnson, Andrew, succeeded the murdered Abraham Lincoln. He began his presidency with a whirlwind of major legislation. But he ended it by announcing he would not run for a second full term. He hoped his decision would reunite those who had become so bitterly split over a war that engulfed him, all of us, a war he could not shed.

Vietnam was his curse. We knew so then and we know more so now. The war kept the country from knowing the better parts of him. He was a unique figure. But Vietnam dominated our lives and obscured the richness of his character. He was colorful, his humor earthy, his heart big and unpredictable. He might have been a popular and admired President, but the young turned against him and he was all but abandoned by his own party.

He was never an easy man to label. His critics were never quite sure if he was a liberal or a conservative or just ambitious. In a way he was a Texas populist, one of Franklin Roosevelt's most loyal New Dealers. In truth, he sought power and found it. He relished the exercising of it. No man ever had a surer instinct for how to pull the levers.

When the ruin of the Johnson presidency had been long apparent, I used to hear learned men around Washington say, in a sympathetic way, that if the parliamentary system had existed in America LBJ would have been a gigantic figure as a Prime Minister, a man to stand with Pitt and Disraeli and Churchill. One senator who felt that way had supported him for President in 1960 and worked to unseat him in 1968. Eugene McCarthy said, yes, LBJ would have been a great Prime Minister, but there is no one to tell the President that he is wrong. Except, of course, the people.

Everything about him seemed magnified. He would laugh louder, get angrier faster, hold a grudge longer. When he was sad gloom spread like smog. He encouraged that impression, I thought. He wanted to be larger than life. But somehow he never struck me as a modern man. I never really believed the stories about his success with women. In that arena I rated him good field, no hit.

A mild flurry of gossip was created when Doris Kearns, who had worked at the White House briefly under a Harvard fellowship and later wrote a book about him, said that Johnson told her he loved her. He might have said that. But he did not invite her to the nearest hayloft, apparently, and carry her off to paradise, and I found that interesting.

He flirted too openly to be very active privately. He pictured himself as gallant and he needed the admiration of women. Lady Bird tolerated that side of his nature. She gave him more than the benefit of the doubt. "Lyndon was a people lover," she said. "I couldn't expect him to exclude half the people."

Frankly, you could not prove by me that Johnson loved people. I can't say I really liked him. I thought I understood him. At times I enjoyed my encounters with him, even respected his ability to maneuver people. On occasion I wished I had known him better.

It is a pity, I always felt, that he never convinced himself that Austin was as good as Boston. He held off doing a televised news conference for the longest time because, with good reason, he feared the contrast to John Kennedy. But how curious that was. No one had ever accused Lyndon Johnson of lacking confidence about anything. About most things he was balls out, let-me-at-it. But still he kept postponing his first TV news conference. Instead, he had what he called pop quizzes in his office and on his strolls around the ellipse. But nothing on television.

Then, finally, he held his first television meeting with the press, in the State Department because he didn't want the East Room contrast with Kennedy. That news conference was my first as the CBS White House correspondent. And I didn't get recognized, didn't get a call to ask a question. I left feeling puzzled and dejected.

I had just been assigned to the beat and I didn't know my ankle from third base. About anything. I thought I knew a little about politics but this was the big leagues. The biggest league. There was Lyndon Baines Johnson at the podium, live and in color, talking to his *fellow Americans,* and my job was to ask him a question.

Instinctively, I marched right back to the White House. I said to myself, Okay, that was a message. The only person I knew on the President's staff then was Jack Valenti. I didn't know him well, but he had been in advertising in Houston, and our paths had crossed. I went directly to his office, and his secretary tried to put me off.

I said, "No, that won't do. I have to see him, right now," and I really gave her a heavy sell. So she let me see him. I said to Valenti, "The President didn't recognize me during the news conference. I can tell you, right off, that's important to me. And I know that you know it's important to me. And I know it was no damned accident."

Valenti cocked his head. "Oh, no," he said, "nothing could be further from the truth. I can assure you, first of all, the President's problem is that he can't see ten feet without his glasses and, for a lot of reasons, we don't want him to wear his glasses on television. As a matter of fact, Dan, I *know* the President was looking for you. He was groping, trying to pick you out."

Well. My own vanity and ego tend to surface now and again. I am asking myself, Can that be? And some tiny voice tells me, No, even as country as I am, I can't swallow that syrup.

I knew quite well that, in Johnson's theory of operations, he pegged people quickly. It would not have been unlikely for him to say, "This kid is new. We can train him right, break him like a bucking pony. It'll take a little while. He's coming on a little salty. But we'll be able to bring him around."

Shortly thereafter I was ushered into Johnson's office. One thing about LBJ, you asked to see him and you usually got your wish. No one ever said so, but I'm sure Valenti arranged the meeting. Johnson could not have been nicer. A very big hello and, "I'm glad you're up here, Dan. *You,* of all people, will understand what I'm trying to do. Anything you need or want, you let me know. And I'd appreciate your letting me know directly." When he wanted, LBJ could charm a handkerchief out of a silkworm.

At the next news conference I was the fourth person recognized. Now,

I don't believe that was accidental. But the treatment works on you. A reporter does find himself courting favor with a President. A helluva problem. But what you learn is this: You come rapidly to a time when you have to make decisions. The temptation to court favor is enormous. It is one of those instances where you simply cannot appreciate the enticement unless you have tasted it. I tell you, in a one-on-one situation in the President's office, where he is asking if you would like a Fresca from his private cooler and he's ready to pop the cap *himself,* that's powerful, down-home stuff. I don't care who or what you are, the treatment is hard to resist. But if you want any respect covering politics, you better learn to resist. To a lesser degree, you can remember as a reporter covering city hall that the mayor tried the same technique. Or any governor you ever met. You-and-me, babe.

One pays a heavy price for succumbing. During the Johnson years, particularly, I heard people say, for example, "Gee-zuz, Nancy Dickerson is going to tear your ass up because she *knows* Johnson and he lays a lot of inside stuff on her." It didn't happen. I have been beaten by many competitors on many stories, but I have yet to be beaten by a reporter who went that route. They do learn things, many of which they are not free to report. Once a politician takes you into his confidence, it can be hell getting out. The only way to fly is to say, "I'd like you to respect what I do. But I'm not running any popularity contest." You have to make that point, early on. If you don't, you never will.

Long after my breaking-in period on the White House beat the three network correspondents were invited to LBJ's hospital room after surgery on his vocal chords. Obviously, the visit was arranged so that he could report on his swift recovery. The occasion was not unremindful, I might add, of that day at the ranch in 1955. But as we chatted, idly, a cake was wheeled in for Ray Scherer of NBC, a birthday surprise. The President then presented him with a gift, a pair of pajamas.

As I filed out, behind Scherer and Frank Reynolds, of ABC, the President signaled me to wait. In a paternal tone he assured me, "Son, you stay in Sunday school and keep your nose clean and maybe someday you'll get a pair of pajamas, too."

Johnson could say more in a sentence than most politicians could in a filibuster. I never got my pajamas. More often what I got was a phone call from the President himself, moments after the Evening News, demanding, as only he could, "Rather, are you trying to fuck me?"

This happened even before the war in Vietnam blew out of control and before students were being tear-gassed in the streets for saying the war was wrong. Johnson would be returned to office in a landslide that November, 1964, while preaching peace. And with the help of leftover John Kennedy aides, he would get us deeper into a war that seemed to have no end and no point.

But Washington was not a bad place to be. It was pleasant to be settled for a change. My daughter, Robin, had turned six and had already attended three schools in the *first* grade. That pattern could not continue. So when summer came Jean and the kids moved and we were together again in one house, even though it was a campaign year and I was gone much of the time.

No sooner had the '64 campaign ended, with Johnson's crushing win over Barry Goldwater, than CBS asked me to move to London. That offer hit me like a brick. Yes, I had wanted to work overseas. I had always wanted to be a foreign correspondent. But not just then. Not another move.

There was something else, a tiny gnawing thought. Three things could have happened, and two of them were bad. One, Johnson had applied pressure to get me rotated; two, I had not been very good at what I was doing; or three, CBS had decided my work was done in Washington, and God needed me in London.

I thought Bill Small looked uncomfortable when he brought up the assignment. My head was muddled. Frankly, I did not feel 1964 had been a good year for me. I had arrived with no sources in Washington, where you can't operate without them. I was just beginning to dig in. I was not anxious to pack up my family again, and this talk of London made no sense to me at all. Why London? I mean, World War Two was over.

But what I wound up saying was, "Look, I'm not sure I want to move and I'm a little shocked by the idea. I've moved an awful lot in a short time."

In fairness, Ernie Leiser, one of the people who had hired me, and a man I trusted, laid it on the line. "Dan, when you came here you said you wanted to be a foreign correspondent. We think it would be good for you. In fact, the network's position is that you will never develop into a fully rounded correspondent unless, and until, you get a wide variety of experience, including a tour overseas. You said when you came here that policy was one of the things you liked about us."

Fred Friendly was the president of CBS then. Salant had moved from CBS News into the corporate structure. Up to then I had few direct dealings with Friendly. I was reluctant, to put it gently, about the whole idea.

Fred Friendly is mercurial, a great hulk of a man, large hands, quick mind, a short attention span, intense, a born salesman. I always thought his name sounded like one of the classic show-biz inventions, like Marjorie Morningstar or Dick Darling. Fred Friendly.

But Fred's contributions to this industry had been gigantic. He had been with Ed Murrow at the beginning of "CBS Reports." Friendly had been the film maker and the salesman, Murrow the journalistic heart of it. Friendly now had the job of revitalizing CBS News. Huntley and Brinkley were in their heyday at NBC. CBS, not accustomed to being second in anything, was trailing in the evening news ratings. A strong second, but still second. Friendly's mandate was to lead us back. He was flaying in every direction.

So I went in to see him. He looked me right in the eye and said the single most persuasive thing you can say to anyone in that spot, "Dan, you have got to get overseas. And you're going to London." He spoke with trumpets in his voice. Then he ticked off the names . . . Murrow, Smith, Collingwood, Kendrick, all London-schooled newsmen, a line of excellence. And he said, "I think you have it in you to be the next Ed Murrow."

That phrase, of course, gets vastly overworked. What you learn after a while is that any time anyone is trying to get his hand on your leg in this business, he will tell you that you can be the next Ed Murrow.

But it sings. And Fred may have meant what he said in all sincerity. He felt so strongly about Murrow, he was *always* looking for the second coming, for someone who might measure up, knowing in his bones that no one could. As Sevareid said, Murrow was a shooting star.

This was December, 1964, and that was his argument. I came back and said to all of them, Small and Leiser and Friendly, I wasn't happy about going. They made it clear I had no choice. As it turned out, what they wanted to do was bring back Alexander Kendrick from London and move Harry Reasoner from New York to the White House.

Reasoner was then the second man at CBS News, filling in at times for Cronkite and anchoring the Sunday night news. Friendly felt they did not have Reasoner in the most effective role. So he planned a chain reaction of moves that would, not necessarily in order: give some of the newer people more experience, and put such better known names as Reasoner in places where they would get more daily exposure. He wanted to build the White House as a "star" assignment. Looking back, I suppose all his ideas made sense; certainly they did to Fred Friendly.

My impression was that Reasoner did not look with much joy on the idea of leaving New York. He was sort of in my position, willing to go but not sure the move was really best for him. (Five years later he went to ABC.)

I called Friendly on the phone and tried to bargain. "Okay," I said, "not that I have any choice, but if I'm going overseas, to get experience—at my age and at this stage of my career—where I ought to be sent is Vietnam. You know, and I know, that the war is going to get bigger. It is going to be the only story that matters."

Friendly said he wasn't all that certain, but, yes, that could be. I could almost hear him warming to the idea on the telephone. So I bore in. "One, it's going to be one of the most important things to happen in my time and I want to see it. Two, I don't have combat experience and reporting is what I want to do. Most of the really great reporters have covered wars. Third, well, London sounds like backwater to me, and that's not what I think I'm cut out to do. I don't want to be reporting stories about thatch-roofed cottages."

Friendly said, "You and I may be the only ones who believe the story is going to be that big. But there is a lot to what you say and if you want to go there, let me check around. Maybe we can arrange something."

I let myself get excited. To say the least, Jean was not. I had promised her that once we got through the campaign we could settle down and have some semblance of normal family life. London still offered that prospect. Not Vietnam.

After the conversation with Friendly, Jean said, "What is it with you? A move to London is one thing. That's a class move, whatever their motives. Maybe Johnson did ask them to get you off the run. And, yes, it may be that you haven't done a very good job. London, that can be a family experience. But *you*, no, you want to go off to some God-forsaken jungle and risk getting your head blown off."

I really had no answer for her, so things were uneasy at home.

Fred and I talked again a day or two later. He had gone from hot to warm to lukewarm. He said, "Look, the problem is, there is a series of moves being made here. We're bringing Kendrick back from London and we need to replace him with just the right person. Some people, including me, think you're it. The big thing is, we don't want to send anyone to Vietnam who has a family."

I broke in at that point and said, "Well, it's still what I want to do. And I'd like you to fight for me."

Friendly was sensitive to feelings of that kind. After a pause he said, "If you feel that strongly, I'll do what I can. I admire you for it and I know you'd be great there. It would be a worthwhile experience for you."

The next time we talked, he said flatly, "It isn't going to happen. I think you're right, but the more we talk the more obvious it is that you have to go to London. That's the next step. If the story in Vietnam gets as big as you and I think it will, you'll get there one way or another."

I don't claim credit for being clairvoyant. In 1964 the talk had been of turning the fighting over to the Vietnamese, or of pouring in more troops and ending the war. But few people envisioned then that the war would drag on past 1965, much less another eight years.

We went to London.

It is quite easy to become enchanted with the England of your mind's eye: Westminster Abbey and the white cliffs of Dover, Buckingham Palace and the changing of the guard, Big Ben and Mayfair and Hyde Park. Even the Beatles.

But my introduction came through Alex Kendrick. I had not known a great deal about him, but I was aware that he had covered the Russian front during the war when few others had. In the later stages other reporters poured in, but Kendrick had been there during the toughest going. He was the classic foreign correspondent, and this was the man I found myself succeeding.

One of the first and best pieces of advice he gave me was in reference to the English people. He said, "Because they speak the same language, it is difficult to remember that this is a foreign country. The easiest thing is to be taken with the upper class, or those who have pretensions. And class *is* still a factor in England. It is easy to make the judgment that these are the can-do people. But keep in mind, they are *not* the ones who won the war."

What he meant was, whether you were dealing with office personnel or camera crews or whatever, the easiest course would be to give the edge to the guy with polish. He was simply cautioning me against making judgments based on whether they dressed snappily and had that clipped, aristocratic accent. We had a mixture in the London bureau of very talented people, some who had that upper-class polish and some who did not.

I had not been in London long when Kendrick invited me to lunch at a restaurant called the White Tower. He introduced me to the Americano, a concoction of Campari, lemon and soda. Just after we got the order settled—baked fish—he removed his glasses, buffed them with his napkin and said, "Well, it's going to be very interesting to see, young man. Your being a child of television."

Really, I wasn't. He was a trifle early. But I knew what he meant. So many young people go to college today and it is all settled in their minds. They want to be Cronkite or Sevareid or Roger Mudd or Mike Wallace. I'm not very good at reading people's heads or their hearts, but what so many of them really want is to be a small-bore movie star. And there is nothing especially wrong with that. But you have to understand what television is to them: a cheap way to be in the movies.

That's the trend today. I blame the colleges and universities in part. But television has just exploded, in a way that doesn't lend itself to blame. The medium is such a powerful presence in our lives, it creates stars and mini-stars even among people who resist, who don't want, don't need or don't deserve stardom. Even bad exposure in television makes you something special. In America today used-car salesmen who do the most wretched commercials become local celebrities.

I corrected Kendrick very quickly and as respectfully as I could. I told him I did not consider myself a child of television. There was, in my background, newspaper, wire service and radio experience. He heard me out and, in fact, seemed relieved. But he added, "Nonetheless, you are the next wave and you are here partly because you have a pretty face." That cut. And I hoped his conclusion wasn't entirely true.

I really felt that I belonged to a group that bridged the two eras, between those who grew up as print journalists and those who were television-bred.

Kendrick said, "What I will be interested to see is whether you have any gawd-dam sense." It was meant in a friendly spirit and I took it that way. But there was just enough grit in me to think, fair enough, mister. I'll do my best to show you and I'll compare notes another day.

He was a straight talker, candid, even blunt, but never insulting. No one could have been more helpful. To relieve Kendrick in London, you don't just walk in and join him for lunch at the White Tower and have him pass the baton. Kendrick was too much a professional for that. He took weeks, I mean weeks, to introduce me to every source he had. To those who were out of town or the country, he gave me handwritten notes.

There is a pride in men like Kendrick and Collingwood and Winston Burdett. They not only do their best to pave the way for you, they are saying, in effect, if you blow this chance, if you tarnish what we have established, we hold you accountable. You will have only yourself to blame.

Kendrick even walked me through several days of what his routine was like. "Everyone has his own," he said, "but this is mine."

I was still figuring out my own working methods when a mine cave-in was reported in Wales. The disaster quickly disabused me of any romantic notions I might have had about my new job. When the first bulletin chattered over the ticker I turned to Patricia Bernie, who had worked with Murrow in the London bureau during some of his television years, and said, "Charter an airplane for me." Then I walked back into my office to use the phone.

Patricia followed me and said, "I'm going to do what you asked, but you *did* mean you want to charter an airplane from London to Wales?"

I said yes and puzzled over why she would ask. Only much later did it dawn on me that chartering a plane in Britain was not that easy, or common, or done quickly. They have far less flying weather than we do in the States. Fog, mist and pelting rain are not just backdrops for Jack the Ripper movies. And the distances are such that the British mostly go by rail or car or maybe a ferry or boat.

We reached Wales even before the BBC. They had a stringer in the area, but before their main force arrived we were on the scene, thanks to the chartered plane.

For U. S. television, a coal-mine disaster in Wales is at best a marginal story; never mind that thirty or forty lives were lost. For that story to play on CBS as a film piece, with a report by our London correspondent, a lot of chips have to fall in line. Among the factors are, can you get in, bring out the film, and feed it back to the States in time for the next Evening News? And will we alone have it or will our competition have it too? Freshness is one of the tests of what makes news. So reaction time can be the difference. The quicker you get there the better your chance of getting a picture before the p.r. people move in, cart off the dead, tidy up the scene and lay out their stories.

This was one film that did make the Evening News, but that isn't why I remember it. One of my favorite movies is *How Green Was My Valley*. Part of the reason the memory stays with me is the portrayal of the young crippled boy. I had seen the movie in the early 1940's, during the time when I was ill with rheumatic fever, and in a way I identified with the boy. There was an unforgettable scene in which the miners were coming to work in the morning in the mist and fog, a terrific piece of film.

It had been a pell-mell day—a mine cave-in, catching the plane, getting there and even beating the BBC—and when we reached the mine the feeling just swept over me. The scene was identical, I thought, to the one frozen in my mind from the movie. Perhaps it wasn't. But at that moment what I saw stopped me in my tracks, and I sort of fixed the picture in my brain and thought, Yes, it's exactly as I had seen it on the screen.

Our British cameraman was just behind me and when he caught up I started talking excitedly about the resemblance between this scene and the movie, *How Green Was My Valley,* how it had the same feeling, how symbolic it all seemed to me.

He was very British, and one of the lasting sights my mind will hold is the totally mystified look on his face as I rattled on. It was all Swahili and high Norse to him. And after a bit I shut up and said, "Well, let's get on with it."

Postscript: I'm not sure how this all ties together, but after I had returned from Vietnam in late 1966, I was in the newsroom one day in New York and a question arose about Lyndon Johnson. One of those questions someone shouts across a room, just letting it hang in the air like a weather balloon. I fired an answer right back, almost a reflex. Emerson Stone, who had asked the question, said, "Are you sure?" And Alex Kendrick, who was there, spoke up and said, "Listen, if it's about Johnson and Rather says so, you can believe it." He turned around and went about his business. A small moment, but I found myself hoping Kendrick's snap reply might have been at least a tiny stamp of approval, an answer to another question raised over lunch one day in London.

Out-Take

7

THE PRESS SECRETARY

Of all the men who have spoken, and misspoken, on behalf of the Presidents of the United States, the model for the job ought to be Ike's man, James C. Hagerty. This opinion is shared by reporters who dated their experience to Woodrow Wilson. Hagerty was the best of all press secretaries.

My one working contact with him took place in May, 1960. I had been assigned as a pool reporter for the Corinthian stations to travel abroad with Eisenhower. What was to have been an historic trip to the Soviet Union and Japan became something much less. A U-2 spy plane, flown by a man named Francis Gary Powers, was shot down over Russia in a dismal piece of timing. There went the Soviet Union trip. Student riots erupted in Japan. We would not be welcome there either.

Instead we touched down at Korea, Formosa and the Philippines. On the way home we stayed in Honolulu for nearly a week, which I thought was extraordinary. But Ike was nursing a cold. It was the end of his presidency. The trip had been a fiasco. And he wanted to play golf.

All through this disaster Hagerty had been remarkable. There was an entire press plane of people along for the trip. But when I applied for my credentials it was not some underling who saw me. It was Hagerty. He made a point of saying glad to have you. He asked questions about my background, made an effort to get to know me. Every other day—and remember, I'm a nobody from nowhere—he would check to see how I was doing, if I was getting what I needed. This was Jim Hagerty in 1960, who had been there.

In Honolulu I began to feel pangs of conscience. My company had spent a tidy sum of money to send me along and all we had done was bounce around the backwater of the Far East. I had not been sending the

Corinthian stations any material that could be described even as semiexciting. I was lamenting about that one day to Cleve Ryan, the White House lighting man. He was paid on a co-op basis by all the networks, in order to have one light man the Secret Service knew. Ryan was a Boston Irishman, one of the seldom credited people who make things work.

"This trip has been a lot of fun for me," I said, "but, I dunno, when we get back I'm going to catch hell. There hasn't been much news on this trip."

Cleve was no Harvard graduate but he had a gift for cutting through the grist. "What you need," he said reassuringly, "is a big interview."

I cocked an eyebrow. "Well, yeah, that would be nice."

He nodded and touched my shoulder. "Let's work on it. Lemme see, who can we get? Ike? Hmmm. We could show up when they tee off and . . . naw, that's too much and the other guys would bitch."

Well, Cleve made it his business to go to Hagerty. He said, "Listen, what about this kid from Texas? He hasn't been getting any news. What can you do for him? What he needs is a big interview. Now you arrange that, Jim."

Not every press secretary would take that kind of talk from a lighting man. Years later, in the Nixon Administration, Ryan was treated like a White House lighting man, to their loss. But with Hagerty he had another kind of relationship and that was to Jim's interest. Cleve Ryan knew everyone, and what most of them were thinking.

The next day Hagerty came to me and said, "Look, I should have thought of this myself. It's true the trip hasn't turned out as we thought it would. We've sent everybody who was anybody back to Washington. But if you want to do an interview with me, I'll give you a little news."

I stammered, "Well, I couldn't do it any sooner than twenty seconds from now, Mr. Secretary."

That may sound small potatoes. But in 1960 it counted, especially to a fellow working for a chain of local stations. Hagerty gave me one of those this-is-how-the-President-feels-about-the-trip interviews. There was some pickup on it and the wire services asked for a transcript. All I can tell you is that it salvaged my trip.

If Hagerty was good at his job, that spoke well for Eisenhower. He had Ike's complete confidence. There were no games. He was very secure, in contrast to Ron Ziegler.

Pierre Salinger was the press secretary when I went to Washington in 1964. He was still on the scene, feeling his way with Lyndon Johnson but not yet decompressed from Dallas. I was not one of his favorites. I was new and not very good. And from Texas.

It is also true that the Kennedy people played favorites. ABC's Bill Lawrence, a former *New York Times* man, was often beating me on stories. Some of those stories I thought were special gifts from Salinger. This got me into a row or two with Pierre. I said, "Look, I don't know very much, but I know enough to know that you lay stories on people and I resent it."

He was honest enough to say, "Damned right. I've known Bill Lawrence a long time and I sometimes lay stories on him." He paused and smiled. "Of course, if you quote me I'll deny it." Then he chewed the end of his cigar and said, "If you ever show me anything"—which I took to mean, if you play ball—"I may lay a story on you from time to time."

I don't believe that in his heart Pierre respected television reporters as a group. He considered most of us to be more announcers than journalists. For whatever reasons, we never got along very well. It may have been as much or more my fault as his.

Salinger sometimes played the jester's role in the Kennedy inner circle. He had the best sense of humor of any press secretary I have been around. There also was a kind of trenchant cronyism about him. He played poker, drank, and smoked cigars with a small group of favored reporters. Even those outside of that group liked Pierre, but we regularly cursed some of his ways.

Among the other press secretaries who served under Johnson (remember that Salinger also was LBJ's spokesman for a while), George Reedy had an academic mind, Bill Moyers was an especially quick thinker, and George Christian, the last of the line, had the best sense of when to say how much. He did not hesitate to say, "That is all we want you to know, gentlemen."

Ziegler, whatever his shortcomings, was as hard a worker as ever held the job.

President Ford's man, Ron Nessen, was a solid broadcasting reporter whose temper and lack of organization skills hurt him in the White House job.

If press secretaries were given I.Q. tests—and that might not be a bad idea; a minimum score of sixty ought to be required, as it should for correspondents—George Reedy would score the highest, I think. He was an intellectual, in the best sense of the word. But in the press secretary's job, a sensitive mind is not always an asset.

Chapter
8

A GREEK CHORUS

LONDON HAS THE SMELL of old tweeds. It is a place where you hear the word *civilized* at least once every day, used as readily in reference to death, divorce or war. London was to be my jumping-off place to that half of the world, my way station to international politics and, if you will, foreign intrigue.

But first I wanted to hit the ground running. I had established one point at CBS. I might not have as much finesse as some would like, the edges were rough, but the scouting report on Rather was: He will get there and he will turn something out.

That was the reputation I had and that was the one I wanted.

The immediate problem in London was figuring out what the story was. It is one thing to be shipped into Selma, Alabama, or Washington, D.C. You knew what you had to cover.

But London was a whole new and different puzzle, literally a new world for me. As the bureau chief you were responsible for the budget, for allocating your resources, and so I plunged into it. One of my tasks was to reorganize the office. Almost the last words Fred Friendly spoke to me were in the form of a challenge. "You are going to be measured," he said, "by how many pieces for television you turn out of that bureau. It is not the only way you'll be measured, but that's one of them."

The emphasis in London then was on radio, and had been ever since CBS had put in a bureau in the days before World War Two. "We have got to plunge into the television age," Friendly had said. "We have all been derelict about doing this and now the satellite is going up."

We tend to forget, today, the revolutionary steps taken in television during the last fifteen years in terms of news coverage. The use of videotape and the launching of the first commercial space satellite, called Early Bird, and later, TelStar, were creating new horizons.

Friendly was a visionary. I sometimes thought his vision outran what was practical. But he foresaw a day when you would have the CBS Evening News with a dual anchor, one man in London or Paris and another in New York. And possibly a third doing the weather from Moscow. That day may be coming.

But they were still radio-oriented in London, and why not? All the people who had been there were trained in radio, were products of an age when radio had the force to move millions. But now we had a new direction. CBS wanted picture stories. I was determined to develop them.

The day I arrived I met with my two cameramen, Johnny Tiffin and Cyril Bliss, both British. I had been warned that the British, like the rich, were different from you and me. They were slower paced, given to long lunches and quiet nights. I made a point of going out to Tiffin's home. I'm not sure his wife, Wendy, appreciated my barging in, but I was eager to get started. And, as it turned out, so were Tiffin and Bliss.

This was another case of building an organization, and that has been among the joys I have known in this business. Certainly, we were not starting this time from the ground up. We were, in fact, in the offices once occupied by Ed Murrow, broadcasting from some of the studios Murrow had used during the war, a location he "could not identify" for reasons of security.

I could get goose-bumps just staring at the gray walls of those rooms. I often listened to old recordings of Murrow. Sometimes he would begin, "This is Edward R. Murrow," quickly, matter-of-factly, slight pause. "This"—long, dramatic pause—"is London." After that sentence became his trademark and the voice was so well known, he was shrewd enough to realize what was needed. He would come on cold, with no signature, just, "This is London," and sign off at the end.

So we were rebuilding something. The joys I had felt in Houston and in New Orleans, where I had created my own teams, I began to know again in London. We cranked out pieces. And, by working around the clock, we did gear the bureau to servicing for television. The pace was difficult for some of the staff. But news is a twenty-four-hour business. I don't want anyone working around or for me who doesn't feel that way.

In effect, we put through a production-line speedup. I could say to myself, okay, buster, you're going to get a chance to show what you can do because there are no ongoing stories here. So we produced a lot of what are known in the trade, and in England, as "civilization" pieces.

The people with their dramas and their survivals are always there if you dig and find them. We did one such story on a group of children who had lost their mother and father. The oldest was sixteen and they were fighting to stay together. They had held a family council, had refused to be divided and sent to foster homes. They wanted to remain a family.

Cyril Bliss made what proved to be a beautiful, touching film. They were British, but you could speak Chinese and understand that story. As a result of that piece being on the air we received hundreds of contributions sent from the States to the bureau in London, more to CBS in New York and some directly to the kids. The story demonstrated to the British the impact of television, American style. This was 1965 and I don't mean they were provincial, but the reaction raised their eyebrows. As reserved as the British are, they were impressed that a short burst on the Evening News would attract so much attention.

By midsummer of that year, 1965, it was obvious that London's air service made it the ideal jumping-off place for all of Europe, and much of the world. We now had the satellite, which made it so much faster to transmit stories from abroad. We had a sense of some new power, and we began to play around with it over the phone, in conversations I had with Friendly and Bob Little, our overseas editor, and Ralph Paskman.

We all agreed that if something happened in, say, Africa, the best way to get there was from London. We began to train our staff to react quickly. To think jet planes and satellite feeds. Travel light, move fast, work lean.

So we were ready when trouble developed in Greece, the beginning of the toppling of the monarchy. I flew in and stayed a month to cover the story. With me were Tiffin and a sound man, Peter Morley, and the two of them formed a splendid British crew, quick and heady. Furthermore, they knew Greece.

Constantine, not yet twenty-five, recently had ascended to the throne on the death of his father, King Paul I. The country was torn by the civil war between Greek and Turkish forces on the island of Cyprus. In Athens there were demands for general elections. Behind the scenes some military muscle-flexing was taking place.

We arrived when demonstrations against the monarchy were mounting and there had been clashes in the streets. Repeatedly, before leaving London, we had been warned to be careful, that Greece was a very tough scene.

I thought to myself, if it's any tougher than Selma or Jackson, I don't want to go. But I didn't really expect it to be.

The difference was that the disorders in Greece were scheduled, and with precision. If we were told that a demonstration would occur at 2 P.M. and last for forty-five minutes, we could count on it. A newsman could file his story and, for the rest of the day, go to the beach and enjoy the Adriatic sun, or find a bar and spend the afternoon drinking ouzo, the Greek propellant.

It was a relaxed assignment as pre-revolutions go. But the street action was deceptive. Centuries of Greek tradition were unraveling. There were so many factions—the loyalists, the military, the anarchists, the Communists—no one could learn all the secret handshakes. It very quickly ceased to be fun and games. We soon discovered we were under surveillance by the government. I never quite understood which agency—their version, I suppose, of the CIA or the FBI or military security. But it was obvious we were being watched. We would see characters taking notes and photographs.

In due course a government courier called on us at the Grande Bretagne, where we enjoyed a superb view of the Acropolis from our window. In human terms Greece, even for one month, was a great and humbling experience for me because it drove home how little I knew. In the schools where I spent my childhood you learned a good deal about Texas history but not much about the world.

Our visitor was not uncivil. He told us we were operating without a permit and would have to see the deputy minister of the interior. He made it clear that no one was pressing us. But it would be wise to drop around and apply for proper credentials.

We probably should have done so. We had already bumped into the law at various points and bluffed our way out of a spot. When asked for our press credentials we would mumble something about being Swedish and pretend we didn't understand. I suppose that act had worn thin.

So we went around to see the appropriate bureaucrat on an errand I thought would be routine. When we arrived, his secretary told us the minister wanted to see us personally and had asked us to wait. Johnny Tiffin and Peter Morley were with me and we seated ourselves in the hall and twiddled our thumbs. Tiffin, who knew his way around Europe, remarked that this was all a bit unusual. As a rule some clerk filled out a card and you left.

Finally the secretary ushered us into a large and rather ornate office. It was obvious that the deputy minister intended to impress us. The walls were made of what seemed to be Greek marble; a high ceiling, windows of leaded glass. The minister sat in an oversized leather chair and, something I noticed later in Dr. Kissinger's office, every other chair in the room was below the level of *that* chair.

He looked like a minor character out of the movie Z. Swarthy, full moustache, dark suit, white shirt too big in the collar, a cigarette held more than smoked. He spoke English with a Greek accent but he spoke with confidence. He asked what I was doing in Athens and, impatient to get on with it, I said, "I'm with CBS News."

"Yes, I know that," he said, "but what are you doing here?" Something in his voice made me hesitate, as if a flag had been raised. I said, "We're here to cover the political situation."

He nodded. "Yes, yes," and now he began to fire a series of fairly probing questions. He wanted to know a great deal about me, where I was from, where I had been, whom I knew. The quiz went well beyond just filling out a form and Tiffin, who was seated off to my right, kept shooting me glances. With each question it became increasingly evident that this was more than what it had appeared to be.

A full forty minutes later he dropped the name of George Polk, a CBS News correspondent who had been killed in Greece in the late 1940's under mysterious circumstances. At the time the war had not been over long, and the battle was on to prevent Greece from falling to the Communists. The partisans who had fought the Nazis came out of the hills, still armed, their motives not always clear. The country was split, the political undercurrents mixed, the threat of civil war growing.

One day the body of George Polk was found floating in a lake. No one ever learned how or why he died, but it was known that he had been trying to make contact with the guerrillas to get their side of the story. A journalism award, the George Polk Award for Overseas Reporting, is given in his memory. I knew the story.

This Greek official just dropped the name in an offhand way, but there was no mistaking that he had mentioned it for a reason. He wanted to see if I knew who George Polk was and how I reacted. A name twenty-five years out of the past. I remember checking myself: Now, wait, this is a new situation for me but I know something is wrong here.

So I said, "Why don't you just get to the point. We have been here for over an hour. We came to get our credentials, which we're entitled to have. Either give them to us or don't, but spare us any more of this"—I groped for a delicate word, gave up, and said—"in Texas language we call it bullshit. I don't know what the word is in Greek. But you mentioned George Polk. I never knew him. But he worked for my company and, in a vicarious way, he's a friend of mine. I'm a colleague of his and . . ."

At that point he held up his hand and said, "Well, what this is about, Mr. Rather," and he paused for effect and went on, "is the danger of too much zeal." There was an awkward silence then and Tiffin's eyes kind of jumped.

I said, "I'm not sure I understand what you mean."

He said, "Well, why don't you think about it."

I said, "Is that a threat?"

He seemed honestly startled. "Oh, no, no, no. Do not be offended. I just say that to you as a friend, that too much zeal can be dangerous."

As we got up to leave, our host told me that he had been on a committee appointed by the government to investigate Polk's murder and submit a report. The probe may have been done under pressure from CBS, or at the request of Polk's family.

Possibly, nothing that was said was meant to sound as ominous as I took it. The government official was, after all, speaking a language foreign to him and my Greek was nonexistent. He may have been saying, We don't want another body pulled out of a lake, and have to spend three months trying to explain what happened. Don't come to our country and try to be a hero at our expense.

We did receive our credentials. At the door the official stuck out his hand and said, "I wish you well." To this day I still have no idea what that interview was all about.

The next afternoon, however, we were invited to the home of a Greek woman who had made a point of bumping into us at the hotel. She invited the crew and myself out for drinks. An older woman, respectable, married, with a family, though I am certain she was involved in some way with whatever the Greeks then called their secret service.

We sat on her terrace in the fading sunlight. She spoke perfect English and she was very interested in what we were doing, what we had seen. She made a point of saying, "I invited you to my home because you are a foreign correspondent, and it is very easy to come in here and misunderstand Greek politics. So often, an American or British television crew comes to Athens and they just see the surface. They do not examine anything in depth, and that can be a great disservice, to your country and to mine. I, first of all, simply wish to entertain you and welcome you to my country. Secondly I implore you to be aware, to look beneath the surface, to work at understanding what is really happening here, what a difficult time this is for my Greece."

It is a hazard of this profession, of course, that one can go nuts trying to read hidden meanings where none exist. But those were, indeed, hard and bitter times for Greece. Perhaps all that was being asked of us was fairness and restraint. The Greek government, then as now, cared mightily about the image that was presented back in the United States.

But the people loved to talk in circuitous ways, a trait I found strange and disconcerting. I can only say that among the scenes branded in my mind is this minor Greek official dropping the name of George Polk and telling us, "This is about the danger of too much zeal."

Tiffin, who was no novice, and I put away several glasses of ouzo that night and tried to figure out what the hell it meant. We never did. We just went ahead and covered the story as best we could.

But the memory of George Polk nagged at me. Still does. Whenever the chance would come along I talked to other correspondents who had been in Greece or had worked for the network when Polk was there. Nearly everyone had a theory.

You began with the fact that Polk had gone off to find the Communists and that, in itself, was dangerous, not unlike later newsmen trying to contact the Viet Cong or the Pathet Lao. Guerrilla fighters do not always stop to ask questions. He might have been killed by mistake or to keep him from reaching the Communists or by either side to create an incident. Or he could have been murdered by highwaymen. I know from my own experience in Vietnam that such scavengers are always around in times of civil strife. Wars ennoble no one. Polk could have died in any of those ways. It was a mystery then and remains so to this day.

We were back in London by the end of July, 1965. The story in Greece would go on, with periodic eruptions, until the Revolt of the Colonels in 1967 and the fall of the monarchy. The country that invented democracy would be under military rule.

From London the world indeed seemed a smaller stage. In August, 1965, at about 2:30 one morning, I had an overseas call from New York. Bob Little was on the line. "There is a plane leaving for Karachi at four A.M.," he snapped. "Be on it."

Rubbing the sleep out of my eyes, I said, "Well, what's going on?"

"We don't have time for that now. It's a long run to the airport. The plane stops in Beirut. Call us when you get there."

I always kept a bag packed for just such a moment, a habit that dated back to my travels through the South. Jean was barely awake when I kissed her lightly, said, "I'm gone," and headed out the door with two dollars and forty cents in my pocket. I remember the amount because it wasn't enough to pay the cab fare to the airport. But I had credit cards, and Little could be counted on to cable some expense money to Beirut, which he did. The important thing was to be on that plane.

At London airport I had a ticket agent pay the driver and add the charge to my air travel card. I made the plane with two minutes to spare. I didn't know exactly where I was going, or why, or what I was to do when I got there. We landed in Beirut and as I walked into the terminal I heard myself paged. Little had left a message with the airline: "Glad you made it, *if* you made it. Pakistan has invaded and pushed into India. We don't know yet how deep the penetration is, or how long the war might last. Call me as soon as you can."

Winston Burdett had been in India and, I learned later, we were trying to get Bernard Kalb to Pakistan. Everyone was scrambling. Hostilities between the two countries had been historic, and now had reached open combat. The Pakistanis were making an armored stab, a la Patton, at New Delhi.

I heard them announce the continuation of my flight to Karachi. Efforts to reach New York by overseas telephone failed, so I reboarded the plane. When I arrived in Karachi I had no passport, no visa, nothing. But I managed to establish contact with New York and the message came back, in effect, "Congratulations on getting there. You did a great job, but you're on the wrong side. We want you on the India side."

Now, going back and forth between Pakistan and India is a little like trying to shuttle between Israel and the Arab countries. You don't just stroll across the border and say, "Hi, folks, do you mind if I cross over?" I had to fly up to Teheran to get back down into India and, finally, I found my way to New Delhi.

I was to relieve Burdett, who happened to be another idol of mine. You must now be thinking, This guy certainly has a lot of idols, and I am afraid that is so. Burdett had not been one of the originals in the Murrow group, but he had been recruited in the early 1940's and had been broadcasting from Rome since the mid-1950's.

I used to listen to a series of five-minute essays Winston broadcast when I worked in radio in Houston. He had a controlled delivery, very smooth and persuasive. He was not what you envisioned as the *macho* foreign correspondent. You know, the trench coat with the turned-up collar, the dangling cigarette and the big Rolex with the superdial, the three stops for turn-of-the-moon, the time zones and the date in English, Japanese and Arabic, so heavy the guy walks with a slight limp on whichever side he wears his watch.

Well, no one ever saw Burdett wear a trench coat, unless it was tailored. His watch was no Rolex and he wore a narrow, plain black band. He didn't need props, any of them. He was a slender man, frail, almost birdlike. But he had class. What he was stuck out all over him. And he had been there. He had covered the rebels in Yemen, had gone to India probably twenty times, and had written books about his experiences. And he was an expert on the Middle East.

He had now been in India for quite some months, had been ill of late and his relief was overdue. He was returning to Rome. Like Kendrick in London he laid it all out for me, names and phone numbers. And he gave me the history of India and Pakistan and a quick seminar on the strategic situation, realizing I didn't know a damned thing about the region. He also briefed me on everything from the local water (don't drink it), to where I could rent a car and not get cheated, to the exchange rate, rupees and dollars, on both the legal and black markets.

Then he was gone, and a totally strange environment closed around me. Rare is the Westerner who can travel India for the first time and come out unchanged. I didn't. It was for me an adolescent experience. Everywhere I looked there seemed to be something new and riveting. India is almost another planet. The only other time I had anything close to that feeling was on the trip to China much later with President Nixon.

I don't know what most people think of when they imagine India. Kipling. Gandhi. The Taj Mahal. Sacred cows walking loose on dusty roads. Or Sam Jaffe in an oversized diaper playing Gunga Din.

But the central fact of twentieth-century India is overwhelming poverty. Poverty and the arrogance of self-styled Indian intellectuals, those who, for example, love to harangue Americans about what is wrong with us when all about them are chaos and suffering. Nothing in my previous experience had prepared me for such pretensions amid so much filth, disease, decay and corrupted leadership. And the war, that was completely new to me, too.

Once I had covered a coup. I had been to Guatemala City in 1962 and had seen a tank roll up to the Casa Blanca in the wee hours of the morning. An officer stood in the turret of the tank and shouted, "We want you out of there in five minutes!" The president raised his bedroom window and looked out, saw the tank and the soldiers, and in his nightcap with the tassel dangling over one eye El Presidente said, in effect, "It looks like you got me high-carded. Can you give me ten?" And he was out. That's the way it was done in Guatemala.

But this was India and Pakistan with hatreds that went back into antiquity. This was war, on a large scale. From New Delhi, an Indian stringer and I rented a car and drove to a place called Lahore, whose name was unknown to me then, I am ashamed to say. I soon learned Lahore was an historic city. Alexander the Great had once marched through it.

Actually, it is a divided city—Lahore on the Pakistani side, and Amritsar on the Indian side.

So here was the flashpoint of all the old tempers. The violence between the two sides had been escalating for some time. Both armies were American-trained and -equipped, as crazy as that still sounds, but the Indians followed more of the British tradition.

We raced to the battle lines in our rented car. It was a little like being taken to a small movie theater and asking for the next feature. Except that this was no movie. It was real. We stopped someone and asked, "Where's the front?"

And he pointed down the road and said, "Across there, a few miles outside Amritsar. I'll take you there for a price."

You paid cash and you paid everybody. We made contact with an Indian army officer, British-trained, who offered to take us the rest of the way in his jeep. Everything had moved so fast I didn't have a full crew with me. I had gone on without Joe Masraff, the staff cameraman who had worked with Burdett. He had left New Delhi after us and had been held up by roadblocks outside of the city.

Two days later Joe caught up with us. That is a little like going on a honeymoon without your wife, but the first step, always, is to be where the story is. In the meantime I could file radio reports. I did have our Indian stringer, Ramnik Lekhi, who shot some silent footage, and I did a voice-over as narration.

A pitched battle was in progress when Lekhi and I reached the front. It was wide-screen stuff, with jets dogfighting overhead and tanks dueling in the sand. We were within a mile of the heaviest shooting, with rounds from both sides falling in our general area. My deal with the army officer was that he would take me with him and I would follow his orders. He didn't want me to get hurt and I'm sure he felt the same way about himself. So we dropped into a ditch. We had a good field of vision and could move freely up and down the trench.

Of course, it takes a while before you work up the nerve to move. The fear comes the first few times you hear a shell going over, whistling, landing with a thud. A curious experience. Someone once said that if you could hear it, the shell was in your vicinity. I accepted that information as fact and the first few I heard, I dived for cover. The army officer didn't laugh. He dived as well. But after a while your nerves seem to adjust and you do your job.

We could plainly see the Indian armor was much older. The Paks possessed more modern tanks with computerized firing; they could quickly calculate the range and find the enemy target on the radar screen.

The Indian tanks had smaller guns with less range, but they were better able to maneuver. This was classic mechanized warfare. One side had more mobility, the other had the firepower. The Pakistanis had the big jet fighter-bombers—but the Indians had the faster, smaller interceptors. It was the battle between the mongoose and the cobra.

In the field the Indians were using jeep-mounted bazookas, concealing them in a treeline. The Pakistani tanks would come ripping and roaring along the road to New Delhi in a desperate drive to get there, and the Indians would bait them with their smaller tanks, planted off to one side. They would lure the Paks off the main road, run them into the mud and the sludge, if they could. Then the Indians would move the jeeps with the bazookas to close range and knock a hole in the Pak tanks.

While the Indian planes were slower, they could outmaneuver the Paks' American-made fighter-bombers. Another thing, while the Paks had done well at the start with all their sophisticated equipment, when the crunch came they forgot a lot of what they knew.

In a single day I counted more than forty destroyed Pakistani tanks. Much of this happened in full view of our positions, where we sat crouched almost on the fifty-yard line. This was a long way from my bedroom in London. It must have been like the storied tank battles in North Africa in World War Two, except that here the equipment was more modern.

In the end the difference was in leadership. The Indian officers were better trained, used their equipment more efficiently and, of course, were fighting on their home ground. The Pakistanis outran their fuel supplies and were stopped short of New Delhi. The Indians began to pull together a counteroffensive, and the Paks were through.

All of which covered several weeks. Near the end, word came that the

Chinese, who were on friendly terms with the Pakistanis, were planning to take some of the heat off them by marching across the Himalayas. A Chinese invasion of India had been threatened for decades. It was a prospect India feared greatly.

True or not, that would be another story in another place. Literally, I would follow that story to the top of the world.

Out-Take
8

THE BRITISH LION

One day in 1965 I traveled by train with Harold Wilson, the Prime Minister of England, from London north to Manchester. I welcomed the chance to compare the trappings of government, ours and theirs.

In the wake of the Kennedy assassination I had gone through a year in which everyone in Washington was so security-conscious that if you opened a tin of aspirin you tried not to slam the lid.

So I boarded the train in London and there was Harold Wilson, this portly, white-haired, dowdy little man sitting in a public compartment. Near him sat only one security person—at least, only one was obvious to me. If there were others, they were disguised as empty seats. Wilson was traveling just a little better than the average rail passenger.

The train was clean, the compartment pleasant, but *Air Force One* it was not. The train was not even the *Wabash Cannonball*. It struck me as remarkable that the Prime Minister, the head of the British government, could move routinely, on a public conveyance, with virtually no restraints.

You hear frequent references to a quality called "British understatement." It is not just the way they talk and dress but also the way they think and live.

One imagines London and what one sees are two old men dozing over a chessboard. As a people they are patient. Thorough. Fastidious. Dogged. Jack the Ripper disemboweled seven whores and a hundred years later they discuss the case as though he were still at large.

Of course, the Queen, the royal family, the Palace Guards, all of that is for show, for pomp and circumstance. But it may be worth pondering that the head of government travels among the people with no frills.

Chapter 9

TO THE ROOF OF THE WORLD

THE RUMOR had spread and grown among the Indian troops as rumors do among any army, through a network unseen, unheard, unfelt. Chinese hordes, the old "human wave" number, were pouring through the Natu La Pass, creating an awful racket of gongs and bugles and their own unearthly shrieks.

I asked Lekhi, our Indian stringer, what he made of such talk. He thought, shook his head, said, "I hardly think so. No, the Chinese are not pouring into India. Possibly they have troops on the border. A feint, maybe. They have done so before."

I said, "That's good enough. Let's go."

Lekhi gave me one of those "crazy American" looks and said, in effect, you can't get there from here.

But I was already heading for the jeep, thinking ahead. Remember, this was 1965, years before the Nixon trip to China, before people started to look up the word *détente*. If any one part of the globe could be said to have still held a romantic fascination for newsmen, it would be what one might call *Lost Horizon* country: the high mountains where China, Tibet and India guard the secrets of centuries past.

There are, of course, assignments that pull you in such a way that it is hard to tell whether you have made an honest news judgment or surrendered to some misplaced yen for adventure. And, sometimes, if you are lucky, you have done both.

I tried to explain some of my feelings to Lekhi. I needed him, he knew the way and I trusted his caution. I was saying, listen, nobody, but nobody, has any film of the Chinese army doing anything. And who knows what we will find once we get up there and begin to operate. In the first place we might even get into China. Secondly if there actually is any combat going on up there, well, what a helluva story that would be.

Lekhi shrugged his shoulders and began collecting our gear. He could not understand traveling a thousand miles to look for trouble when we had it all around us. But he was not the kind to say no. Ramnik Lekhi was killed later, in Vietnam, working for CBS.

Our destination was the Natu La Pass, 14,000 feet above sea level, one of the three or four corridors through the Himalayas. The Pass was fifteen miles northeast of Gangtok, the capital of the small mountain kingdom of Sikkim, then an Indian protectorate.

I have long known that, for me, snap decisions are often best. Given time I tend to delay, analyze, wait for signs. Even then, however, I am often uneasy with decisions reached slowly. But I never second-guess the moves that must be made on impulse.

By this time, on our way back through New Delhi, we had picked up a new cameraman, a Dane named Carl Sorensen. We were now a really mixed crew. What I didn't know, but soon learned, was that Sorensen was the type who can get you killed. He was superb with a camera and courageous in a way that took me a long time to define. What I mistook in the beginning for courage may have been something a little different. Courage, I came to decide with more experience, was being afraid but going on anyhow. Sorensen was one of those people who never seemed to know fear. That quality is admirable in its own way but carries with it a danger. Carl would stick his head up *anywhere.* It was one thing to recognize, to calculate and take a risk and hope that whatever you were doing was worth the price. But Sorensen was strange in that sense. He was absolutely unafraid. It was as if fear were a language he had never learned and with which he now couldn't be bothered.

We three flew to Calcutta, then to Katmandu because that was where the mysterious "CIA Lady" was supposed to be. Lekhi had been told that the one best source on anything happening in the area was a woman at Katmandu known as "the CIA Lady." When we arrived she was out of town, probably at Gangtok, so that's where we headed. We never did find her.

From Katmandu, we eventually made our way by air to Siliguri. There we rented another jeep and drove straight up the base of the Himalayas to

Gangtok, through the purest kind of jungle. Monkeys dashed across the road in front of us. We saw what Lekhi said were tiger tracks, and when we got hungry we stopped and ate wild fruit off the trees, made soup from leaves and drank from the water cans we had stored in the back of the jeep. I'm not sure why, but the trip was wonderful.

The road was not as rough as we had expected, paved most of the way, almost untraveled, at least while we were on it. We drove to Gangtok in one full day. The village sits on a shelf of the Himalayas at an altitude of around 6,000 feet. In the distance we could see the three tallest peaks of the Himalayas, including Mount Everest. According to the local folklore, this is where the gods live.

Lekhi had been to Gangtok but not in many years. We were uncertain about our next move when we pulled in around two in the morning. We had been on the road since midnight of the previous day, and the only food we had eaten was the fruit we picked from the land. We were famished.

Now, Gangtok is straight out of *The King and I,* the Yul Brynner movie. It was like nothing I had ever seen before, with little pagodalike houses and mountain peaks looming in the distance and cotton wisps of white clouds visible below. A city in only the loosest sense, Gangtok had a population of maybe five thousand.

Sorensen, a blunt talker who spoke English with a Danish flatness, was not charmed. "Dammit," he said, "we can't go to bed without something to eat." We had brought bedrolls and puptents with us, figuring to sleep on the ground. The idea of trying to find a room had struck us as laughable.

At that hour the prospect of a hot meal wasn't exactly promising either. When we rolled into the village with Lekhi at the wheel everything was dark. No one was in sight, and nothing appeared to be open. We turned onto a dirt street that looked wider than the others around.

We had decorated our rented jeep with a diplomatic flag—a CBS shipping bag. That was an inside joke. Back in New Delhi we had been advised that no one was allowed to travel except under special orders, either military or diplomatic, because of the war. So I rented the largest limousine-looking car I could find, a black, 1950-ish Packard. We put a flagstaff on the fender and attached a CBS shipping bag, one of those yellow grapefruit sacks with the words stamped in red across the side, "CBS NEWS, RUSH, URGENT, HOLD AT AIRPORT." And that was our pass to roam all over India.

The trick worked so well we had decked out the jeep the same way.

Now here we were high in the Himalayas on a dusty road in Gangtok, and the only thing moving was our grapefruit bag, fluttering in the breeze with the CBS Eye in the middle, known to airport shipping clerks the world over. It was 2:30 in the morning and deader than Dodge City, and it was obvious to me, if not to Sorensen, that we were not going to find anyplace to eat.

At that moment a wild little man darted out of an alleyway and began running toward us. The Sikkimese are a small, wiry, bony people, physically not unlike the Vietnamese. He was flapping his arms and babbling away and I thought at first we were about to be robbed. I imagined we were being set upon by someone with a knife or a blowgun.

Then I realized he was shouting, "Hey, CBS, me CBS." He was waving a square of yellowing paper, folded so many times it was torn along the creases. He handed it to me with a toothy, triumphant grin, and I almost fell out of the jeep. Signed by Ralph Paskman, written years and years ago, the letter said:

"Dear Mr. ———— [he had a long Sikkimese name, one I couldn't pronounce then and can't remember now], Yes, we would be pleased to have you represent us as the CBS stringer in Sikkim. We will be happy to pay you for any footage we can use on the air at a rate of $5 a foot."

This was similar to the deal I had once made in Houston with a taxi driver named Dick Perez, only for less money and with a higher expectation of results. This was Sikkim's version of Dick Perez. He had written to CBS inquiring if they could use a stringer. I'm sure Ralph had decided, well, we need people worldwide and, who knows, this guy may run onto something. Paskman had shipped him two one-hundred-foot rolls of film, two CBS shipping bags with labels and the cover letter I had just read. That was the last contact anyone had with him. He had long since ruined the film, but the shipping bags were among his proudest possessions. They were proof that he was the accredited CBS News correspondent, meaning that he got into all the soccer matches for free.

He had been sleeping outdoors, under a lean-to, when the noise of our jeep awakened him. Of course, he had recognized the grapefruit sack and came ripping out to greet us. He was the kind of hustler-scrounger-climber that you could drop any place, at any time, and in a matter of hours he would be in on the action. It turned out he also claimed to be the stringer for the London *Daily Telegraph,* and a paper in Rome, and no telling what else. He didn't make any money, but he was loaded with prestige.

He spoke Hindi—better than he did English—and he and Lekhi conducted a little business right in the road, in the middle of that sleeping village. The next thing I heard was, "Food? I fix. Oh, yes, yes, yes." He made clear that we were very special guests. Indeed, he regarded us as his employers, having come at last to inspect the field office.

He assured us that he would explain the full story about the Chinese troops, but the first priority was to get us fed. He began pounding on a nearby door and woke up several women, not to mention most of the dogs in the neighborhood. The Sikkimese women, for the most part, are dainty and graceful and when they move you can almost imagine the tinkle of bells. Their voices are chirpy. They are obedient in the Oriental tradition.

The women proceeded to kill a chicken, being very careful to wring its neck right in front of us. That sounds gross, I know, but this was their way of assuring their guests the meat was fresh and hadn't been hanging around on a hook. They cooked a really delicious meal of chicken and rice right on the spot.

Our excitable new assistant—I'll call him Sabu—was a rare find. He was the perfect combination of houseboy and press agent. Sorensen, who had spent most of his life on the road and was always looking for a better place to stay, patted him on the head and said, "Say there, little friend, I don't suppose you could arrange a room somewhere instead of these bedrolls we have here?"

Indeed he could. He rushed off, ran around in very determined circles, then reappeared to tell us we had rooms at the new hotel. Still unfinished, the hotel had never been more than partly open but had been used for the royal wedding. I remembered that story. Sikkim was a remote country, with more or less artificial boundaries, not unlike the principality of Monaco. The news media discovered it in the early 1960's, when the maharaja, Palden Thondup Namgyal, married a New York society girl, Hope Cooke. They had met in the garden of a Buddhist monastery while she was visiting his country. It was a romantic story, the soon-to-be king and the American commoner, of different race and culture and class. His coronation had taken place in April, 1965, only a few months before our arrival.

The hotel had that strange new-but-rundown look of not quite completed buildings. Sabu led the way and woke up the guard and got us our rooms. There was no running water and we were the only guests, but we slept there, gladly.

Early the next morning the CBS man in Sikkim appeared to say he had arranged for us to meet the *Chogyal* (king). In a country so isolated, visitors of any station were not that frequent and, to be sure, the king was eager to receive us. We drove with Sabu to the palace, a beautiful, almost storybook place, with the fragile look of a hanging lantern.

The king led us into his back garden, with its rows of exotic flowers and lush greenery and tiny pagodas—the equivalent in this country, I guess, of gazebos. Our little hustler was in all his glory. I saw him whispering to the king's protocol man, and although I could hear none of it, and would not have understood anyway, his manner and expressions were unmistakable. He was saying something to the effect that we cannot have representatives of the United States government here and not invite them to dinner!

All of a sudden, with the power invested in him by no one, Sabu had made us representatives of the U. S. government. Sure enough, we were invited to dinner.

I wore a bush suit, the most formal attire I had and, in fact, the only change from my fatigues. The royal couple wore traditional silk gowns. Hope Cooke was a thin, intelligent young woman who took her role as the *Gyalmo* (queen) seriously. She was pale, with brown hair, reminding me of the studious girl who made the highest marks in her class and might have been pretty if she had the time. In the summer of 1973 she returned to the United States and applied to have her citizenship restored. Her husband had been forced into exile by the Communists.

I had no way of judging their marriage but I thought there was genuine affection between them. I have few other specific memories of that dinner, possibly because I was so eager to resume our trip, partly because the evening seemed not quite real.

The whole experience had been an eye-popper for me, especially watching Sabu operate. What a stroke of luck to run into that little character. He was obliging and willing and we paid him, but I must admit that as a stringer he was virtually useless. He had a camera, which he barely knew how to turn on. But no one could fault him on effort. Whatever you wanted or needed, he was boom-boom, can do. And he was proud to say that he understood the American way; that is, he was not part, he said, of this slovenly Indian system. He delivered. He seemed to know everyone, and before we left he introduced us to the only general Sikkim had. In truth, they boasted a general but no army, just a local militia. Sabu's man introduced us in turn to the Indian general in charge of protecting the Natu La Pass and that, after all, was where we wanted to go.

We left Gangtok and drove almost straight up the side of the mountain to reach the Pass. We traveled as far as we could by jeep to the general's tent, to an altitude of about 11,000 feet. Eventually we would reach almost 20,000, but by now we already had varying cases of altitude sickness. Lekhi suffered the worst. I wasn't far behind. Sorensen, damn him, could have cured his sickness with a Rolaid.

The symptoms were dizziness and queasiness of the stomach. When we got there the Indian general laid on a meal consisting of chutney and curry, Indian-style, thick with spice and grease. My insides already felt as though a bunch of squirrels were doing a folk dance. But I said to myself, I'm gonna get this meal down and it's gonna stay down. But it didn't. I was terribly embarrassed. I tried my best not to let the general know of my discomfort but I am sure, from the number of times I excused myself, that he guessed the problem. He understood, though, and was gentleman enough not to take special notice.

He was a polished man in every sense of the word, British-trained, tough, a good military man. But he had a curious obsession. He carried with him a tattered paperback copy of *Battle Cry,* the Leon Uris novel about the marines in World War Two. He loved that book, read and reread it, could quote you page after page and, in fact, recited long passages to his men. It was his Bible. He used excerpts to make a point about courage and military conduct. Many of the pages were dogeared, and he had underlined whole paragraphs in ink. He was a true aficionado of the Marine Corps.

The general went to some lengths to explain to us the tactical situation at Natu La Pass. The Chinese had made a couple of feints, he said, threatening to come across into Sikkim. He was unsure how many troops were now poised on their side but felt certain that Chinese troops had been massed there on more than one occasion. Keep in mind, intelligence and reconnaissance capabilities at that height were limited.

He later escorted us all the way to the Pass. We drove to a certain point by jeep and then transferred to horseback. And after another point we were issued oxygen equipment, as a safety precaution.

It was an eerie sight. Above us, in some nooks of the mountains, there were soldiers on both sides of the border, who couldn't really move around much because the air was thin and their oxygen masks and other high altitude gear were awkward. They looked like combat astronauts on the moon, sucking their oxygen tubes and sizing up one another. We could see the Chinese on their side—which was Tibet—wearing mountain-climbing gear with heavy fur-collared coats and square fur hats. One whom we took to be the commanding officer of the post had a red star on the front of his hat.

The Chinese had occupied this part of the country in 1959. Tibetan refugees fled through the mountain passes, struggling against the cold and the gales, to reach safety in India or Nepal. They brought out their ailing god-king, the Dalai Lama, straddling a *dzo,* part cow, part yak. During the long trek they unbraided their coarse black hair and pulled it across their eyes to keep from being blinded by the sun and snow.

All of that was now part of the lore of that lonely pass. A pile of rocks now marked the border between Sikkim and Tibet, and that was the picture: the Indian soldiers on the forward post on this side, the Chinese, in the distance, on the other side, both taking air and moving as little as possible to keep from wearing themselves out. Then there were the eerie sounds, the echoes. There is no echo anywhere in the world like an echo in the Himalayas. You could fire one shot up there and the noise would sound like World War Three, the shot bouncing off the mountain-tops and coming back to you, going on seemingly forever.

In this curious tableau some of the guards had been up there so long they sort of knew each other, yelling across the border to one another. I doubt whether any shots actually had been fired in anger. Each side had done a little of what the military people call recon-by-fire, but nothing more.

Still, I was certain we were going to get a fairly dramatic story. The doors are open a crack today, but in 1965 China was completely closed, as mysterious and forbidden in some ways as it had been a century and more ago. Excitedly, I told Lekhi and Sorensen what a terrific scene I thought we had—at the top of the world, with the Chinese and the Indians face to face, and the question still hanging in the air: Are the Chinese going to come pouring through Sikkim, into India, to relieve some of the pressure on Pakistan?

We began to speculate among ourselves about how to approach the story. If we could get right up to the border, maybe even a few feet over into their side, we could shoot pictures right down into Tibet. And as we talked, it slowly occurred to me that Sorensen, whom I didn't know all that well, was walking steadily forward, toward the Chinese lines.

The Indian general had turned us over to a British colonel. By now we were only a few feet away from the last Indian guard. When we drew even with him, the colonel said, in effect, "From this point, you are on your own." He gave us a quizzical look and dropped back.

Sorensen had a big sound rig on his shoulder, not one of the small, hand-held silent-film jobs, and I was working the separate sound system. Lekhi had stayed behind, still sick. So the two of us kept walking, with me attached to Carl by this electrical umbilical cord. I was saying, "Carl, um, Carl, I don't know whether we should go any farther or not. Carl?"

Sorensen just continued to move toward the border, and the last Indian guard was dropping farther behind us. We could see some Chinese soldiers clearly now, the lower half of their faces covered against the below-zero cold. They just did not know what to make of us. We weren't Indians. Americans? What would Americans be doing here?

We could have stopped at any point. I could have simply pulled the plug or said, no, hold it right here. The proposition was risky. But it was risk-versus-gain, and while I hesitated, Carl carried us along. His idea was, look, we just keep on walking and we get some really close-up pictures of these Chinese and then scram, before anyone gets nervous.

I knew what he had in mind. It was an old technique I had used myself. You just keep moving, gambling on the other side's indecision, and you bluff your way wherever you want to go. But I wasn't at all certain that this was the time or the place to be playing that kind of game. Yet the ruse seemed to be working. We were only a few yards from the top of the ridge. In a moment we would be able to look down into the other side, take film of that mist-shrouded Chinese valley in Tibet, get those closeups of the troops.

Unknown to us, three Chinese guards were much closer than we realized, kneeling behind rocks to our left. One of the Indian soldiers called out to warn us. But Carl was still walking forward, the camera grinding, focusing on the border outpost twenty yards ahead. I was growing more uneasy with each step.

Then I heard the very distinctive clack of a shell being rammed into a magazine, no more than ten yards away.

The sound startled me. And Carl as well. My immediate hope was that they recognized the object on his shoulder as a camera, but what the hell, it had a barrel, it could have been a weapon. So the first thing I did was put my hands up to indicate I was unarmed. Carl tried but couldn't, and in his confusion he knocked off his camera. He fumbled for it, had to sweep it off the ground. A kind of comic, madhouse moment. Without a word, we began to walk backward, almost in lockstep.

The Chinese guard didn't level at us. But his rifle was loaded and cradled across his chest. He shouted to one of the Indian soldiers, just some calling out back and forth. I could imagine the dialogue was along the lines of, hey, who are these people? Well, they are Americans and they are not going to tarry here.

I had a feeling that the Indians did not want to see us shot, but they would not worry unnecessarily if we were.

On the other hand, they seemed to be caught up in the tension. No doubt *spellbound* is too stagy a word; it was not unlike watching a car edging back toward a cliff. You want to call out, but a cry might startle the driver and send him over.

So the Chinese didn't know what we were about, and there was this very clear, ominous click. Sorensen got the camera on his shoulder again and we backpedaled, the film running. When we had returned to the last Indian guardpost and what I thought of as "safety" Carl said, evenly, "Hand me the tripod."

I thought, That's smart. We'll set up right here and shoot some more footage. Good thinking. I handed him the tripod and damned if he didn't tuck it under one armpit and start moving up the trail again.

This time we walked to the peak of the ridge, right up to the rocks on the border. Sorensen held the camera steady and I held my breath. The Chinese soldiers who were bunched there did not fall back. They just stirred a little, and watched, and let us *know* they were watching. Slowly, Carl set up the tripod, attached the camera and ran his film, panning part of Tibet and the great valley beyond the Natu La Pass. The view was spectacular, but there was not a great deal else going on, and we settled gladly for what we could get.

We eventually were able to ship a film story for the Evening News and say, "It isn't much, folks, but it *is* a picture of China." Life is a series of small victories, and pluses, and I count that journey as one of them.

No, there was no combat, no invasion, no particular drama except, possibly, what our presence created. But we had tracked a tough story almost to the roof of the earth. Through whatever enterprise that involved, we had shown the strange confrontation on one of the remote borders of the world, had come away with a film which, to our knowledge, no one else had tried to get.

I may be attaching a greater importance than this story deserved, I don't know. It might have been more productive, in fact, if we had stayed at the India-Pakistan front. But you win some and lose some, and this one I felt was well worth the effort.

If I wavered at all in my conviction, it was only on the trip back down the mountain. Our last guide, the British colonel, had assigned us a driver and told him to take us back into Gangtok. Sorensen wanted to take a different route on the return trip, and kept insisting, but the driver, a corporal who spoke a little English, refused. He had his orders.

Sorensen was an adventurer, as most cameramen are. As a breed, they are usually more adventurous than the correspondents, like it or not, and most times I did not. They are either intrepid, brave or whacko, which has to do with the nature of the job, I suppose. Carl insisted we go down a different way, take some side road. I still felt woozy from the altitude and drained from our experience with the Chinese. I just wanted to get the hell down.

Sorensen had lived for a time in Mexico, had traveled throughout South America and Africa and was schooled in the "great payoff." The corporal kept saying, "My instructions are to take you to Gangtok." I half pleaded, "Carl, leave the guy alone."

So Carl stuffed an American twenty-dollar bill in the soldier's shirt pocket and said, "Oh, now, I think we can work this out."

But we did not. The corporal let the bill stay where it was, but he shook his head. "It is not the money," he said. I was surprised that he kept it, and was disappointed with myself for being surprised.

When we arrived back in Gangtok the driver went to his superior, a lieutenant, and reported what had happened. The lieutenant marched briskly over to where we stood and addressed himself to me. His anger was real. "You have insulted all of us," he said. "You would not think of offering an American soldier twenty dollars to disobey an order. He would have shot you, and I wish my man had."

There was no point in my saying, hey, Sorensen did that. I would not have passed the buck even if I thought it would have helped, which it would not. The responsibility was mine, after all. So I just stood there, gazing at my feet and sort of pawing the ground, while the lieutenant read me off, up one side and down the other. I could only say, yes sir, and no sir, but the entire time I was thinking, man, wait until I get that Sorensen alone. I will wring his neck like that chicken we had been served so many hours before.

To his credit, Carl tried to butt in a couple of times, but his approach was like putting sandpaper on a blister. "What the hell are you talking about?" he said. "This is done all the time. We didn't mean to insult anybody. What's the big deal?"

The officer ignored him. He kept pacing a few steps in either direction, steam all but rising from his ears. "You know," he said, shaking his head, sadly, "that is one of the major problems we have, trying to discipline our troops and instill in them a high standard of integrity."

For the third or fourth time I apologized, told him how much I regretted the incident and promised it would never happen again. Finally he paused, frustrated, his cheeks puffed with words that wouldn't come. I was just trying to break off and so was he.

And then he thought of the last, appropriate words. In one final, exasperated, painful flourish he waved one hand and declared, "I will tell you this, NO ONE IN *Battle Cry* WOULD HAVE TAKEN THAT MONEY."

Well, as I recall the novel, there were at least a few characters who would have, and then have gone back for more. But even so, it was a splendid kicker line, and the moment we got out of his sight Sorensen and I doubled up with hysterics. We traveled a lot of miles together later, including parts of Vietnam, and in any number of situations one of us would wink at the other and say:

"No one in *Battle Cry* would have done that."

Out-Take

9

CHINA

There is an endless quest in television for the "perfect" job, much as surfers roam the world in search of the perfect wave. I'm not sure what it would be, except that it is never the one you have at the moment.

On the trip to Red China with President Nixon, I met a writer for a Toronto newspaper, one of the few Western correspondents then accredited behind the Bamboo Curtain. I remember saying to him, "God, how I envy you."

"Don't," he replied. "The luck and loneliness of it no one understands."

Here was a guy on the cutting edge of history, a quote—dream assignment—unquote. What I didn't know was that he was single. He got out of China only once every nine or ten months to Hong Kong, as a fallback R and R (rest and recreation).

He confided that he went virtually every night to a folk ballet produced by the Red Guards in Peking. The reason was that the lead dancer performed in Bermuda style shorts and knee socks and you could see her bare knees. He said, "That's the only exposure you can get to the female anatomy in the whole blinking country." China is a Cromwellian society and they dress accordingly. And that was the extent of his sex life.

There was no point in trying to tell the reporter from Toronto what a dream job he had.

Chapter 10

THE TELEVISION WAR

WHEN THE CHANCE came to go to Vietnam I took it, with no misgivings and very little guilt, but with an impatience that soon served me badly.

By that time, November, 1965, American involvement in the war had mushroomed. CBS vice-president Bill Leonard was passing through London. I stood gazing out my office window into the rain and said to him, "Bill, I've got to go. Help me. This war is becoming the most important story of this generation. I want to see it, report it."

"You're crazy," he said. "You have a good spot here, one of the best in the company. You have a family and . . ." The sentence trailed off. He looked me in the eyes for a few seconds, then said, "All right. I understand better than you may think. I'll do what I can."

Two days later, a telex came from Fred Friendly in New York: "Provided your wife approves, I'll send you to Saigon."

I already had Jean Rather's reluctant approval. "It's only for three months," I reminded her, referring to the fact that this was now the network's normal rotation. But Jean was smarter than that. She said, "Listen, this war is not going to be over in three months and if I know you, and I do, I'll be lucky if you come back, period, much less before it's over." On that she was wrong. The war outlasted all of us.

One of the first things I had been told about Vietnam—it had become an article of faith—was how difficult it was to see "the enemy." This was as true for journalists as for the infantry. Vietnam was not like India and Pakistan, where you could look out and observe an entire panorama of the battlefield. There were any number of correspondents who came to Vietnam, served their time, spent months, maybe a year, and never saw anyone they *knew* to be a Viet Cong or a North Vietnamese regular. That is the nature of guerrilla warfare in the jungle. You could see a lot of fire and hear a lot of shots. But you could travel far and stay late and never find the enemy.

In less than twenty-four hours after my arrival I had an eyeful, and more. I was literally up to my ass in VC.

I had determined that whatever mistakes I made, and I was to make many, I would not hang around the office and attend the military briefings, the so-called Saigon Follies. At that point a lot of newsmen did. In fairness, a print journalist could do so and, in some ways, on some days, be better off. But you can't get pictures sitting in a press tent.

So my first day in South Vietnam I flew to Da Nang, found the headquarters for I Corps and arranged a meeting with Gen. Lewis Walt, later to be the commandant of the marine corps. This was not a good day to be calling on him. The general had malaria, and I'm not sure he knew how ill he was. His eyes were watery, his face flushed. It was obvious that, physically, he was not at his best. So I tried to make my point and get out.

I said, "Sir, I don't want to hang around the CBS office in the Caravelle Hotel in Saigon. And I don't want to hang around the marine press center in Da Nang. I want to get out in the field."

He nodded and said politely, "Some do and some don't and I appreciate your telling me. I'll put you in touch with our people and you can go out immediately."

I said, "Sir, to me, immediately means now."

He didn't blink. "Well, let me see." He picked up a phone, asked a few questions, put the receiver down and said, "We have a helicopter leaving in about ten minutes for a place called Tam Ky, just below here, along the coast. You can be on it if you want."

As poorly as he must have felt, the expression on his face was kind, but it said to me, hope that's quick enough for you.

In a few minutes I scrambled aboard the helicopter and we were gone. With me was a French cameraman named Alex Bauer. I had my own man coming in, Jerry Adams, who at my request had been borrowed by CBS from the staff of Channel 11 in Houston. But Adams was still in Saigon, getting outfitted and briefed.

I had crossed Bauer's path a few times in Europe and knew who he was. You would peg him as a fellow who enjoyed wine and good food, a true Frenchman. He was on the portly side, young, with dark, slightly receding curly hair. Alex had been in and out of Vietnam over the years and, as matters developed, I was damned lucky to catch my first foray with him.

It was as if my inner clock had gone haywire. I couldn't slow myself down. I had rushed pell-mell to get to Vietnam, to find out where things were happening, and to get wherever the action was. All in the first twenty-four hours. I have no idea what I thought I had to prove, if anything, but I knew I had some catching up to do.

I will say this. I was getting my wish, with interest and double bonus stamps.

The helicopter did not even touch down, just hovered a foot or so off the ground. The door gunner said, "Go," and gave me a good shove in the back. I went sprawling out the side and the helicopter fluttered away. They always worried, with good reason, about staying too long on the ground and catching a mortar round, or crossfire.

We were dropped in an open field, no camp or base in sight. But a marine patrol was in the area on a search-and-destroy raid. From the air we had spotted them, made contact with their radio post, and the chopper put us down within reach of them.

I stood up to brush off the dirt and instantly Alex grabbed the shirt-tail of my fatigues—they were new and not too well-fitting; the shirttail was already hanging out—and yanked me down. He blurted out something in French, which translated meant, "Don't be an idiot, get your head down." My command of French was poor to failing, so I didn't understand. Alex spoke English then, and speaks it better today, but he often resorted to French under pressure. This time he said slowly in English, "Listen, you are going to be here a long while. Why don't you just watch me at first. N'est-ce pas?"

I said, "Fine, but what's going on?"

Alex said, "Well, my friend, you will stay here a very long time and not know the answer to that question."

We caught up with the marines as they swept through an outlying area of what I guessed was Tam Ky. It was rice-paddy work. They were moving low and tense through the paddies and they ran into a heap of trouble. I heard gunfire, saw the dirt kick up close by, and hit the ground. Ideally, you fall on your stomach, but I landed on my back and was pinned down for about an hour and fifteen minutes. There was heavy fire from mortars, automatic weapons and some small arms. I had the strange sensation of lying on a river bank in Texas and daydreaming, watching the sky. Except for the noise.

Because the gunfire was continuous, I was afraid to raise up the four inches or so that would be required to roll over on my belly. Sounds silly now. But four inches could be the difference between getting and not getting hit. And I didn't want to find out.

By that time I was already separated from Alex. Eventually he got back to me, flopped down and said, "We don't want to get caught out here overnight."

The shooting had moved away from us and I now felt confident enough to dig in an elbow and turn on one side. But what Bauer said didn't sit well with me. My intention had been to stay overnight in the field, possibly several days, and turn out five or six stories. When I said that, Alex just rolled his eyes. "Oh, no, my friend," he said. "You nev-air stay on the ground overnight if you can avoid it. Take it from me, what we need to do is get a helicopter and get the hell out of here."

I said, "But we haven't been able to film much. I can't see that we have a story yet."

He said, "Forget it. There will be other days, other times."

I was not trying to be hardheaded, but I had just arrived on the scene and wanted a little more taste of what combat was about. It wasn't a question of courage, his or mine, but I was reluctant to leave.

The decision was settled for us when we heard the helicopters flapping overhead. This was the way you covered the war. By hitchhiking. We were at the whim of the helicopters. Whenever a reporter needed to get somewhere and he could find a whirlybird, he ran for it and tried to talk the pilot into taking him there, or at least to whatever base the pilot was headed for, knowing that other choppers would be leaving from there. Eventually you got where you wanted to go and you would run into a story, maybe.

There was no system. We could wave, try to signal the helicopter from the ground. Sometimes the pilot would land and sometimes not. There was no cab service. You couldn't ask one to drop around at six o'clock.

Over a period of months we developed a technique to get the coverage we wanted. We learned to stay close to the Medevacs. Those were the Medical Evacuation helicopters, with red crosses painted on the front and sides. We would hang around with a crew and wait for an emergency call. When it came, I asked the pilot if we could ride along. Sooner or later the call always came. We had the advantage of having not only a way in, but a way out. We knew that something was going on in the area or they wouldn't be calling for medical help.

I'm not sure the public ever fully understood how different the war in Vietnam was because of this capability. At that stage the morale of our troops was much higher than had been pictured. The reason, as one veteran of the Korean War explained to me, was that if he got hit he knew he was no more than fifteen minutes away from first-class medical help.

Every other war had been fought before the helicopter age. Oh, there were some choppers in Korea, but not many. In the days of Ernest Hemingway and the civil war in Spain, for example, hours or days might pass before the wounded reached a hospital. They had to wait for an ambulance and drive mile after mile. In World War Two and, to a large extent, Korea, it was still a case of having to be driven or carried to a rear position and receiving first aid.

But in Vietnam, unless the circumstances were extraordinary—say, the Green Berets were cut off somewhere on a night strike—the Medevacs could always reach the wounded quickly.

So something about the urgency in Alex Bauer's manner told me that when I heard the helicopters, I had to *move*. And that was the way it was at Tam Ky. We did not see the choppers land, but we heard them and had a sense of their direction. They had put down away from the rice paddies, back behind a row of thatched-roof huts.

We could hear the blades beating and coughing, and Alex gave me a quick tap on the shoulder and said, "Run for it, let's go." He said it so suddenly that I wasn't sure I actually had heard him right. Before I knew it he had ducked into some brush and was out of sight.

I paused a moment to take in the picture. In front of me were the rice paddies, with the built-up beds of orange soil, and at the edge of the paddies sprawled a thicket of thin trees and lifeless bushes. Then came the thatched huts and beyond them a small, open area, which was the LZ, the landing zone for the helicopters. Alex had ducked into the bushes and picked his way along a path.

I couldn't see exactly where he went in, so I headed for the cluster of huts and started running right through them, as though they were connecting cars on a train. Just in one open door and out the other until I came to a large hut at the end of the row. It was dusk now and through a crude window I could see the helicopters, about 175 yards beyond this hut.

Then, suddenly, I was aware of a woman standing right in my path, in the middle of the room. Mind you, I had not seen a Vietnamese woman other than in my swift passage through Saigon and Da Nang. They were city ladies, dressed in the long flowing robes called *bao dai*. This woman was wearing the black pajamas of a peasant, and she had a child about ten months old in one arm and a French-made rifle of undetermined age in the other.

I slammed on my brakes. It must have looked like one of those old cartoons in which Bugs Bunny is running like mad and then he comes to a *screeeeching* halt. You know, click, try that as a still picture. My first reaction was, well, black pajamas, Viet Cong. This is how the world ends.

This was the dress of all the rural people of Vietnam. But I didn't know it then. And she had a rifle in one hand, and to her eyes, at least, I'm dressed like your average newly landed G.I. in my ill-fitting fatigues.

When I stopped she raised the rifle and gritted her teeth. To my amazement, her teeth were completely black. The peasants chew betel nut, another piece of trivia I learned later.

Instinctively, I understood the situation without knowing a great deal about Vietnam or the culture or the war or this peasant lady. Face it. Her life had been disrupted for God knows how many days by troops from all sides. The Viet Cong were probably operating out of her neighborhood. Maybe she was one of them and maybe she was not. The North Vietnamese and South Vietnamese regulars probably had been there the week before and the U. S. marines had swept through that very day. Now me. She was not in a mood to be messed with and she had this incredible antique pointed at me. The rifle looked like something the French Foreign Legion had left behind in 1850.

In my own mind I am reviewing at a fairly rapid clip the highlights of my life and toting up my last regrets, of which I had a few. I could not very well say to her, Madam, I am sorry to be dashing through your house. It is all a terrible mistake. Nor could I say, hey, I just got here. I'm not what you think I am. I'm Dan Rather and I do the weather on Channel 8. Would you like to see my press card?

For how many seconds my mind simply raced I can't tell you. I only know that we stood there for all the ages. Finally, and for what reason I still can't conceive—it is not a sign I am given to—I clasped my hands and placed them under my chin in what I hoped was a kind of international sign for mercy. It did not occur to me then, but that was the kind of peace sign once associated with Gandhi and Nehru.

I was desperate to make some signal to her that said, I mean you no evil and please don't kill me, even though my presence in your house must strike you as strange. Other than to show her teeth, she made no motion.

At that point I figured the next move was up to me. So, making the sign with prayerful hands, I backed out the way I came in. In the meantime several of the helicopters had taken off. Once I got through the doorway I was, as we used to say in East Texas, hightailing. Up to then I had been confused and not quite certain I wanted to leave. But once out of that hut, I was the most decisive human being you ever saw.

I mean, if there was no helicopter out there when I reached the landing zone I was going to invent one. They were going to see the damndest autogyro heading back to Da Nang anyone had ever known, because I was going to be aboard *something*.

When I hit the clearing the only helicopter left was already cranking up. In fact, the props had never stopped. When the choppers take off they hover a few feet off the ground, turn the nose down and sort of gin the motor for a minute. That is what this chopper was doing and I thought, Gee-zuz, he's going.

I had maybe fifty yards to cover and I was carrying a large pack with web suspenders and a pistol belt on the front and my typewriter, which I had hauled a lot of miles and considered fairly valuable, a tape recorder, a change of socks and a letter from home. Sorry, Jeannie. I just unbuckled the pack, dropped it right there and turned on the speed, waving and shouting all the way.

Of course, they couldn't hear me above the noise of the blades. But I got there and I never slowed down. To the people on the helicopter I must have looked as if I had been shot out of a circus cannon. I sailed on board with a dive that almost carried me out the other side.

I no sooner sprawled aboard than the pilot said, "Hey, you can't go with us." I didn't say a word. I merely thought to myself, friend, you don't know what *I* know, and what I know is I'm going with you. He repeated himself a few times while I sat there, breathing hard. After a bit he gave up and took off, to my boundless relief.

But I wasn't with them long. They were on their way to make an equipment drop to marines still in the field. A unit had fallen back from the sweep area, planning to establish a camp for the night a few miles beyond Tam Ky. When they reached the area the pilot turned to me and said, "Look, we gotta take on a lot of equipment and some more people here, and there just isn't going to be room for you."

I nodded and said, "Understood. I appreciate the ride this far. It's just that back in that other area I didn't see anybody else around."

It had been a spooky feeling. At one point marines were everywhere, then suddenly no one. They had all fallen back and moved out. Alex and I were not attached to them or to anyone else. Most likely, the marine commander didn't even know we were out there. So they were just gone before we knew it. By then, of course, I assumed that Alex had cleared out on one of the other helicopters.

Here, in microcosm, was the confusion of the war and it said a lot to me. I had still not come to the end of my first day.

They dropped me off again and by that time it had turned dark, I had lost my pack and had no gear, but I wasn't all that worried. Another chopper showed up not long after, dropping off more supplies. I climbed aboard and said to the pilot, "I'm trying to get back to Da Nang. I got cut off from my cameraman and I'm stuck."

There were six or eight marines sitting on the floor and he said, "No problem. We're headed back for Da Nang right now."

But then he had radio contact from a marine unit that was in trouble. Another helicopter had been downed, and the marines had set up a circle to keep the Viet Cong from getting the radio. So we sat down in a field a couple hundred yards from the downed chopper and we caught some fire as we came in.

The word was that the VC had been reinforced with North Vietnam regulars, but who the hell knew. The point was, the small marine force was now badly outnumbered, it was getting darker, and there was a real danger that they would be wiped out.

So the helicopter I happened to be on had to get them out. The marines came hurrying in the classic fallback procedure. One group would lay down a base of fire while some others fell back and established a position. Then the forward ones would retreat while the others covered for them, sort of leapfrogging backward toward the helicopter.

They kept coming and finally the pilot said, "Hey, I don't think we can take all these people." There is a limit to what any helicopter can carry, and it sticks in my mind that this one could handle eighteen. Someone did a head count and we already had twenty-two. And there were two marines still out there. One had been hit and another had hung back to help him. Some were firing out the door of the helicopter to protect them, and the pilot was saying, "We gotta go. We gotta get out of here."

The marine in charge of the ground force, a young first lieutenant, snapped at him, "Don't you dare move until we have all our people."

And the pilot said, "Hell, I'm not even sure we can take off with what we're carrying."

Now put yourself in my position. I'm the only guy aboard, in effect, without a ticket. I'm sort of hunching down, getting smaller and smaller. It was a bad, confusing time. Finally some of the other marines jumped off the chopper and hauled the last two into the cabin.

That was an impressive demonstration of a lesson pounded into recruits back at boot camp: You never leave a marine in the field; you come out of there with your dead, your wounded and your equipment. I remember someone in the helicopter saying words to that effect, and someone else answering him, "Damned right. Either everybody goes or nobody goes."

Once we were all aboard the pilot ginned his motor for what seemed forever. In the dark I could see the outlines of several dozen Viet Cong rushing the downed helicopter and firing at ours. Not wave after wave, but it *was* several dozen quick little men in black pajamas, with sandals made out of old tires. They had at least two automatic weapons with them.

This time I had seen the enemy, to paraphrase Pogo, and they wasn't us.

The helicopter just sort of hung there and the pilot tried to gain momentum. He hovered longer than normal in order to rev up power to offset the extra weight. I began to doubt that we would ever take off. He did make a long run on the ground instead of rising straight up, to give the VC less of a target, and finally we were gone.

We had people literally hanging out the door. I thought of that after a good deal of derision greeted a photograph of a South Vietnamese soldier clinging to a helicopter skid, when the Laos operation turned into a debacle. Well, I didn't laugh. I just put myself in his situation, remembering that flight, and I thought, I would have hung onto a skid. I would have hung onto a nail to get the hell out of there.

That was my introduction to the war in Vietnam. It was sobering and vivid.

By the time we returned to Da Nang, Alex was fairly nervous about me. He had brought in a roll of film, I did a narration and we filed my first report on the war. In that instance the piece was far easier than the process by which we got it and moved without problems. A lot of them did not.

Always, we were in the begging business. We packed everything into one of those trusty grapefruit bags—our film, sound, script, dope sheets of what was in each can—we taped them all together, tied the sack and found the nearest helicopter clearing or air base. Then we sought out the next plane leaving for Saigon and tried to talk someone into carrying it. Sometimes they wouldn't. Sometimes they did, adding, "But I can't promise it will get there."

The system was hit-or-miss. The heartbreaking thing was that sometimes a correspondent risked his life, literally, or the lives of the camera crew, marched twenty-five miles out and fourteen miles in, slept on the ground for three days, shipped the film—and then it disappeared. Maybe the film would be buried in the back of a helicopter. Or maybe it got pitched out in an open field, with the C-rations and spare radio parts.

That was Vietnam. And all these years later, I have trouble sorting out what I felt about the war, how I feel even now. I am not easy with moral judgments. It is one thing to say the war was immoral. Most wars are. That is not the issue in terms of what those Americans gave up who went, and served, and who left behind pieces of themselves.

It is not hard to look back now and see the unfairness. To the Vietnamese, North and South; or to us as a people, to those who had to play games to stay out of the service on what they saw as moral grounds, and to those who had to fight the war.

Once, when the country was going through a kind of epileptic fit, a magazine writer came to Washington, asked me what I thought, and said he had expected to find Jean Rather in an antiwar demonstration. Well, he didn't know much about the Rathers, Jean *or* Dan. I still find the senselessness of the war, the confusion overwhelming. I used to shake my head when I heard people who had been in Vietnam for three months, even a year or longer, pontificate on what the war was about, the deep, root causes. There might be a few Arnold Toynbees who could put the war in perspective, but those I heard talking were not among them.

India and Pakistan, ancient hatreds, religious and historical wars, I can understand. Vietnam I cannot. I didn't go there with preconceived notions. I didn't come out with absolute answers.

I do believe it is one thing to have opposed the war on whatever grounds —emotional, philosophical, religious—and another to make those who fought and bled pay for our divisions. Of the veterans I encountered, few went because they enjoyed war or wanted to be helicopter gunship cowboys. Oh, sure, there were some. There have been in every army on every side of every war. But many of those I encountered in Vietnam wanted badly not to go. They simply were not sufficiently wired into the power structure to stay out. Many simply went in and did their damndest, and frequently those who had the toughest time had been given the least by society.

When you get down to cases I suppose it has always been that way, beginning with Alexander's army. In the basic infantry outfit there is a disproportionate number of people from Harlem or Appalachia. I am haunted and angered by the immense waste, in human and material terms.

I saw the unfairness of the system firsthand. And I am appalled that we did not have an effective national program for making sure that every Vietnam veteran got a job. We still don't. I know that's preachy. As a practical matter, how do you make sure veterans get jobs? I don't know. But I don't see anyone working to find out.

My colleague, Eric Sevareid, once wrote that the essence of youth is believing things last forever. For many of us who were there, the essence faded in the reality of such scenes as: A kid from Tennessee, marching back from a Thanksgiving Day dinner of turkey from a can, who stepped on a land mine. There was a muffled "ba-room," and his legs were gone. South Vietnamese soldiers, in a rage, pushing a blindfolded prisoner out of a helicopter at three thousand feet. And the bodies of villagers disemboweled by Viet Cong or North Vietnamese, strung up as a warning to other peasants.

There was so much intellectual fiction about the war that we lost sight of another critical point. Most Vietnamese, pro- or anti-Communist, North or South, were just trying to make another day. That message came through to me loud and clear. The real struggle in Vietnam was for survival, not ideology. In that light how we got there, why we stayed, the way it ended, must seem even more confounding today.

When I landed in Da Nang in late 1965 the American combat role had begun to escalate. I felt I should spend most of my time obtaining the television record of Americans at war. I saw the American push as the developing story.

I may have been wrong. I did receive some criticism, in and out of CBS, for spending too much time in the field covering combat instead of what to many was a political war. I did some politics. Perhaps not enough. I think the complaint was fair, but I do not apologize for it.

For the first time, after all, war was coming into our homes. For the first time people could watch actual combat scenes while they ate dinner. I don't say that is necessarily a good thing. But the war changed the way we think about television. And TV changed the way we think about war.

In retrospect Vietnam for me was a sergeant named Nuñez, a pathfinder and good at his job. Those were the scouts who were sent into hostile jungle territory to select landing zones for helicopter assaults. A mean assignment with a high attrition rate. I never knew Sergeant Nuñez. Nor did I ever see him alive.

We went in with a group that was looking for Nuñez. We got there about an hour too late. He had run into a fire fight, had stayed with another pathfinder who was hit, and both were overrun and killed.

He was a Filipino. In working the story, we found out that Nuñez had joined the army because he wanted to become an American citizen. Everyone we talked with mentioned that about him. He said the one thing he was proud of was his American citizenship.

I can't tell you why, exactly, but I still recall Sergeant Nuñez when I think about the craziness of war. He was a Filipino, in an American uniform, who died in Vietnam. He considered it an honor to do so. That is a rare and precious thing for this country. But his life was squandered, for what?

Another time, another place, cameraman Jerry Adams and I saw a G.I. perform an act of heroism that won the Congressional Medal of Honor. It was one of those bigger-than-death things that happen even in unpopular wars. An American sweep had been held up a day and a half by a machine-gun nest concealed in a trench in a heavily wooded area. Our soldiers couldn't move.

Without anyone's ordering him, this soldier suddenly charged, single-handed, and cleaned out the nest. All we could see was this figure racing through the trees, a grenade in his hand, vaulting into that nest and pulling the pin, blowing up everything there, including himself.

My three months in Vietnam grew to four, and the four months turned into nearly a year, and Jerry Adams went the distance with me. That is a story in itself. When it developed that we would have to go outside CBS for a cameraman I asked for him. Some on the staff had already been there, some didn't care to go, others I just didn't know.

Adams had worked for me in Houston. He had been a combat photographer. He had lied about his age, served in World War Two and fought at Bastogne when he was eighteen or less. My rule still was, when you move into rough waters, know your cameraman.

I not only knew Adams and had confidence in him but considered his experience under fire a huge plus. He took a leave of absence from his job and his family to join me. It was a gamble for him in a lot of ways.

There were no stars in his eyes. Working for the network was not his life's goal (though he later did and is now a CBS staffer in Washington). He came as a favor to me. I leaned on him.

It was another new world for me. I discovered a contradiction in being a combat correspondent. Genuine though it may be, you never quite earn the fear, the discomfort, of whatever pain or grief you feel. This is because you are aware, barring a misstep, that you can leave at a time of your own choosing. Meanwhile you are dry and fed and safe more days than not. You stay a year, observe the war, intrude upon it, but you do not really, fully, share the daily risk.

I tend to believe that this is true of most wars, but more so of Vietnam, a war that too often no one could seem to find, except when they were not looking for it. One moment you saw nothing, heard nothing. Then a pop, and the next you knew a marine was in a ditch with a hole in his back.

In a way you could never know at home, you felt a closeness to people you met only once, or not at all. You heard about them on your rounds. Their names came up in other places. You asked about them, wondered how they were. And each day brought a new reminder that America had never fought in a war quite like this one.

There was a day when Jerry Adams and I heard about a big operation shaping up below the delta. At times the military made a point of letting you know: "Operation Cedar Balls will jump off in the morning." They wanted the coverage. At other times they had operations they were not so sure would succeed, and they didn't want you around.

We were hitchhiking that day and had gotten word that something big was about to break in an area difficult to reach, but we finally begged a ride.

This was the background: A colonel was in charge, bucking to make brigadier general. His unit had attracted the wrath of the Pentagon, through no direct fault of the colonel's. But he was not exactly offended by publicity. He liked reporters and he knew the value of a tough reputation. That sort of attitude hadn't hurt Patton.

At any rate, the colonel's unit was one of the first outfits linked to atrocity stories. They had been accused of cutting off the ears of enemy troops and keeping them as trophies. I have reason to doubt that they ever did. But this was in the early part of the war. (Later, there were specific orders against such practices.) The colonel, or someone around him, decided that this story, true or not, should be published. Good *macho* image. Give the VC something to think about.

And the roof had caved in, at least from the colonel's standpoint. After a national magazine picked up the story of the ears being cut off and kept as trophies, the brass descended on the colonel. There was the devil to pay. He had been moping around for weeks, thinking, God, my career is ruined; I'll never make brigadier, it wasn't my fault, what a crappy thing to happen.

Of course, I knew none of this until we talked to the troops. I didn't know what to expect when Adams and I ducked out of the helicopter, Jerry with his camera gear. A second lieutenant saw us and was puzzled: Who are you and what is this? I quickly introduced myself.

Then the colonel stepped out of his tent and spotted us. His eyes lit up like the jackpot on a pinball machine. He said with a kind of gasp, *"Television."*

What I couldn't know then was that he had to be thinking, God has sent you, and if we're lucky we'll wipe out all that unfavorable publicity . . . who gives a shit about that cheap rag of a magazine . . . CBS Television is here! His actual words were, "Come into my tent. You're mighty welcome." He beckoned to us with his hand and then, to no one in particular, "Get these men a hot meal, they must be hungry."

A sergeant said, "Colonel, we don't got no mess facilities out here."

The colonel ignored him. "I said get these men a hot meal." He held the flap of the tent open for us. As we ducked through he added, "And wine. We must have a bottle of wine."

It was the "colonel's table" treatment. He could not have been nicer. We were just somewhat dazzled. We had never had such a warm reception. To the colonel, redemption had descended from the skies, landing right on his doorstep.

The operation was bogged down and the colonel was in a quandary about what to do. He knew, or thought he knew, where the enemy was concentrated, among the densest jungle anyone had seen.

He briefed us, then said, "You looking for a story? We'll give you a story. What kind do you want?"

I said, "Colonel, we're just checking out the area. If it's all right with you, we'll just look around."

"No, no. Tell me exactly what you're looking for."

"Well, combat."

"Ah, combat. A fire fight?"

For an instant I had the goofy feeling that he was about to snap his fingers and shout to his orderly, "The man wants a fire fight. Crank up a fire fight. Crank up a fire fight."

It was strange and confusing, as if at any moment we would find ourselves the butt of a practical joke. Jerry and I exchanged foggy looks. We had wandered into outfits and been welcomed politely, or turned away rudely, and had no complaints either way. But this was something else.

Another reason the colonel's outfit had fallen into official disfavor had to do with a band of Mao tribesmen, who had worked with the Americans, when they were not working for the other side. They moved freely back and forth across the Cambodian border. In recent days some of the colonel's artillery shells had, quite accidentally, fallen into their ranks. It wasn't clear to me that anyone had been killed. But it was clear that the tribesmen regarded this incident as a less than friendly act. A meeting between the Mao and the colonel had been arranged.

We were there when the tribal chief and his party came riding up on these small, Cambodian elephants. All they lacked was a sword swallower and the bearded lady. A small footstool was produced and the elephant kneeled so that the chief could descend with great dignity and consult with the colonel. The two leaders disappeared into the tent and the chief's grievances were soon redressed, at what cost I don't know.

But the colonel still had the problem of how to get his operation underway. A West Pointer, in his early forties, he had a crew cut, and a lean and outdoorsy look. I had the feeling he would not be a bad fellow to serve under, the ear trophy story notwithstanding.

Now he unfolded a large map, spread it across a table, jabbed with a finger and said, "We know they're in here. We've been pouring in artillery but it's so wooded you can't see a thing. Now, we plan to jump off in the morning."

I never knew whether he had originally planned to begin operations that morning, but my strong suspicion was that the decision had been made at roughly the moment he saw the camera come off the helicopter and into his camp.

"The difficulty is the lack of light," he went on, speaking, I think, for us as well as his troops. "You can't believe how dark it is in there."

Indeed I didn't. We later saw the area and it was dark as a dungeon. There were three layers of overgrowth. There were trees too, quite large for Vietnam, vines as thick as a man's leg, and heaven knows what else.

The Viet Cong were hidden in there, secure in their tunnels. They were almost unreachable. Even an artillery shell, heavy as one is, splintered away and could not be aimed with accuracy.

The colonel said, "The problem is going to be the light. Now this area right here"—and he pointed to the map—"I think is our best chance. It's not quite so heavily overgrown. We'll try to put you down in there by helicopter. That would be a good position for you to take pictures of us moving in."

He was giving us the kind of break you dream about. I only regretted that I could not work up more enthusiasm for it. I kept thinking how weird the situation was. But our job was taking pictures, and we were game, if he was.

Jerry Adams had said little. That night, after we had bunked down, Adams turned to me and said, "Don't kid yourself. It's going to be hairy in there."

We didn't know how hairy.

The next morning the troops moved in and the colonel tried to drop us by helicopter, ahead of the foot soldiers, with what is called a blocking force. Though we made several passes, we couldn't get through the dense, three-layer overgrowth. It was like trying to drop through an ocean of kelp.

The colonel was on the radio to the helicopter. "You got to find a way," he exhorted. "We've got to get these fellows in there." He was speaking of Adams and me, not his troops.

And I was saying, "Hey, look, don't push it too far." Having seen what was out there, we were not all that eager to land.

Finally he sent out a helicopter with a winch, the kind used for bringing out the wounded or equipment when ground movement is restricted. The plan was to hover and lower a guy on the winch, who would try to hack a hole through the cover, maybe clear out enough to get the helicopter down. The plan was insane. It was like a man trying to chip away a rock with a Boy Scout knife. After a while the fellow on the winch signaled the pilot to crank him back up.

The colonel's level of frustration rose with each new attempt. He was growing desperate as he realized he could not get us in.

When we flew back to the camp he had the maps spread out again. The operation had been placed on "hold." The troops had moved up and dug in. They would have been slaughtered if they had continued into the jungle. So far nothing had worked. They had tried to find a landing zone, had tried to hack their way in.

When we entered the tent the colonel was rubbing his chin, staring at the map, saying, "There has *got* to be a way. Now, there is a clearing over here. That's up ahead but—"

"Colonel," I interrupted, "look, I think maybe we ought to fall back and check with you again in a few days."

He said, "No, no, don't go. We'll figure out something."

Suddenly he whirled around and said to me, "Do you jump?"

The colonel had been a paratrooper. As it happened, Adams had qualified to jump during his time in the army. But when I turned toward Jerry he shot me a very dark look. At that time I knew of no Americans other than a handful of Green Berets and special medical units, who had parachuted into a combat zone.

For a brief moment I considered the idea. Then I said, "Colonel, in the first place I'm not jump-qualified. Secondly I have no intention of jumping. And third I'm not going to tell you how to run your business, but I am telling you that we're going to leave."

(Later I did jump once, with the Vietnamese, a dumb and scary thing to do.)

I think I had a strong sense of what was going through the colonel's head and heart. I could have been wrong but I don't think so. We left and he was visibly sorry to see us go. But we did get a short piece on the air about his mortar outfit, a sidebar feature about mortars. I heard later that he had been pleased.

I also learned that he had weathered the rough seas of publicity, had survived and made brigadier. I was happy for him. He was an unforgettable character.

A colonel for the television war.

Out-Take

10

THE BRIEFING

When I returned from Vietnam in November, 1966, Bill Moyers suggested I visit President Johnson and chat with him about what I saw and what I experienced. LBJ's whole operation was geared that way. He often met with reporters on an individual basis. It was partly his way of picking brains, and partly the White House way of trying to bring you into camp.

Moyers said, "But I do believe you ought to see Rostow first." So it was arranged for me to meet with Walt Rostow, the President's advisor on national security, whose job later went to Henry Kissinger under Nixon.

Rostow is a genial man. His credentials as a scholar are impressive. I had read and admired many of his writings, particularly about regionalism as a force in world politics.

I was led down to a small room in the White House basement designed for military briefings. Rostow yanked down a wall map with the kind of authority that suggested to me at the start that he was not in much of a mood to listen. I had gotten the impression from Moyers that the White House wanted to hear a fresh viewpoint. I had spent a year in the field in Vietnam and was naive enough to think my report would actually be welcome.

Rostow proceeded to give me a briefing that I knew to be inaccurate in a number of ways. He talked about an area near the Cambodian border known as The Hook, where later, under Nixon, the so-called incursion would take place. He said the reports from The Hook were encouraging. We were beginning to see some very good uses of armor in that area. He tapped the map.

I was no expert on tanks. But I had been to The Hook. I knew that even the die-hards had long since given up trying to employ armor there. Even the Armored Personnel Carriers, which the army had persisted in testing in terrain for which the APC's had never been designed, had bogged down and in some cases had been abandoned.

It was all I could do to keep my mind from wandering, comparing what I was hearing to what I had seen. Then I heard Rostow say, ". . . of course, we are not bombing on this side, the Cambodian side, of the border." The reality was that the bombing runs crossed that border every day.

Historically, there were some arguments about where the boundary existed. You could pick any three maps at random and you would probably find the line drawn in three different places. But the main factor wasn't geographic. If you were near the border and your outfit was taking fire and you called for air cover, nobody got very picky about where the planes went in to knock out the enemy guns. If a few bombs landed on the Cambodian side, tough luck, Jack.

Once or twice I disagreed with Rostow. He did not like my comments. His attitude was not quite haughty. But he made it plain. "This is the White House and this is the way it is." And I retorted, in effect, "That's fine. You're the ones with the map. But I just came from there. I was on the ground. And I know what I saw."

I walked out of there thinking the briefing had been a disaster. Either the President's principal advisor on the war was shockingly misinformed, or I had just been through a blizzard of snow. Probably, I decided, some of both. But if Rostow believed what he had said, it wasn't hard to understand why. By the time the information is passed up the chain of command, everyone puts the best possible face on it.

Several weeks went by before I actually got to see the President. He listened, and asked questions, but I had the feeling he was putting little stock in what I said. No doubt it was presumptuous of me to think he would. But among the points I tried to make was a suggestion I felt then, and think now, would have been useful. Once a month, or every three months, the President should send a direct order to Vietnam and say, "I want to see one hundred company commanders. Pick them at random and fly them back here." Then let them sit down with the Commander-in-Chief and tell him what is going on.

In my experience I had never known a single person in any branch of the military below the rank of colonel who lied to me. Sometimes they were mistaken. But they never tried to bullshit me. Any number of times I sought out a major, or a captain, or a lieutenant, or a sergeant, and I said,

"Look, it's hard for me to tell, I've only been here a day. What's going on?" And he would say, "I'll tell you, we're just getting creamed."

Then I would walk into the command tent and I would be told, "We're having a very effective operation. The body count is two hundred enemy dead and . . ."

This is where the sugar coating starts, the lies that eventually provide the President with what he wants to hear. When I mentioned my idea about bringing in the company commanders Johnson's ears picked up a little. "Well, that's not a bad thought," he said. Of course, nothing ever came of it. Nor was I invited back to meet with Walt Rostow.

Chapter 11

THE UNMAKING
OF A PRESIDENT

I HAD KNOWN H. R. Haldeman for possibly ten minutes when he informed me that he knew who I was and what I stood for. I found this quite remarkable, since most of us spend our entire lives searching for the answers to those two questions.

"You," he snapped, "are a Lyndon Johnson, Texas liberal Democrat and we are going to be watching you."

Bob Haldeman shot me a look that would have exterminated a house. I sat there on the other side of his desk, uncertain whether to laugh or cry. What the hell was this? Having just lived through a period in which Lyndon Johnson himself had said that Dan Rather had failed him, had not been fair, had not been a *friend,* I was more than somewhat taken aback.

That day in January, 1969, was my introduction to the new President's chief of staff, a whiff of what the next six years would be like. Haldeman had a sort of set piece he practiced on reporters. The refrain would become familiar but it was new to me then: "You guys have held a grudge against Richard Nixon ever since he first came on the scene in the Alger Hiss case."

As a matter of fact, I was in junior high school at the time. I had to go back and read a history of the Hiss case to learn what it was all about, including Nixon's role, and to comprehend the emotions that are fanned by it to this day. I tried to explain, but Haldeman cut me off. "You won't get anything out of us," he said. "And you had best watch your step."

I left that meeting with a feeling of puzzlement. I finally shrugged my shoulders and decided, well, you hang around city halls and courthouses and state legislatures and you meet all kinds. Maybe that was just part of his act, to throw me off balance.

But I did reflect on life's small ironies. I had been offered a chance by CBS to be rotated before the new administration took office. I was tempted. The last year and a half of the Johnson regime had been tumultuous and, especially near the end, acrimonious. Increasingly, the hardening of feelings about the war in Vietnam had made the job a bitter one.

Yet I still had a sense of unfinished business. I had spent only a year on the beat before the move to London in 1965. I didn't see the White House as a place where I would live out my years, but instinct told me I should stay. When I sorted out my feelings I said to Bill Small, "Frankly, I'd like to cover the White House when things are a little more tranquil."

Small said, "Fine. We were hoping you'd say that. We'd prefer not to make a change."

Like so many people, I could not pin down all I felt about the election of Richard Nixon, by a wafer-thin margin, over Hubert Humphrey. But part was relief, in a purely professional sense. I didn't know Nixon, had no passionate impressions of him. But there was this feeling of a new wind blowing through the capital. I was curious to see what the men around him would be like. I looked forward to getting to know them.

I had heard that Haldeman was, one, very brainy and, two, a reasonably good source if you could develop a relationship with him. I should add, the latter information was campaign-trail hearsay and turned out to be dead wrong, even for reporters who courted Haldeman's favor. From that very first session he came on strong. Still, given time, I felt I could convince the President's men that, while everything I did would not be favorable, I would be fair. I would win their respect, which is the most a correspondent should expect.

The temptation at the White House, especially for a new man, is to look for friendships. In the first place he is working in a cage. It is such a restrictive geographic beat. Keep in mind, for security reasons he can't wander outside the pressroom unless he has permission. So each day he is working in one small room and, very quickly, the most important person in his life, his best link to information, is the press secretary. The temptation is very strong to ingratiate oneself.

All else being equal, a correspondent wants to be liked. That's only human. But for a reporter, especially one covering the White House, that need can be damaging to his work. Ideally, if another newsman calls the press secretary and asks, "What about this story Rather had on the air last night," I want the press secretary to say, "Look, if Rather has it, all I can tell you is he didn't make it up. He got it somewhere."

Ron Ziegler and I went through some strained and difficult times. He was held up to a fair amount of ridicule, much of it justified. He was not the best choice for that job. But to the very end Ziegler understood that the good reporters worked not for his favor, or to be popular with him, but to gain his respect. He was able to say, "I don't care for you, not one iota, but I do respect the way you go about your work."

We—the press corps—seldom saw much of Nixon, not even at the start, when the slate should have been clean. Within six months it seemed obvious, at least to me, that Haldeman and John Ehrlichman were running interference for the President, whether he wanted it or not. For a while I held out hope that he did not, that he was unaware of the hard line they were taking. It is reasonable now to say they were reflecting his attitudes. The record shows they were more calculating and cunning about whatever they did than many of us knew at the time.

Looking back, I can count no more than a half dozen times that I had a feeling that I was seeing Richard Nixon in an unguarded, unrehearsed moment. I believe one of the mistakes he and those around him made was not allowing Richard Nixon to be shown enough as a human being.

Part of the answer rests, no doubt, in a nature made lean by early poverty and turned inward by the long climb to political power. Nixon was, is, essentially a loner. But I felt I had a glimpse for the first time of another Nixon, who wanted to mix and be casual if only he had known how, aboard *Air Force One* in late July, 1969.

There is something about being aloft, in that cocoonlike atmosphere, a feeling of being above it all that seems to intoxicate every man who holds the country's highest office. The sense of escape, of privilege, of power in motion, seduces him into letting his hair down just a bit more.

To begin with, this airborne feeling is *very American*. There is no other way to describe it. There may be things we don't do as well in this country as we would like, or believe we should, but when it comes to producing and flying airplanes no one in the world can touch us. A correspondent on *Air Force One* has a captain who has logged forty thousand miles and can land that baby like a penny dropped on a bed. The crew is hand-picked. He can ride the press pool one year and order his coffee white, with one lump, not fly it again for a year and a half, step aboard the plane and have a steward greet him: "Coffee, Mr. Rather? Cream and one lump of sugar?"

That day we were flying across the Pacific to greet the moonmen of *Apollo 11,* who had just splashed down from their historic lunar landing. I had never seen Nixon, and wouldn't again, in a mood approaching his that day. He had been in office six months, had begun to get the feel of the job. It was just the right moment. Soon after, some things would turn sour, including the war, which became Nixon's war.

On this day, however, there was a plaque on the moon with his name on it, a triumph of good timing. Tomorrow he would continue on to Vietnam and around the rim of China, winding up in Romania to—symbolically— send the Soviets a message. Enjoyment was written all over him: I'm in this job, the job I always wanted, and I'm beginning to get a handle on it. By God, it can be fun. Glorious. After all, I'm flying across the Pacific to welcome back the men who walked on the moon.

In that mood he strolled to the rear of the plane, to the cramped section where the pool reporters sat. It was not unusual for Presidents Kennedy or Johnson to wander around the aircraft and hold an impromptu press conference, just visit, or engage in a little badinage. But it was a rare thing for Nixon to do. Later, as his troubles were building, he would become the first President to bar pool reporters, even the wire services, from *Air Force One* on a regular basis.

Ron Ziegler, who had preceded him, assured us that "the President just wants to chat. Nothing really of substance. I mean, necessarily of importance. Just small talk."

Nixon was smiling. Not a tight, brittle, politician's smile. A genuine, open, surprise-party smile. I thought then, and have reflected any number of times since, that what followed had to be one of the strange and memorable conversations to which I have been privy. To be sure, I didn't say much. None of us did, because Mr. Nixon just sort of rambled on. There was a non sequitur quality that sort of spun me, but on the whole I found it engrossing.

The President declined an invitation to sit down. He stood awkwardly in the aisle. He looked no one in the eye. He didn't seem to know what to do with his hands.

Almost at the start Helen Thomas asked a question about Vietnam. Ziegler nervously shifted the weight on his feet. Haldeman glared. *He* looked you right in the eyeball. You could almost feel your pupils contract. But the President got a distant look as though he were pondering the question. Then he said, brightly, "You know, the Senators and my friend Ted Williams have gone into a little slump. What they ought to do is make some trades. They could get a lot for Epstein."

It is fair to say that there were several people at the press table who had no idea who Epstein was. They probably thought he was an attorney for the Civil Liberties Union. But Mike Epstein was a first baseman for the Washington Senators, a left-handed hitter with power but not very effective against left-handed pitching.

A reporter hesitated, then asked if Mr. Nixon had a particular trade in mind. It so happened that he did. "They ought to trade Epstein to the Yankees. They need the power. Especially left-handed power. They have that short right-field porch. And they could afford to platoon him. And you know he would be a very good draw in New York."

Anyone who kept up with baseball knew what he meant. Epstein was Jewish and New York, according to legend, was a city starved for a player who could appeal to the large number of Jewish fans. The tradition of the "Jewish Hope" dated back to the 1920's, when the Giants brought up a second baseman named Andy Cohen. Whatever, this was pretty sophisticated baseball talk.

Another reporter broke in. "Mr. President, on the economy, can you—"

THE PRESIDENT: "Ted could probably get a couple of good prospects for him, including a decent pitcher."

The dialogue went on in that vein for several more minutes. Someone else asked about the Soviet space program. And Mr. Nixon observed that Sonny Jurgensen, the Redskins' quarterback, was getting a little age on him, had a problem with his arm and seemed to be saving his long throws for those times when he really needed one and thought he could connect. The President approved. He thought Jurgensen was playing a very slick game of concealing the fact that throwing deep hurt him.

With that comment he disappeared back through the door leading to his own quarters. Followed by Haldeman. Followed by Ziegler.

I did not come away with any negative feelings, certainly not disappointment. I felt mostly confusion, as I often did in the presence of this complicated man who, even in moments of supposed leisure, would be photographed strolling on a beach in summer wearing a suit and tie with his coat properly buttoned. Though the visit was short and unproductive, I believed this contact offered a fleeting insight into what the man was like.

As a reporter, I try not to engage in the psychoanalytical game. I depend on what I see and hear and can touch with my fingers. But those moments struck me as revealing. No doubt, I thought, he does many things well, but being at ease making small talk isn't among them. That was unfortunate for us, meaning the press and, by extension, the public.

Here he was on a day swollen with clear cause for joy and pride, a day when he was obviously jubilant, wanting to be friendly and needing that warmth reciprocated, but not quite able to completely unbend. And I recalled Norman Mailer's description of Nixon at the 1968 Republican Convention, "The most disciplined man in American politics."

It was obvious that on matters of importance he would not answer questions in a visceral way. Lyndon Johnson frequently did. I'm not passing judgment either way. If one wanted to argue the point, one could build a strong case that the Nixon style could serve a President better. But the contrast was there. Johnson, particularly when he was airborne, riding the big sky, didn't hesitate to answer from the gut. Nixon, no way. Not even in that golden, mellow moment of flying to meet the men who had explored the moon. And, believe me, the questions were not tough. On the Soviet space program, I had reason to think he could have held a seminar. It was simply part of his nature and personal discipline not to answer questions if he had not prepared for them. He didn't realize how severe this attitude made him look and that, of course, was one of the bottom lines on President Nixon. He was tone-deaf on how things would appear, how they would look and sound to others.

The seven or eight reporters who had observed the session on *Air Force One* all had much the same quizzical reaction. A shrug, an exchange of what-was-that-all-about looks. We agreed the interview had been awkward, but not unpleasant. The President had not given off vibrations of dislike. He was merely uncomfortable. Ziegler had been nervous. Haldeman hostile.

No one attempted to describe the scene. If someone had written it verbatim for, say, the *New Yorker,* the effect might have been devastating. But it wasn't the sort of story I could step off a plane and give a minute and fifteen. It would have been unfair to everyone.

One point that did get across was that the President avidly followed sports. He watched the games on TV. He was a fan. We had been told that he did not read the newspapers. But a member of his staff assured me, "I don't know if he reads the front pages or the back, the stock markets or the editorial page. But I can tell you he reads the sports page." The President was filled with the sort of insights you can only glean from a daily habit.

Nixon constantly thought in sports metaphors. He had made at least a loose connection between himself and those who were in the arena. I'm not suggesting that he saw himself as Sonny Jurgensen with an ailing elbow. But I do know he identified with the underdog winners of sport, coming from behind, clinging to that winners-never-quit doctrine of the locker room. He thought those beliefs helped him survive the losses to Kennedy in 1960 and to Brown in California and brought him finally to the White House.

I have one other memory of that flight across the Pacific: President Nixon aboard the aircraft carrier *Hornet,* peering at the moonmen, Neil Armstrong, Buzz Aldrin and Michael Collins, through a porthole of glass in their quarantine cubicle and telling them, "This is the greatest day since the Creation." I thought, that must come as a shock to the followers of Moses, Muhammad and Jesus.

In ways that were not always subtle *Air Force One* became a showcase for Nixon's use of symbols in the exercise of power. Special flight jackets had been designed for the White House staff, with the presidential seal on one side and their names stitched on the other. In a kind of ritual, Ziegler, Haldeman and Ehrlichman, and often the President, would peel off their suit coats and slip into the flight jackets. That act made them members of a very small club.

The space for the press shrank considerably under Nixon. The President's quarters very much resembled the lounge car on a railroad train, and when he closed it off there was complete privacy, so that only one other restroom was available for the other VIP's, the press and the galley crew. This situation made for some fairly comical scenes of, say, a Henry Kissinger hurrying toward the back, not wanting to confront the press but having to go to the bathroom.

Nixon was a student of the kind of symbolism practiced by Charles de Gaulle and Chairman Mao. In private he talked much about the uses of such things. He was not, however, able to implement them very well. So it was that on his first trip to Europe he was impressed with the operatic uniforms of the castle guards in Brussels. He returned with the idea of dressing the White House police in those Nelson Eddy *Student Prince* costumes, a symbol of the Nixon presidency. The police rebelled and the public laughed and the cartoonists had a field day. The idea was dropped.

Then there were his appearances on television with a bust of Lincoln behind him. The Christmas scene with the President sitting on the floor, stroking his dog, while the First Family trimmed the tree. The American flag in the lapel. Suddenly, everyone belonging to the inner circle appeared with such a pin, and the message was clear. The flag was synonymous with support for Richard Nixon. He had tried to appropriate the most visible symbol of all. Only Henry Kissinger refused to make that gesture. Kissinger did a great deal to please Haldeman and Ehrlichman, as well as the President, but not that time, to his credit.

Of all the attendant lords Haldeman best understood the symbols of leadership. My becoming known as The Reporter the White House Hates had less to do with Dan Rather, I think, than the way CBS operated. My guess is that from the outset the Nixon people wanted to establish a kind of authority over the networks. They said, in effect, all right, television is important to us. Of the people covering the White House, Rather is in the position to do us the most harm because CBS has the largest audience and because the network tends to give more time to its correspondents. Also, Rather is incorrigible (which is to say that in their philosophy any coverage not judged to be favorable was judged to be unfair). Somehow, some way, we have to bring him around.

Such thinking wasn't new to politics or, for that matter, to the institutional life. In a football game, in an army barracks, or in a prison, you pick out someone with a potential for causing trouble, crowd him, put on the pressure, and the others will get the word.

What was new was the zeal with which the Nixon people pursued this tactic and the scale on which they practiced it. I never knew with any certainty what Richard Nixon thought of me. We had him on the record as saying, in general, that he thought reporters looked at him, quote, *with hatred in their eyes.* But my guess is that he did a lot less thinking about individual reporters than the reporters sometimes imagined, this one included.

But the fact is we went through a fairly long, carefully orchestrated campaign to disrupt and discredit the press. Nixon, and especially Spiro Agnew, sold their line hard—to be fair, that coverage had to be favorable—and they found some willing buyers. I would argue that totally favorable coverage would be the unfairest of all because it discourages free thought.

The Nixon people would also use the carrot-and-stick approach, what lawmen refer to as the tough-cop, good-cop treatment. A reporter would get a tongue-lashing from Charles Colson and later Ron Ziegler would sidle up and say, "Now don't take that as a reflection of how people here really feel."

Then they would try the wedge. They would hand a few stories to Bob Pierpoint, the other CBS correspondent, hoping to create some rivalry, some dissension—in their terms—"to wedge us." We laughed about it. The laughter was a little hollow at times, but to a lesser degree we had gone through the same thing under the Johnson Administration. My impulse was to play the game with them. We were in the news business. All stories were welcome. But we had to keep the lines open between ourselves, and Bob always did. We worked closely. He would walk into the office or hang up the phone, grin and say, "Here they come." The more they tried, the less successful they were and the harder they pushed.

All of which led in time to an odd conversation over breakfast in the Edwardian Room of the Plaza Hotel between John Ehrlichman and my boss, Richard Salant, the president of CBS News. I do not know all of the subjects discussed, but one of them was me, and Ehrlichman made it explicitly clear how he and the White House felt. "Rather has been jobbing us. [Half smile.] Aren't you going to open a bureau in Austin where Dan could have a job?" He went on to suggest that possibly I could be given a year's vacation.

In short time, details of that meeting were in print. I demanded an appointment with Ehrlichman. We met in his office, in what came to be known around the Rather household as The Meeting in the Upper Room. His office was located upstairs at the White House.

Ehrlichman met me at the door and suggested that I sit in a particular chair. The thought occurred to me at the time, I wonder if he has a tape recorder going. This, however, predated the revelations of Watergate by a full year, and I immediately dismissed the notion as absurd. In retrospect I would guess that my suspicions were probably right. He had taped almost everyone else in his office. I don't know why he would not have taped that meeting.

In a curiously loud, purposeful voice Ehrlichman said, "I simply want to say to your face what I said to your boss—"

I quickly broke in. "Oh, I appreciate that. What I don't appreciate is what you tried to do, and I have to tell you that I consider it a cheap shot and unworthy of you and unworthy of an assistant to the President."

Then Haldeman walked in. The conversation ranged afield and Haldeman impressed me with how much he knew about my business. Somehow we got off on the subject of standups, which are just what the name suggests: a reporter stands on the White House lawn, hair blowing in the wind, posed against that famous backdrop, and briefly tells the day's story.

Haldeman, who had one of the last crew cuts left in America in the 1970's, remarked that he would not have the problem of unkempt hair. But he knew how and when the standups were done.

We soon cycled back to the reason I was there. Ehrlichman said, "I don't know whether it's just sloppiness or you're letting your true feelings come through, but the net effect is that you're negative. You have negative leads on bad stories."

I could feel my temperature rising. "What's a bad story?"

Ehrlichman said, "A story that's dead-ass wrong. And you're wrong ninety percent of the time."

I said, "Then you have nothing to worry about. Any reporter who is wrong ninety percent of the time can't last."

At that point Haldeman interjected, "What concerns me is that you are inaccurate and unfair, but your style is very positive. You sound like you know what you're talking about. People believe you."

Ehrlichman piped up, "Yeah, people believe you, and they shouldn't."

I said, "Well, I hope they do, and maybe now we are getting down to the root of it. You have trouble getting people to believe you."

We kicked that thought around and finally I said to both of them, "Of course, it must be easy for you, being on the inside, to spot things that are off in terms of tone. Outright mistakes. And I accept my share of the responsibility. But you have to accept yours, Mr. Haldeman and Mr. Ehrlichman, because you don't tell us a great deal about what goes on in here."

We settled nothing. Nor did we clear the air. But I had a chance to study the two men closest to the President. Haldeman, I knew, was the kind of person who makes a studied practice of looking you straight in the eye and drilling you hard. He talked slowly, precisely, without fidgeting. By contrast, there was a softness, a blustery manner to Ehrlichman. He often talked with his hands, and a couple of times he lamely tried to break the tension with a small wisecrack. Not so with Haldeman. He was all grimness.

Another revealing sidelight developed out of that meeting. During the hour I was with them we were interrupted by a secretary who rushed in with a brief story off the news ticker about Senator Edward Kennedy. Keep in mind this was April, 1971. I did some checking later and learned there were standing orders for anything that moved on the wire about Ted Kennedy to be brought immediately and directly to Haldeman.

Many of us overlooked that connection in trying to trace the seeds of Watergate. It is hard to exaggerate how concerned President Nixon, and the people around him, were, from the beginning, with the Kennedy legend and the threat of a Kennedy candidacy. The effect of Chappaquiddick on the reelection of Nixon and on the history of this country should not be dismissed lightly.

Before Ted Kennedy's car plunged off the bridge, the Nixon presidency attempted to project an image of being more centrist than to the Right, more moderate than conservative. They were talking about tax and welfare reform and solving the problems of the environment. After all, Richard Nixon was a minority President. The Republicans were pointing toward 1972, and there loomed the present danger of Camelot Revisited, another chance certainly, some romantics thought, to redeem the losses of the 1960's.

Then came Ted Kennedy's ill-fated midnight drive and the drowning of Mary Jo Kopechne. Look at the Nixon record, before and after, in terms of the mood, temper and direction of the Nixon presidency. Perhaps it would have gone that way in any case. Who can say? But the post-Chappaquiddick change was dramatic. The White House had concluded that Ted Kennedy, in July, 1969, was finished as a presidential contender.

Then after the midyear elections in 1970, after the Republicans had taken a beating—to my surprise, and I know to theirs—the polls began to show the last of the Kennedy brothers with a slight comeback going. The polls turned out to mean little, but more important was how the White House perceived them: Hey, we just came out of the '70 elections, we took a beating, lo and behold, Ted Kennedy is on the rise and Gallup and Harris have the President trailing Ed Muskie.

Therein was the genesis of much of Watergate, the Department of Dirty Tricks and what was to follow. People continue to say, I just can't believe they were so stupid, knowing they not only had the 1972 election won, but that they were going to win it so big.

The answer is they didn't know, not at the time those forces were set in motion. Throughout the spring of 1971 the country had been stunned by the disclosure of the Pentagon Papers, the leaked secrets of the Cambodian bombing and the SALT talks. The stock market was reeling and the polls showed Muskie, the craggy, understated senator from Maine, the man favored to become the candidate of his party, leading Richard Nixon.

In 1972, after the fiasco of the McGovern-Eagleton campaign, it was easy to see Nixon as a sure winner all along. But in 1971, viewed through the prism of their fears and prejudices, that outcome was by no means a sure thing. And so the Liddys and the Hunts came aboard and the Colsons were given carte blanche to operate. Now you add the reality of what happens when all the cages are unlocked—once you hire a former cat burglar for the FBI such as Gordon Liddy, once you hire a spy and soldier of fortune such as Howard Hunt and once you turn loose an unprincipled Chuck Colson. At the very least, a different moral climate was created. A President could say, "All right, do whatever is necessary, but get it done," and the scrambling that followed would leave footprints on the Constitution.

Certainly, the attention of President Nixon was focused elsewhere: trips to China and Europe, attempts at détente with the Soviet Union, the economy. But all the while the momentum of the Hunts and Liddys and Colsons and the Dirty Tricks squad was building. It is no good asking, who would have been so stupid, in mid-1972, to turn all that loose? You had to do a time dance, eighteen months into the past.

And their paranoia began not with Muskie but with Kennedy. This was one of the lost stories of Watergate. As fast and thick as they came, stories that in other times would have stayed in the headlines for weeks lasted only until the next edition. So it merely went into the Dirty Tricks column when Anthony Ulasewicz, a colorful, street-wise, former Brooklyn cop, testified that CREEP, the Committee to Reelect the President, provided more than $100,000 to finance six months of snooping into Chappaquiddick. The idea was to find new evidence to discredit the version of the accident told by Ted Kennedy. Attempts were made to bug the apartments of the so-called "boiler room girls" who had worked on the last campaign of Robert Kennedy and in whose honor a cookout was held on the night of July 18, 1969 (which was, coincidentally, in the week of the landing on the moon).

Regrettably, for those who had hired him, Ulasewicz reported that he had found little evidence to contradict Kennedy's story, and the quest was finally dropped. That may have been as clean a bill as Ted Kennedy can expect to get, and it was paid for by the Republicans. Meanwhile Ulasewicz regaled his Watergate audiences with his description of life as a bagman, paying off various agents, slipping in and out of phone booths while trying to balance paper sacks filled with money.

We would come to a time when one could not remember the Nixon years without thinking of Watergate. It would be like trying to imagine Philadelphia without a slum. His accomplishments, such as his initiatives in foreign policy, his eventual success at ending the war in Vietnam, would be marked down by the crimes that drove him from office.

Whatever feelings I had about Richard Nixon as a person were shaded by the fact that I never knew him very well and didn't know anyone who did. The overriding impression I had was of a man who had been wounded. It was in his eyes. Yet the few times I was ever actually near him and got past the protective armor of the presidency, I can say truthfully that I did not feel uncomfortable.

In January, 1972, I sat across from him in the Oval Office, in a rare one-on-one interview televised for one hour live over CBS. He told me later that he had been surprised when the network assigned me to ask the questions, but said he had not objected. He imposed only one condition, that he be permitted to open the telecast.

The time went by in track shoes. The interview was intense but he came off as being well prepared. The very last question, though, seemed to throw him. It had to do with the women's movement and the use of Ms. as a salutation on White House correspondence. An attempt on my part to end the interview on a light note, the question was asked with a smile. He fumbled a bit and never quite addressed the question.

The moment the lights went off and the telecast was over, he said, "I didn't understand that last question and I know I didn't handle it well." He didn't say that in an uptight way. As a matter of fact, he reached over from his chair and placed his hand on my arm. If anything, the gesture was a lament.

In my view, an interesting cameo. I had not seen Richard Nixon that way very often. I explained to him very quickly what I had sought, and intended, by the question. In an almost classic hand-to-the-forehead gesture Nixon said, "Ah, of course. Well, that was the one question in the whole hour we didn't anticipate. We should have been prepared for it." No one on his staff had raised the subject of women's lib. At the time Gloria Steinem was at her apex and Ms. Magazine was just starting, but in retrospect it was not the sort of subject Nixon would have made a point of following.

When we had finished he rose and said, "I wish we could do that part over again." Then he smiled and added, "But that's the way it is with live television, isn't it?"

In no hurry, he moved around the room, posed for pictures and shook hands with every person there. He made a point of seeking out first Jimmy Wall, the only black technician on the floor. He chatted easily with everyone. One expects a politician to do so, but we already knew that small talk was not a Nixon strength. This night he did it very well. As he circled the room, I asked him finally if there had been any particular reason why he had insisted on opening the telecast.

He said, "Well, you were a guest in my home, and I felt that it was a bit more appropriate for the host to speak first." He was very gracious. There was no one near him, not even Bob Haldeman.

And finally after twenty-three minutes on the clock—I checked it—he said goodnight. Rather jauntily, I thought. And one didn't often have reason to describe him as doing much of anything "jauntily." He walked out of the office, through the paneled glass double doors, over the marks on the floor made by Ike's old golf shoes and across the back portico. No one was around him, not to his left or his right. The nearest Secret Service agent stood twenty or thirty paces behind him. My eyes followed Nixon most of the way. He glanced to his right in the direction of the lighted Washington Monument, and beyond to the Jefferson Memorial. Then he turned sharply to his left and began whistling. I could hear him softly through the open glass doors as he walked along the porch, past the magnolia tree that Andrew Jackson planted, and disappeared into the mansion.

I had never heard him whistle. I came away from that night thinking, if this two-hundred-million-dollar public relations operation that they have mounted here didn't prevent people from seeing that side of Richard Nixon, he would be vastly better off. So would we all.

Six months later, on June 17, 1972, a team of seven men broke into the offices of the Democratic National Committee in a high-rise complex called The Watergate. The telephones had been wiretapped. The White House press secretary, Ron Ziegler, dismissed the break-in as "a third-rate burglary attempt. This is something that should not fall into the political process."

Out-Take

11

SHOVING THE PRESS

If you're a lone wolf in Washington or if you run a small bureau for a group of papers in the Midwest, the message gets through to you early: If you're a good boy, you get favors out of the White House. If you're not, we have a thousand and one ways to eat you alive.

And they do.

It begins with something as basic as the White House press pass. A reporter literally cannot get in the gate without one. Ron Ziegler and his staff had the power to make obtaining a pass a routine matter or they could make a reporter wait for weeks, even months. They could get you instantly through the northwest gate and have you inside the White House in minutes or they could make the clearance take half a day. The intimidation of the press began with access to people.

Take Ken Clawson, who was the deputy director of communications, a one-time Washington *Post* reporter and a man who knew the business. He might get word to your editor: "Hey, next time you're in town let's go to lunch." And over lunch, "You know, I really like your paper. So does the President. You fellows do a terrific job. But it's puzzling to us why you would have a reporter covering the White House who, ah, doesn't know his way around." It was like a kiss from the Mafia.

Some of the ways they kept the press in line, or tried to, were subtle. And some not. On Nixon's trip to China in 1972 a reporter became a captive of the White House p.r. machine. Only a certain number were allowed to go. Ron Ziegler, with the advice of Haldeman and Kissinger (and, possibly, the President), prepared a checklist that determined who qualified.

Ziegler pointed out, "Not every reporter who wants to go to China can go, and we must use some standards for selecting who does and who does not." Not so incidentally, this gave Ziegler great control over a reporter. It happened that *Newsday* had just run an investigative series on the Bebe Rebozo connection with Nixon. And their Marty Schram, a first-rate journalist, who met each of the points on their checklist, was refused a seat. He was simply told, "No room."

Meanwhile Bill Buckley, whose favor they were courting at the time, was allowed to go although he did not meet a number of their own standards. Such as: how often did one cover the White House? How many foreign trips had one made previously? The whole thrust was to give preference to the regulars. Marty Schram was a regular. But he was scratched.

So one may ask, why couldn't a paper say, here's your passport, here's your money, make your own arrangements and be there. Sometimes it is done that way. But not often. And not on a trip to China, a closed society. Another point, a reporter must have security clearance if he or she is going to get anywhere near the President. If the President plans a state visit to England, no one can prevent a reporter from being there. But without clearance and credentials, he won't get within miles of the man he has come to cover.

On the China trip it was virtually impossible to avoid the controls set up by the White House. Where reporters went, whom they saw, what they heard, all were programmed. Given those limits, one had to wonder if Marty Schram's coverage really would have differed from Bill Buckley's. And it should be noted that Buckley worked hard during the trip and turned out the rich, graceful copy you would expect of him. *Newsday* fought the ban and lost. I doubt that the paper's later coverage of Nixon was affected either way.

But a point had been made about the power of the White House and the whole press corps knew it.

Chapter 12

WHERE WATERGATE LED

A MIGHTILY FRUSTRATED George McGovern had tried, and had failed, to arouse the voters' interest. An attempt by the Democrats to open hearings on the burglary of their headquarters was quickly turned off. Only the size of Richard Nixon's reelection margin remained in doubt. As a news story, the Watergate break-in had exploded like a puff of talcum powder.

That was the picture in September, 1972, when I boarded a flight from Washington to New York and found that my seatmate was Edward Bennett Williams. I must confess to being a buff about the supersuccessful defense attorneys. My interest was due in part to having covered the leonine Percy Foreman when I was a young newsman in Houston.

I didn't know Williams well, but I admired him. He was a power in the Democratic party, a liberal, but he had defended Jimmy Hoffa (and, years later John Connally). He is urbane, tough, country-club handsome, with a quick and nimble mind. It would depend on where I was, whether I would send for Percy Foreman or Ed Williams to bail me out of a legal jam.

Williams sat down, loosened his tie, buckled his seat belt and ordered two quick Scotches. He has a habit of picking up conversations as though you had been interrupted in midsentence. There was no preliminary, no two-stepping around. His first words were, "Well, I know you think there is nothing to it, but this Watergate thing is the greatest political story of your time."

I just stared at him. The truth was, I had thought a great deal about the break-in. A half dozen of us at CBS were directly involved on a daily basis trying to match Bob Woodward and Carl Bernstein, the two Washington *Post* reporters who were running hard and often with exclusive stories. We couldn't, but we had made some headway and were still trying. We were, we believed, ahead of the other networks. In the meantime, a duty existed not to be so anxious as to broadcast mere suspicions, and/or Democratic party propaganda. And, fair to say, I did not even imagine the proportions to which the Watergate story would eventually grow.

Now, in my infinite wisdom, I thought to myself rather smugly, Okay, here's Edward Bennett Williams, famed attorney and bulwark of the Democratic party, about to do a number on me.

And then I heard Williams say, "They will never be able to stop it. That, my friend, is a fair bet. The question is, can they contain the damage it does? If they win the election big, they may. But it has to be put to rest within six months after the election. Remember that. Six months. I don't think they'll make it."

I said, "Even if you're right, they'll be able to shut off the water far short of Haldeman."

Williams shook his head. "No way," he said.

From the outset that was the key. If suspicion reached Haldeman, it touched the President. At the time of our conversation, however, the scandal was still largely confined to McCord, Hunt, Liddy and the Cubans. It seemed unthinkable that the coverup could lead to the desk of Bob Haldeman. You had to know how powerful he was. Yes, there had been strong presidential advisors in the past. Ike had Sherman Adams. FDR had Harry Hopkins. And John Kennedy had his Irish Mafia. But they all paled in comparison with Haldeman.

Here was Richard Nixon, a loner, wanting to be insulated from what he considered the harassment of people coming at him from all directions. So Haldeman wielded a power unique in the history of the presidency, a power accountable only to Richard Nixon. I don't believe the public knew, and perhaps still doesn't, the full implications of the fact that when Haldeman spoke, men who were generally perceived to be people of power in their own right quaked. Even Cabinet members instructed by him to do a certain thing had to think hard about saying no, and they seldom did.

Williams and I made a small wager that night, my position being that Watergate—whatever that word meant—would stop well short of Bob Haldeman's door. The stakes were something like two tickets to a Redskins game against a hamburger at Clyde's Restaurant. Williams, of course, owned a controlling interest in the Redskins. He was the man who had brought Vince Lombardi to Washington and later George Allen. One could say he had a sense of what it takes to win.

But at that stage I was skeptical of his Watergate predictions. There were too many ways, I thought, of detouring whatever investigation finally got launched. Still, the encounter proved helpful. Williams proceeded to tell me a few things, not all of which I believed, but out of that conversation came two or three good leads.

The shuttles to New York, where I anchored the CBS News on Sunday nights, were a part of my weekly routine. In December we ran into each other again on the same flight. By then the election was over. The seven Plumbers had been indicted and were under pressure by Judge John Sirica to break their silence. Stories in the Washington *Post* had mentioned such White House names as John Mitchell, former Attorney General and later Nixon campaign director, and his deputy Jeb Magruder. Watergate threatened to go off like a delayed-reaction time bomb.

Again Williams loosened his tie, ordered his Scotches and just picked up the thread of the conversation as though three months had not passed. He said, "Well, they are not going to make it. *None* of them will make it."

I still didn't accept that contention, but by then I had decided that nothing was impossible.

In the CBS offices in New York and Washington, we were now holding almost daily meetings to track the Watergate story. There was no prying the lid with the twist of an oyster knife. No stop-the-press news bulletins. In the early stages my contribution, if any, consisted of raising questions and analyzing whatever evidence we had. I like to think that I was among the first to draw a line from Magruder to Bob Haldeman to the Oval Office. Maybe Ed Williams, I thought, was right.

When it became clear that Jeb Magruder had been involved in a fairly deep way, someone at CBS said, "Assuming that the suspicions about Magruder are correct, we still can't take any reckless leaps. It doesn't necessarily mean anyone higher up at the White House had a part in this."

But based on my experience, that was precisely what the evidence did mean. "If Magruder is in it," I argued, "then somebody very close to the Oval Office had to know."

That was the way the Nixon staff worked. When it soon became apparent that Dwight Chapin had been mixed up in the Donald Segretti, Dirty Tricks business, I said, "That tells us plenty. There is a pattern developing. If Magruder and Chapin were involved, we know Haldeman must have been involved. The question now is, how deeply?"

But the brutal truths of the Watergate story continued to be broken not by television or by the White House press corps, but by a pair of mavericks from the police beat: Woodward and Bernstein. We did turn up some angles at CBS. We did define some of the issues. And raise some of the right questions. But in the important early going our coverage was less than outstanding.

Time and again in the wake of Watergate I would hear the question raised, why doesn't television do a better job of investigative reporting? Often someone would cite the fact that *The New York Times* broke the Pentagon Papers case, and the Washington *Post* produced most of the headlines on Watergate.

Let me say first that I dislike the phrase "investigative reporting." According to my definition most reporting is investigative. But in the current use of the phrase—taking long-shot leads, tracking them down, doing a story in depth—television has not yet found a way to compete with a few powerful newspapers of high integrity and dedication.

It took courage for *The New York Times* to print the Pentagon Papers and talent to reduce them to a form that people could understand. But Daniel Ellsberg and his friends walked in off the street and handed the papers to *The Times*. That did not require great investigative reporting in my judgment. I take nothing away from *The Times'* accomplishment, but it was not a triumph of private sleuthing.

The Watergate scandal began as a police-beat story. The Washington *Post,* in addition to being a national newspaper, is also a local journal for what amounts to a one-industry town. They cover the police beat. We don't. We have beaten them on some stories. But certainly not on that one.

Television as a news medium has some maddening problems, not the least of which is that it can be clumsy and expensive to report a story that requires any degree of secrecy. A newspaper can commit a so-called "investigative team" to a story and tie up the time and salaries of maybe a half dozen reporters. But that's all. If a television network commits to that kind of assignment, the cost can quickly run into six figures and above. One reaches a point where camera crews and technicians are involved, a virtual army of people. Not always but usually we need pictures. To produce a film of people and events, especially if you do not want to let the world know what you are doing, can be mighty complicated as opposed to simply unearthing the facts.

I want to make clear that I am not excusing television, or CBS, or myself, for what we have not done well. I am only arguing that it is not a case of not wanting to do the job. Whatever our Watergate failures, they were not caused by any reluctance on the part of anyone at CBS to pursue the story. Indeed, the opposite is true. The whip was put to us daily. "Get on that story. Stay on it. What the hell is this about? Find out." We spent a great deal of time and no small amount of money trying to do just that. Bill Small stayed after us. Cronkite called regularly.

I came out of this period with a sense of, boy, I better reassess what it is I do for a living and how I do it because covering Watergate was a humbling experience. I had gone along thinking I did a pretty good job, that I was a tough pro and hard to fool. Every reporter wants to think that of himself.

Well, here was a story people needed to know about and we could not really get out in front. Watergate changed me as a newsman. I think it changed us as a people, and the way we think about politics. I am far less likely now to give any official spokesman the benefit of the doubt. I don't believe in cynicism as an approach to reporting. But skepticism is essential. And what I try to do is to give myself a very heavy injection of skepticism every morning before I go to work. A triple dose, now.

It seems incredible today to realize how easily the entire Watergate story might have been missed. I hesitate to use the word *fluke,* because the people who broke the story worked long and hard and creatively to do so. But you can begin with the tape on the door handle. How easily the night watchman might have overlooked it.

Then, to me, the most crucial of all chance moves: The first car that answered the call at the Watergate offices happened to be part of the police special squad, a "Serpico" group. What would have happened if it had been a routine patrol car? The record tells us that the Washington police department is frequently controlled very closely by people in the White House.

Any reporter who ever covered a police beat knows that he sees a Dickensian side of life that most people seldom glimpse. For example, he realizes that equal justice under the law is a nice ideal, and I don't say that lightly, but putting it into practice is damned tough.

If you have ever been around a jailhouse, you learn to look for signs. And in the District of Columbia, the signs told you that the police were controlled, for a long while, by John Ehrlichman. The mayor, Walter Washington, might argue and certainly won't like hearing it. But during the ill-famed May Day demonstrations, Ehrlichman was in radio contact with the chief of police and in virtual minute-by-minute control of what went on. And what went on was the illegal, mass arrest of perhaps as many as fifteen thousand citizens.

In the structure of a local police force, the good special squads are made up of a different breed of cat. It is tougher to choke them off in terms of what they know. If the first car to arrive on the scene had been a routine patrol car, I'm not certain Watergate would ever have made the blotter.

McCord's letter and Judge Sirica's skepticism and toughness made certain that at least part of the Watergate story would be laid before the public. Once the coverup began to unravel, once John Dean came forward to match his guilt against the President's, there was no holding back the truth.

Even now I find it strange that during this time of runaway news I became known among the Nixon people, and elsewhere, as a "gadfly." That was not by design. In my own self-criticism I faulted Dan Rather most for being too conservative in my approach to work, for being less aggressive than I should have been.

Living with a story every day is like trolling on the beach for coins that have fallen out of people's bathing trunks. I would canvass all my sources, some of them in the White House itself. They didn't pass notes to me in invisible ink, but they were people who saw a lot of paper and overheard a lot of conversations. Middle-level aides throughout the Executive Branch often were the most valuable sources. But secretaries, chauffeurs, waiters and cleaning people also sometimes knew more than their bosses liked to believe. Part of every week went into base-touching with every reachable source.

Out of this would sometimes come a tip and perhaps a small break for that night's newscast. In the middle weeks of the coverup I called William Colby, the head of the CIA, and asked, "Mr. Director, there is a story going around that Howard Hunt once worked for a company that was a CIA front."

Long pause.

"Are you there?"

"Yes, I am."

"Well, what about this?"

"That isn't much of a question."

In Washington you have to know the political codes. His language told me, I'm willing to talk and, yes, I know what you are referring to, but I must have specific questions.

So I began ticking off a series of pointed questions. There is a company called so-and-so at such-and-such an address. Are you familiar with it? "Yes." Does the CIA have any connection with that company?

Another long pause. A signal to me that this was still not specific enough.

"Did Howard Hunt work for that company?"

"Yes, I believe he did."

Right on down the line. There is a tacit understanding with certain people in government that you had to follow the form. If it ever got down to a disclosure, the source wanted to be able to say, "He called. He asked a specific question. He had the right information. I wasn't going to lie to him."

You have to recall the mood of intrigue and suspense that dominated Washington in those months. The case was like a huge oil spill, running in every direction. A former Attorney General, a second former Cabinet member, Nixon's own lawyer, staff assistants and members of his reelection campaign were being indicted by a federal grand jury. The CIA, the FBI and the Justice Department all had been misused by the White House in an effort to keep the coverup from dissolving.

Had I been smarter, more aggressive, more alert and less hounded by a conscience that too often makes me do things the hard way, I might have broken more of those stories myself instead of reporting and analyzing the stories of others. I know for sure that I did not take advantage of the one most important break that fell my way during the endless Watergate drama. I was the first reporter to meet privately with Leon Jaworski after he had succeeded Archibald Cox as the special prosecutor, following the "Saturday Night Massacre."

Jimmy Doyle, a pugnacious Irishman out of Boston, a no-holds-barred former newspaperman, had served as press secretary for Cox and later Jaworski. When Jaworski flew into Washington to take over, the first week in November, 1973, Doyle met him at Dulles Airport.

Doyle asked if he knew anybody, meaning anyone in the media. Jaworski said, "Not really." Then he hesitated and added, "I do know one person. I know Dan Rather. And I don't want to see anybody until I see him."

As Doyle confided to me much later two thoughts raced through his mind: One, jiminy crickets, that's going to be a disaster if he thinks he can play favorites; and two, at least, that's a start.

Leon Jaworski was a partner in a prestigious Houston law firm when Gen. Alexander Haig, on behalf of the President, pleaded with him to take the special prosecutor's job. A thankless task before, it was worse now. I knew Jaworski, having covered the courts in Houston. After the Kennedy assassination he was very helpful in a number of ways when I thought I was going to cover the Jack Ruby trial. I was in contact with him all through that time and he even helped arrange for some guests to appear on a broadcast of mine called "The Law and Lee Harvey Oswald."

His credentials were impressive. He had been a prosecutor at the War Crimes Trials after World War Two, had served on the Warren Commission, had been president of the American Bar Association. But on his arrival in Washington he was viewed with disdain by many as "the President's man." His friends believed he had voted for Nixon in 1972. Now he was being called in to clear the man in the Oval Office and *get Watergate behind us.* Or so went the educated thinking.

He had not been in town more than forty-eight hours when Doyle called me and said, "The special prosecutor wants to see you." I have to tell you I thought perhaps it was about the break-in at my home, which was one of the more interesting things to happen to me over the years and about which more later.

The building that housed the special prosecutor's office was under heavy security to keep people from stealing papers and files. If you had not been around him for a while, you tended to forget what a take-charge guy Jaworski is. He's deceptive in appearance and manner, with the sweet, cherubic face of a baby doctor.

Remember that he had just taken command of a group of brilliant and rebellious young lawyers. Jaworski's second greatest accomplishment, I think, was keeping Cox's staff and winning their confidence. Many of them suspected that Jaworski was a Texas sellout. He knew that he had walked into a real pit; those who didn't see in his appointment a Duval County kind of fix figured him for a rube. Those who knew him, of course, thought differently. I had been interviewed on a radio broadcast the morning after his selection, and one of the questions had to do with Jaworski's reputation in Texas. "The record shows," I said, "that whatever his political label, his integrity is oak-solid."

He greeted me inside his office, said, "I appreciate your coming," and dismissed Doyle with a nod. But before Doyle could leave I quickly said, "Mr. Jaworski, I certainly don't mind if Jimmy stays. In fact, I'd feel more comfortable if he did. That's form around here. Also, in addition to being a first-rate professional, Jimmy is a good friend of mine. I can assure you that anything that needs to be said in confidence can be said in front of him."

Jaworski was straightforward as always. He said, "I know I'm taking on a helluva thing here. I haven't got my feet on the ground yet. But I want to talk to you in general terms. I want to ask you about a few things."

I said, "Well, if you want to put it on the basis that I'm not here for a story—of any kind—we can put the whole meeting off the record."

He said, "No, I don't think that is necessary. But if you have any questions to ask, I'll probably have to get someone else to answer them. So let's just make this informal."

He was clearly feeling his way. I told him, among other things, what he had already sensed: that many members of his staff thought he had been hired to take a dive. Those who were willing to grant that he was honest considered him a hayseed.

Doyle broke right in. With a slightly nervous smile he said, "Dan, I wouldn't go quite that strong. There might be some problems here, but nothing that can't be handled."

At one point Jaworski held up a stack of letters. Everyone in town wanted him for something. The pile included requests from such network television shows as "Face the Nation," "Issues and Answers," and "Meet the Press." He grimaced and said, "I can't do all of this."

I agreed with him. I said, "I think it's probably far too early for you to attempt any TV appearances. There is nothing really you can say." I bit my tongue after that. On top of the stack was the letter from "Face the Nation," and they wanted him to appear the following Sunday. Hastily I added, "Of course, when it *is* time for you to do it, you should go on 'Face the Nation.' You'll reach more people on CBS."

He gave an impatient wave of his hand and said, "Yes, yes, I understand all that."

We chatted for perhaps half an hour before I said, "I think it would be better for both of us if we stopped right here." He was very much a gentleman about it. He nodded and said, "I'm glad we could have this visit. I'm not sure how all this is going to go and I welcome your counsel."

I said, of course. And then sounding a little windier than I would have liked, I added that it would have to be within the ethics of my job. I had my precepts to follow just as he did, as a lawyer. He said, "By all means."

I was trying to say, politely, that I would like to keep our lines open. But I didn't want to be an informant or compromise my freedom to go after a story. I'm sure he understood. The fact was, Jaworski didn't need a thing from me. It had been simply a nice gesture on his part, his way of saying, look, I wanted to establish contact with you. We might not be able to speak frankly again, but I didn't want to come into town and ignore you. Also, in a shrewd way he was fishing for information, for other viewpoints and a sense of what the city felt. He was doing his job.

Leaving his office, I felt the stirrings of a conflict. Could I develop Jaworski as a news source? Should I even try? I only knew that I needed all the help I could get.

One of the few people I told about this meeting was Bill Small, who has a gift, rare in this business, of not making a question larger than it is. He said, "Dan, you have to make a judgment. I'll leave it entirely to you and, in fact, I don't want to know any more." And that is the way a good bureau manager works when a correspondent's sources are involved.

There were two special factors to consider. For one, Fred Graham had just moved over from *The New York Times* to cover the Justice Department. He is an attorney by training, an experienced reporter, and I have always made a point of not poaching on someone else's run.

Then my own personal feelings held me back. Given the problems that already faced Jaworski, I didn't want anyone raising the Texas Connection. I resolved the matter by not calling or going back to see him. Later I wasn't at all sure I had done the best thing. A really aggressive reporter perhaps should have said to hell with it, this is the story of the century, a lot of bets are off, what better source could you have than the special prosecutor. Of course, I don't know that Leon Jaworski would have allowed himself to be developed as a source, even indirectly.

In the back of my mind I felt if a question arose, if I needed to verify a point or a piece of information, I might put it to the test. At least twice I literally had the telephone in my hand. Once I walked over to the special prosecutor's office at 1425 K Street on my lunch hour, intending to see Doyle and ask for an appointment. Each time I backed off. As hot as things were getting, as desperately as the President's men were looking for ways to discredit those who were contesting them, I would not risk even the appearance that I had a pipeline to the special prosecutor.

If one were teaching a journalism class, this might pose a worthwhile textbook problem. Assuming that an advantage might have been taken, what should a reporter have done? If I were answering today, I'd say he probably should have gone back, fairly quickly, and at least established a line of communication.

At odd times, in unlikely ways, the Texas Connection continued to surface. There was the clash in Houston and, leading up to that, the incident at San Clemente.

Reporters were milling around the grounds of the Western White House, waiting for the first presidential press conference in five and a half months to begin on the lawn of San Clemente. The date was August 22, 1973. The country was by then obsessed with Watergate. Nixon had mounted a counterattack, with a series of carefully orchestrated public appearances. But the noose was tightening.

It was one of those brilliantly clear, late summer California afternoons. Reporters bantered back and forth as the last chairs were put in place and the technicians checked out their sound systems. Idly, I asked Marty Nolan of the Boston *Globe,* "What is the toughest non-Watergate question you could ask?"

Marty replied, "Mr. President, what do you do all day?"

I smilingly shook my head. "That would be too tough."

A few minutes later I happened to be standing a few feet from the driveway when a husky man in a dark suit, wearing a snap-brim hat, ducked out of a car. As he alighted he glanced in my direction and said, "Got to admire you."

I stopped short. I thought, who the hell is that?

He raised up then, smiled, stuck out his hand and said, "John Connally."

With a foolish grin I said, "Governor, you just startled me." And he had. For one thing, I expected to see the former governor of Texas in a Stetson, a far more familiar piece of headgear. Here he was with a gray snap-brim hat. It was the first time I ever saw John Connally when he actually *looked* like a Republican.

For another thing, around that time, and in that setting, I had not been accustomed to hearing kind words.

Connally laid a little politician's talk on me and qualified it with, "Of course, you won't quote me on this." That was the Connally line on most things, including how the weather was, even when he knew full well you would quote him and, in fact, hoped you would.

"I'm not saying I agree with everything you say," he went on, "or any of it. But I have to admire you. Lot of times I thought there wasn't any *Texas* left in you. But I think there might be some."

It was pure bull's wool, of course, but masterfully done. I fumbled around, not quite certain how to react. I was still embarrassed at not having recognized one of the best known political profiles, but as I say, the hat threw me off. My impression of that brief encounter was simply this: Connally had picked his side, he was supporting the President, but he had reservations and he was letting me know. He was not, shall we say, blinded by loyalty.

The press conference started a few moments later. I knew what I wanted to ask. The question, in fact, had been asked of me by my relatives in Texas, not far from John Connally's own ranch in Floresville. Frequently, during those turbulent Watergate months, I would call my father-in-law, Martin Goebel, in Smithville, and ask what the people were talking about at the Post Office or over at the barber shop. The question that came back to me was, did they try to bribe that judge or not? They meant, of course, the judge in the Daniel Ellsberg–Pentagon Papers trial.

The President seemed to grow more visibly irritated with each question. He had prepared himself on a wide range of topics—six months' worth of news had gone by—but almost all the questions were related to Watergate. Actually, that suited the White House strategy. They had decided it was time to go on the attack. Here Nixon was on his own best ground. And Buchanan, Clawson and others had been spreading the word for days: The President is going to face a *hostile* press. Like Australian wild dogs they are going to be coming at him.

I had worked and reworked my question. I had all summer to get the phrasing down. "Mr. President," I began, "I want to state this question with due respect to your office, but also as directly as—"

"That would be unusual," he broke in.

Startled, but trying not to show it, I said, "I would like to think not."

His flash of annoyance was covered quickly. "You are always respectful, Mr. Rather," he said. "You know that."

I said, "Thank you, Mr. President." Then I went on. "It concerns the events surrounding your contact with the judge in the Pentagon Papers case, Judge Byrne. Now, you are a lawyer, and given the state of the situation and what you knew, could you give us some reason why the American people should not believe that there was at least a subtle attempt to bribe the judge in that case?"

Judge Matthew Byrne, it had been revealed, was visited by John Ehrlichman during the trial and told that he was being considered for the directorship of the FBI. Incredibly, the judge was brought to the Nixon compound—while he was still hearing the case.

To the question, the President reacted sharply. "Well," he said, "I would say the only part of your statement that is perhaps accurate is that

I am a lawyer." But his answer was long and rambling and never really dealt with the question. There was little doubt in my mind that he wanted to come across as combative, fighting back. But he evaded the key questions. The truth by that time was beginning to come clear. *They had tried to bribe the judge.* One of the minor ironies of Watergate, among so many, was that Judge Byrne might have made an excellent director of the FBI.

It may change no one's opinion now to say I was only trying to draw out answers to questions I thought needed to be asked. I was not baiting the President or promoting myself. But some people wanted to read into it more than was there.

Before this news conference, I was not convinced there was any special tension between us. Yet, months earlier, before anyone else had brought it up, Jean said to me one night, "What is it between you and the President?" And the answer was, I don't know. And I still don't.

But where I am is this: I went to my job every day determined to be as fair and as accurate as humanly possible. At the end of each day I didn't ask myself, do they like me, or do they like what I did? I asked myself, did I meet my own standards for this day? And if I had, then I slept well. If I hadn't, I tossed and turned and asked myself, how can I do it better tomorrow?

The single most important question for a television reporter relates to the person watching at home: Does he or she believe what I am saying? One of the troubling tasks for newsmen in general is getting people to understand what we do. We try to be honest brokers of information. In many ways, his acceptance in that role is more difficult for the television journalist. He is often perceived as little more than an announcer. The slander is sold hard by many politicians that we are somehow less ethical, more biased than our counterparts in print. These are among the special problems that cause restless nights.

I had no problem sleeping on that 1973 trip, not in San Clemente, nor in New Orleans, where another strange encounter had taken place two days before. The President was indeed taking his case to the people. But, increasingly, his public moods and reactions were unpredictable.

In New Orleans, as he entered an auditorium to deliver a speech, Mr. Nixon turned and shoved his press secretary, Ron Ziegler. I pursued the story perhaps beyond what it was worth, but I was motivated in part by the insistence of the White House staff that nothing had happened. It was as though someone had claimed to have seen a UFO.

To begin with, any President who physically shoves one of his staff in public has created a story. How often has anyone seen a President angrily push one of his men? I would submit to you that the answer is never. I thought people would be curious. All we required was an explanation. He did it in fun, or unintentionally, or he was demonstrating a new isometric exercise. Anything except a denial that anything had happened.

As luck would have it, a CBS photographer, Cal Marlin, had been alert enough to get the moment on film. I was jammed in somewhere in the herd of reporters trailing behind the official party, and Marlin found me and said, "Did you see that?"

I said, "No, frankly, I couldn't see too well. I know that something went on up there and I . . . I thought the President pushed somebody."

Cal said, "He pushed Ziegler!"

"Aw, you know he—"

"No, I'm telling you. I've got it. I filmed it."

So I followed the crowd into the hall and went straight to the pressroom. I asked one of the White House staff, "Why did the President push Ron Ziegler?"

I was assured that the President had done no such thing.

I said, "I'm telling you, we've got film of him pushing Ron."

"Well, it just didn't happen."

We processed the film, put it on the screen and there it was, the President pushing a startled Ron Ziegler. I called our man on the White House staff and told him I was sitting there, looking at the film. He said, "No, you must be mistaken. He did not push Ziegler."

So that was curious, to say the least. Denied or not, the story would be aired on the CBS Evening News, so unusual was the episode. My description went like this: "By the time the official party reached the hall nervousness was showing and so, for a few seconds, was the President's temper. What you are about to see is a rare glimpse in public of presidential irritation, as Mr. Nixon tries to prevent Ronald Ziegler from entering the hall with him."

On the screen the President wheeled around, placed both hands on the chest of his press secretary and gave a shove, sending Ziegler stumbling a step backward. My report concluded, "The President's aides deny he is nervous or testy or anything."

Even after the film had been televised, the White House insisted it never happened. In the end they cited the piece as one more example of their problems with a news media given to distortion and unfairness.

It was only a matter of time now. The Watergate burglary had been exposed as part of a sweeping campaign of political espionage financed by secret campaign funds. Week by week the President's support drained away, even where it was deepest, in middle America, where the people are slow to anger and slow to forgive.

The coverup collapsed. The denials, the evasions, the deceits—all would fail. Nothing worked, not even a new language, in which Ziegler declared all of the President's previous statements on Watergate were "inoperative." Nixon's anguish, and the country's, kept growing. Spiro Agnew fell in some unrelated chicanery. The White House staff was torn and panicky as various aides marched off to face the grand jury and, some of them, to go to jail. There were missing tapes and eighteen-minute gaps and edited tapes and, finally, one that exposed the President's guilt, the tape that became the smoking gun.

On July 24, 1974, the Supreme Court ordered the release of eighteen White House tapes to the special prosecutor. Among them was one dated June 23, 1972—six days after the break-in at Watergate. In three conversations that day with Bob Haldeman, Richard Nixon had conspired to obstruct justice, commit perjury and bribery and to subvert the powers of the CIA and the FBI.

A transcript of the tape was made public on the afternoon of August 5, three days after John Dean had been sentenced to prison. The transcript proved the President lied repeatedly when he said he first learned of the coverup from Dean on March 21, 1973. The country had been struck a final thunderbolt. Gamblers quit quoting odds on whether he would be impeached. The ten Republican members of the House Judiciary Committee who had voted against the articles of impeachment called on him to resign. He had withheld the truth from his lawyer, James St. Clair, his chief of staff, Al Haig, and from his family.

I had covered the story every day to the bitter end, which came on August 8, 1974, when Richard Nixon went on national television to resign his office.

The night of the resignation the CBS cameras, along with those of the other networks, were set up on the grounds of Lafayette Square, across the street from the White House. It was an incredible scene, the crowds gathering as if by signal, milling and hushed, the mood expectant, time suspended. Against the glare of the lights I could see only shadows, as I waited to go on the air. Then a figure darted out of the crowd and threw something at me. It struck me on the chest. A black felt-tipped pen. I still have a striped shirt with the ink stain over the pocket. The park police rushed up and led him away. He was a member of the Nixon press staff, half out of his head with emotion.

Some of Watergate's questions may never be answered, but this much we know. The news media didn't bring down the President. In the end the country rejected a government run by men with small minds, who wouldn't obey the laws they were sworn to uphold.

I have never fully understood and still don't care to think deeply about the meaning of a night in April, 1972. Around midnight I heard noises downstairs in our home in Georgetown, inside the District of Columbia. I stepped out of the bedroom on the second floor and shouted into the darkness, "I don't know who you are or what you want, but if you don't get the hell out of here I'm going to blow your ass off. And if you don't believe me, listen to this."

With that I rammed a shell into the chamber of a shotgun. There is no mistaking that sound. Within seconds the intruders, or whatever they were, had fled. I switched on the lights and Jean and I began to check the house. Nothing had been touched, no valuables taken. Only my personal files in the basement had been disturbed.

We had not planned to be home that weekend. At my request, the White House had booked reservations for Jean and our two children on the press plane that would follow the President to Key Biscayne. But Robin developed a fever, and Jean and the kids stayed home. I flew south alone on Friday and returned to Washington Saturday night to be with them.

I never knew how many prowlers were in the house, how long they had been there, who sent them or what they wanted. But one does have suspicions. It could have been just another third-rate burglary.

Out-Take
12

WALTER

At a time when the credibility of the news media was thought to be never lower, how do we explain the polls that showed the most trusted man in America to be a news commentator, Walter Cronkite?

If only all questions were so easy to answer.

The honest answer is that you know him as well as those of us do at CBS. He has been at that desk every night for a very long time, with no place to hide. What you see is exactly what you get.

What comes across the screen is a man who is warm, concerned, assured, unflappable, perfectly aimed, with a dignity so pure you cannot imagine anyone's ever calling him "Walt." If a movie were made of Cronkite's life, he would have to be played by someone like Walter Pidgeon.

The point is, he does care. In Dallas, the day John Kennedy died, Cronkite telephoned at least three times, in my vivid recollection, simply to say, "You're doing a terrific job. What can we do to help?" To Dan Rather, thirty-one, with the network two years, a Texan—and on that day conscious of it—Walter's concern mattered.

When I received my assignment to Vietnam, Walter wanted to see me before I left. He didn't contact me through channels. Walter simply picked up a phone and said, "Hey, why don't you come through New York? I'd like to visit with you."

He said, among other things, that he appreciated my going and told me not to be a hero. Then he made a list of points where he felt our coverage had been strong, and where it had been weak, largely because we had not committed enough people in the field. He thought we would need more help, and he would fight to get it.

Walter is a believer in the personal touch, and it is one of the reasons why so many of us would put our hand in the fire for him.

One cannot mention Cronkite without using the word integrity. His is a special brand. He has been criticized by the so-called sophisticates in the business for "reading" too much on the air. This is a misunderstanding of Walter's dedication to the news. He refuses to adorn a story. If there are no pictures, he is entirely willing to read his piece as though it were out of a newspaper. His objective is to deliver as much news as the minutes will allow to the person who turns on his set at night. For a generation of reporters, that straightness may be Walter's best legacy.

Ed Murrow hired him at CBS, for $135 a week, to cover the Korean War. He never got to Korea, but he practically invented the Evening News. For years he did it twice a night, ad-libbing every story from notes scribbled on pieces of paper. Network television was not quite so structured, so organized then. Once he asked Fred Friendly, then president of CBS News, if he had approved a three-week vacation Walter had coming.

"I never approve of vacations," Friendly said.

In 1975 Cronkite celebrated his twenty-fifth year with CBS. His title today is managing editor, but his voice and face are still among the most familiar in America. Some men's eyes reveal their entire life. His are like that. There is no one on the air today that people feel they know quite so well.

Once I was filling in for him during a week of the Evening News, while Roger Mudd, his usual replacement, was off elsewhere. A lady with a refined country-club voice called one night and demanded, "Where is Walter? Why is he off so much? When is he coming back?"

I explained, as patiently as I could, that he was away, that he was at a stage in his career when he received, and deserved, longer vacations, and added vaguely that he was expected back around midweek.

When the week passed and I was still on the air the lady called again. Her voice sounded hurt. "All right," she said, "when are they going to tell us he has died? That *is* what happened, isn't it? And they're afraid to tell us."

Morbid though it was, I found the experience fascinating. I think it tells us something about how suspicious people are about "They" in this country. And it tells us how protective Cronkite's fans are of Walter: that CBS would try to shield the news of his demise does not strike them as unlikely. That fear, that suspicion, surfaces periodically when Walter goes on vacation. It is a weird compliment, one usually reserved for kings, race-car drivers and pop singers.

Chapter 13

SHOW AND TELL

THE MOMENT I walked into the room for Richard Nixon's first White House press conference, I sensed that something was, well, different. Then it hit me. Instead of LBJ's lectern and TelePrompTers, the stage was bare except for a single stand microphone.

The thirty-seventh President wanted to make clear that this was a new day, that he could handle himself on his feet. Johnson sometimes had a briefing book in front of him. I can't recall a time when he actually turned to a suggested answer, but the book was there, a kind of Linus blanket.

So here Haldeman and Ziegler had applied their advertising skills. They felt that one of Nixon's strengths, and they were quite right, was his ability to speak without notes. They wanted to drive home the point that the President was engaging his audience live, direct, naked, except for his own intellect and courage.

They wanted a clean-line look and they had one. A stand microphone. But lo and behold, we got about three questions into the press conference when one of the White House waiters, holding a silver tray with a silver pitcher of ice water, appeared on the stage, off to the side, just out of camera range. He happened to be black. Surely, no one planned it that way, but it appeared for all the world like a classic Uncle Tom situation. The thought crossed my mind, If there is a picture of that anywhere tomorrow, whatever they intended, certainly every black person in America is going to *think* he understands the symbolism. It would prove devastating.

The waiter stood motionless behind and a little to the left of the President, almost in the folds of the curtain. Of course, White House staffers are among the best at just fading into the scenery. That is what they are trained to do. And make no mistake, this man was no Tom, he was alert and sharp. But the clean-line look didn't allow for the use of a small table or a chair. So what do you do if the President gets thirsty? You had some-one stand there. And stand he did, off camera, for the entire news conference.

When it ended, I walked into Ron Ziegler's office, thinking I might do a story later about the changing style of the press forum. I was already picking up the vibrations of a heavy dose, yea, an overdose, of ad-man psychology at work.

But I couldn't imagine who would send a man out on that stage to hold a pitcher of water. I sat down in Ron's office and, in an offhand way, began to probe. After a moment or so he shifted in his chair and gave me a quizzical look. "What's the purpose," he asked, "of all this talk about what would have happened if the President had wanted a drink of water?"

I felt like an actor delivering the punch line to an unprepared house. I said, "Well, I'll tell you straight out. I thought the symbolism of that black man standing there the whole press conference, holding a silver tray of water, was not exactly the kind of symbolism we've had around the White House in recent years, and that might represent a change."

Ziegler came unglued. He said, "Gawd awmighty, I never thought of that. No one did." He immediately understood the implications. "Believe me," he said, "I don't know who put him there but I'll find out and it will never happen again."

At the next news conference they had a very small table on the stage, holding the pitcher of water. Still later, for reasons unknown to me, they went back to using a lectern.

I can think of few things as important to the American system, with so much potential for game playing, as the presidential press conference. Again this is another area where we, as newsmen, have done a poor job of explaining to the nation why it is important. This is the only time and place in our political process where a President has to face—live, in front of people, in front of God—questions at random.

If you believe as I do that it is essential to have a high degree of trust between the leadership and the citizenry if the system is to work, then there must be a forum in which questions can be raised. The press conference may be imperfect, but right now it is the only forum we have.

The critical point is that a President must stand up, *stripped of all his protection,* and field questions coming at him from various directions in an unprepared context. Thus the viewer can see how he reacts to the unexpected when he catches a snowball and, sometimes, what he really thinks.

Certainly, television has unmistakably changed the format, for the better. The cameras first came into the room under President Eisenhower, whose conferences were filmed, and edited, before they were released. John Kennedy, whose wit and grace were made for the medium, was the first to hold them live. He understood how powerful television would become in politics. Johnson wrestled with it, and lost. He was so sensitive about the prominence of his ears that he had the TelePrompTers positioned to his left and right so the cameras would not catch him head-on. One night my father-in-law called and demanded to know, "What's wrong with the President? He looks turkey-necked all the time." Nixon liked television and feared it. Ford came across as exactly what he was, a good shoe.

In Jimmy Carter, we saw a candidate not yet at ease with television. The patterns of his speech did not fall as gently on the northern ear as snow on a New England rooftop. But Carter has a quickness of mind and eye. His voice seemed to deepen within days after his election. The feeling was strong that, as President, he would use the medium effectively. The question was, would he come across with authority or conceit?

All of which I think makes a point. There have been increasing complaints that TV now has a dangerous influence on how we elect our leaders. I don't believe it. The telegenic quality of a candidate is vastly overrated as a decisive factor in a campaign. I do not buy the idea that a Lincoln couldn't win today because he was ugly; that a Robert Redford kind of candidate would beat a quality candidate who had an ax scar down the middle of his face.

The press conference is one of the tools, maybe the best, for character exposure. My theory is, if you are on television often and long enough, there is no place to hide. You are going to come across for what you are.

How does it work? Begin with what you see: a roomful of people. A glare of so-called "klieg lights." That, by the way, is a passé phrase. The technology has gone way beyond that since the dawning of color television. A fellow walks into a studio and says *klieg lights* and it is like walking into a football locker room and saying, I like your *togs.* Today they are simply called lights.

The assumption is that everyone in the room is a reporter and likely to ask a question. Not so. Out of, say, two hundred people—a low figure—fifty will be White House staffers who have come to observe. Another twenty-five will be technicians. Now, of those left, ninety will be reporters with White House press passes who have no intention of asking a question and, in fact, may not have a story in their next day's newspaper.

They come because it is important that they be seen. There is an editor at home who may be watching. He may have only a one-man bureau in Washington but he, the editor, likes to think that his guy is involved in all the big stuff.

I'm not putting down that attitude. If I ran the Washington bureau for the Elkhart *Truth,* I'd damn well make certain I showed up at a news conference and would be praying that the camera picked me up, so my editor and others would say, "Hey, there's Dan. He's alert, he's taking notes, he's doing his job. It's nine thirty in the East and he's awake."

But that reduces the number to no more than thirty-five who would be classified as regulars, who travel with the President, who will ask the questions and who, in a real sense, represent the White House press corps. It is important to understand this fact if we are to put in perspective the charge used against us by Haldeman and Pat Buchanan and others on the Nixon staff that a so-called "circus" atmosphere was created.

The scene is far less circuslike than may appear on your television set. I'm not blaming anyone at home for thinking otherwise. You see us jumping up and down like pogo sticks, the waving hands, the constant lights. But the picture that comes across the TV screen often reflects the need of a director—at least in his own mind—to look for shots that will be visually interesting. Crowd color. So if he can show shafts of light catching the portraits of George and Martha Washington, and the President framed against that backdrop, it tends to give a show-business look to the proceedings. If you are there, and into it, however, you don't smell the sawdust.

What you do feel is the pressure to pay attention, to listen, to concentrate. I tried to go into a White House press conference with five basic questions I would *like* to ask, then a backup list of five more. But I had to be ready to jump out of my own pet list and follow up the last one. All of a sudden, boom, I am on my feet. I am dealing in microseconds. There isn't a lot of time to think about what is moving across the TV screen or the look on the President's face or the tone of his voice.

The seating, you should know, is not by accident. Again, on television you see this mob of people pile into the room and they all plop down. Not quite. The regulars will have marked seats in the first three or four rows. Beyond that the seating is on a first come, first served basis. In a way that no one talks about, this allows a press secretary to let you know about his or the President's displeasure. A reporter walks in one day and finds he is sitting five rows back. He works for, say, the *Sun-Times* in Chicago, and for a year and a half he has been on the front-row wings. He goes to the press secretary and asks what the hell is going on.

"Aw gee, Joe, you know, we just like to mix things up a little."

But Joe from Chicago knows well what has happened. And the press secretary knows that he knows. But what does he do? No reporter wants to be in the position of crying, "Hey, they took my seat away." It sounds silly. But it is a deep finesse game.

The fixed seating allows the President to know who is sitting where. Johnson studied the charts. Nixon always knew where the reporters who mattered in his view were seated. He knew the reporters and their tendencies. His staff prepared him, the way a coach tells a linebacker, don't forget, their tendency on third and five is to throw to a halfback rolling out of the backfield. He knew where he could go if he needed to change the subject and, most often, that was to Sarah McClendon. She was the relief valve, the reporter most likely to ask a question that came out of nowhere; on telephone poles in Vietnam, or whatever.

For my money Sarah McClendon is an all-right journalist, original and sharp. She could be a pain, but that was part of what made her effective. She was fiercely independent. And Sarah never had behind her the muscle of a CBS network or the Associated Press or the Washington *Post*. She represented a string of fairly small Texas newspapers and radio stations.

She had to scratch. I heard other reporters say, "We really ought to hold down the numbers to keep out people like Sarah." I found that attitude intolerable. I feel strongly that anyone who was accredited had a right to be there; they *ought* to be there. One of the things that makes the system work—the system of news, as well as government—is the fact that the people in power have to answer as much to the Biloxi *Bugle* as to *The New York Times*. Possibly, the obligation to the former is even greater.

However, Sarah's famed independence made it highly unlikely that she would ask a followup to anybody else's question. She was noted for the tough question the President hadn't thought about when he walked into the room. The White House could have Pat Buchanan prepare a list of five hundred likely questions and you could bet that Sarah's would not be on it.

So if you were Richard Nixon and you were thinking, I need to change the subject, your best hope was Sarah. There was no guarantee that the question wouldn't be tougher than the last one, but at least it would be different.

The lack of followup has always been one of the flaws of the press conference format. The press corps has never done a good job of it. Too many individuals locked into their own visions. But at least once a sequence of three questions, nicely done, was prepared to deal with that shortcoming.

After the May Day demonstration of 1971, the last really major antiwar rally in Washington, the D.C. police made massive arrests, knowing they were illegal but determined to clear the streets of anyone who got in their way. A command post had been established by John Ehrlichman, who sent down the word, *arrest them all*. His point man was Egil Krogh, not long out of law school, with roots in Seattle. You could argue whether Ehrlichman was talking to the President or acting on his own, but no one doubted that the shots were being called from the White House.

The event passed, some fifteen thousand jailed demonstrators were turned loose and the President held a news conference. This time three reporters got together and decided not to let up on him. They were Jerry terHorst, who later became Ford's press secretary (and resigned after the Nixon pardon), Forrest Boyd of Mutual Broadcasting and James Deakin of the St. Louis *Post-Dispatch*.

The question was posed first by terHorst: Does the legality of these arrests concern you in any way? Nixon parried, bumped off and went on to the next questioner, who happened to be Boyd. He came right back: The illegal arrests of so many people could not have been an accident and what did Nixon have to say about it?

This time the President began to get that look we all came to recognize: I don't like this question and I think it is dangerous for me. He began to perspire. He slid off again. Then Deakin was on his feet and he rephrased the question a third time. Nixon knew he was cornered. Whereupon he went clear across the room to call on Sarah McClendon. She asked a good question but unrelated to the illegal arrest of the demonstrators and, as Nixon hoped, she broke the chain.

Still, a purpose had been served. Anyone watching at home, with an open mind, knew the question had been ducked. A furious Bob Haldeman walked out of the room muttering, "We're never going to go through *that* again." He added that the press conference had been a circus. As a result we didn't have another news conference for six months.

But that kind of effort was rare. Most reporters realize that what may be teamwork to them will look like collusion to others. For the same reason many of us will not accept a "planted" question. Some do. They take the view—one I don't share—that if the question has merit there is no harm. They very quickly get to be known among the White House staff.

Once, during my early months with Johnson, I agreed to take a planted question. This was during a time when I had no contacts, no sources and no standing. I was trying to feel my way and I gave little thought to the ethics of what I was doing.

A situation had developed late; steel prices were on the verge of being raised and the President did not want to address the issue directly. He wanted the question to come from the floor. Half an hour before the news conference someone in the press office who knew me came around and said, "This is an awkward situation for us. We don't plant questions. We tried to talk the President out of it. But there was no way around it. We know you are new here. That you feel you've had some difficulty in getting recognized. I want to say to you that today you *will* get recognized if you ask a question about the price of steel. It will make news and will probably lead *The New York Times* tomorrow."

I stuttered a bit. It didn't sound quite right to me.

He said, "Well, look at it this way. You are here to ask questions that may elicit some news. This is a question that I guarantee will generate news."

That logic is hard to resist. And the truth is I did not resist. I went into the press conference prepared to ask that question. I said to myself, I think there is a matter of ethics involved but I don't have time to analyze it. Other thoughts ran through my mind: It wouldn't hurt for my bureau chief, Bill Small, to see me on my feet and getting recognized and asking a question that produces a substantial answer from the President, one that may even be the lead news item the next day. Small doesn't know me all that well. I'm still trying to cut it. Then there was peer-group acceptance. Yes, it might be nice to have a Tom Wicker or a Bill Lawrence notice that I had asked a useful question.

And finally: No, I don't have any contacts in Washington. It might help if the word spread that, yes, we can do business with Rather. Looking back, I find that shameful. Your mind should not work that way, if you call yourself a reporter. But the pressure, if you are a new man on the beat, can be persuasive. You have a need to get your name known.

The Johnson men were not sure they could depend on me, however, so they laid the question on three other reporters. It was asked before I could be recognized. My jaw fell open like a pelican waiting for a fish when the other fellow asked *my* question. But in the end I felt a surge of relief and soon I sat down to think about the ethics of it. What I arrived at was this: Any time they invite me to ask a question they have a reason. Now, their interests may parallel my own. But I don't think I can stay in business, going into a press conference, asking someone his own question. I am not being fair to the viewer. The game is fixed.

Lyndon Johnson was never comfortable with television. He let the machinery of it shackle him. But more than any other President of the Television Age, he held a lot of press conferences in many different forms. He held them walking around the ellipse, aboard *Air Force One,* in his office, or yours. At those times, at least, he was more likely to be himself. On TV he tried to pose, the worst mistake anyone can make. He listened to people who encouraged him to play the role of a rancher, a teacher, a businessman, and went through one phase in which he was a kind of cross between J. Frank Dobie and Will Rogers.

What one begged to hear from LBJ after he threw out the Tele-PrompTers and got rid of the wire stays under his collar was something like this: "Listen, I ain't John F. Kennedy. I'm no longer a teacher from Cotulla, Texas, and I'm not a cowboy. What I am is a wheeler-dealer politician who knows where the levers of power are and how to use them. You may not like the way it's done, but it will work and you are going to like that a lot. Watch my smoke." Dynamite. I can't say he didn't try it. But he never succeeded, or we didn't, in getting that Lyndon Johnson on the screen.

Where you did see that side of him was in the air. He reveled in the flying press conference. Not everyone can do that. A man might own his company plane, but he doesn't have the press there, representing the largest news agencies in the world, hanging on his every word. If they can't really hear above the engine noise, too bad.

Sometimes the news conference would wander for hours, on the record and off, over thousands of miles. Johnson had arranged the configuration on *Air Force One* so that he could get aboard a desk similar to the one he had in the Oval Office, with a push-button bar. He would pour his own drink, a Scotch—he claimed he drank bourbon and branch water because it fit the western image, but he preferred Scotch. Then he would lean back, lift his feet on the desk and say to George Reedy, "Gawge, bring the boys in here."

Without fail, when Helen Thomas of the UPI heard him—and this was well before the heyday of the women's movement—she would correct him, directly and respectfully. "We're not all boys, Mr. President."

Ideally, a news conference should be no big deal. One should be held every ten days to two weeks, televised, live, in an unstructured setting, inside the President's office, for example, with the cameras coming in as just another pad and pencil. Television works best when it puts you *there*, in a situation where the camera has the least influence on the person or the event. Given the improvement in our technology, we are coming to that point fairly soon. The new mini-cams spit out broadcast-ready videotape on the spot.

President Kennedy had the know-how and charm to use television, but only half the will. It was still uncharted water and he felt a sense of caution about trying to orchestrate and control his every appearance. Johnson was willing but lacked the know-how. In Nixon, for the first time, we had a President who understood and had the will to manipulate television. That was what the Nixon White House set out to do, and in some ways they succeeded. Nixon made more prime-time TV speeches than any President before him, forty in his first term, five times as many in one term as Eisenhower made in two. And those appearances did not include a guest shot on "Laugh-In" during the '68 campaign.

On the night of our one-on-one CBS interview in 1972 he walked into the room, sat down and asked, "Where's the *key* light? Oh, there it is." Now, I don't know of another politician able to pick out the key light, that being the principal light on the subject.

As his Watergate troubles deepened, Nixon turned to television so extensively that he wore makeup much of the time. One day I was walking toward the White House with Pete Lisagor of the Chicago *Daily News*. The president of the Congo was arriving for a routine ceremony on the south lawn. The marine band would play "Ruffles and Flourishes," parade briefly, and then the two heads of state would retire to the White House.

We were moving up the driveway, chatting, not paying attention, when we realized we had nearly walked right into the dignitaries. We stopped and moved back, but Nixon spotted us and with a wave motioned us over. Lisagor went immediately, but I wasn't certain the President had meant for us to join them and I hung back. He waved again and I realized he wanted some help in saving him from what had become a rather awkward scene.

There was President Nixon, wearing heavy television makeup, and the president of the Congo, a very strong, robust man who spoke nothing but French, and his interpreter. The president of the Congo could not take his eyes off Nixon's face. It was obvious that he was thinking, What is that stuff?

Nixon was nervously trying to make small talk, and the interpreter was working away. "Mr. President, this is Mr. Lisagor. He's one of our better known correspondents. This is Mr. Rather, he's from Chicago. You know, they have a lot of money in Miami." The interpreter dutifully translated all this while Lisagor and I stood there, looking at one another. The president of the Congo wasn't listening. He was too busy looking at Nixon's television makeup. And then the party walked off and moved on to the West Wing.

Thinking back, I can see that my problems with most, if not all of the President's men, were related to press conferences, starting with his first in January, 1969, at the Hotel Pierre. Nixon had not yet taken office. There was to be a routine appointment, which could be filmed, and a question period that could not. I objected to this directive as censorship. I was told if we insisted on trying to film, our lights would be cut off.

When I heard that order I just brought in a second camera crew. When they switched off the lights, as they said they would, our backup camera filmed the blackout scene. It ran just like that, *cinéma vérité,* on the Evening News with Walter Cronkite.

On October 26, 1973, after Spiro Agnew had resigned and Archibald Cox had been fired, I walked into another press conference expecting to ask a question on the Middle East. I did have a backup question, however, based on the rumblings of impeachment talk. I had met earlier with my CBS colleagues, Bob Pierpoint and Bernard Kalb. We guessed that the first question asked would probably deal with the subject of resignation or impeachment. We thought a followup would be in order. Kalb said he would like to know what went through the President's own mind when his removal from office was discussed. I wondered, too.

Then the news conference began, and impeachment was not the first, or the second, or the third question asked. I began to think that our backup idea might be a good way to broach the subject. When the President recognized me I dropped whatever question I had planned to ask about the Middle East. I rose and said: "Mr. President, I wonder if you could share with us your thoughts, tell us what goes through your mind when you hear people who love this country and people who believe in you say, reluctantly, that perhaps you should resign or be impeached?"

I am told that no reporter had ever asked such a question of a U. S.

President before, not in the history of television, not in the history of the country. There had been no need to do so before.

Nixon answered by saying, "Well, I'm glad we don't take the vote of this room, let me say."

Leaving the news conference later, a member of the President's staff told me that I had asked a good question, one that had to be asked, one that had been put in a gentlemanly way. Beginning the next morning, however, seven different Nixon lieutenants sought me out and filed their objections.

So be it. A reputation for asking hard questions is not one I regret. No reporter would. Yet in my time at the White House I can think of a dozen, possibly more, who were better. It is in the character of television that a Dan Rather can ask a tough question and people will know who posed it and perhaps take sides. But a John Osborne, of the *New Republic,* can pose a question that makes news and only the answer will be remembered.

In terms of my personal likes, attending a press conference would not rank among my favorite things to do. Most newsmen prefer to work alone. In that situation the only risk is the interview might just stop dead, as happened once with Mike Mansfield, the taciturn former senator from Montana. He is a master of the yes-no answer. Often with that type a reporter can outwait him. The dragging seconds, the echoing silence, will inspire him to go on. Unfortunately, this tactic didn't work with Senator Mansfield. He would sit there, sucking on his pipe, perfectly content to let the time pass as your film ran out.

The press conference format guards against that kind of stalemate. The question that can't or won't be answered is quickly replaced by another, sometimes too quickly. There are other weaknesses, of course, among them the fact that 99 percent of the questions are political. Such issues as genetic engineering, overpopulation, the global economy, do not get raised. We have not figured out yet what our responsibility should be, in electronic journalism, to report these issues faster and better, before they get to be such immense problems.

For that matter, we probably give too much air time and too much attention to politicians. When did you last hear an interview, in depth, with a poet or a philosopher, or a master of the dance or music? These are brilliant people and we don't do enough on them. Also, we probably talk to journalists too much. Even on the air we wind up interviewing one another.

Walter Cronkite has said that the Evening News is at best a headline service. We have tried over a long period of years to make it more but, in the final analysis, a headline service is what we are. Television tends to be two-dimensional. Anyone who depends on it entirely for his news is not doing his job as a citizen.

But having said that, one needs to repeat that in times of crisis, television has the power to hold this country together. We do not, after all, have a national newspaper. So the whole idea of the Roosevelt fireside chat on radio has carried over to the era of the small screen.

In my lifetime Franklin Delano Roosevelt was the Chief Executive, one of the few in our history, with the strongest sense of that role: the President-as-communicator. He relished news conferences, met the press often. FDR played favorites, liked some reporters, disliked others. But he saw the value of the press as carriers of the message, his message, his hopes for the country.

In a lesser way so did Truman and Ike and Kennedy. That was part of what we began to lose during the Johnson years, and then the relationship came tumbling down, like some ancient ruin, under Nixon.

You think of FDR in his wheelchair, crippled by polio, and you ask, how would television have treated him? Lovingly. He would have been even more effective. He had a strong air of command, of leadership. What was obviously at work with Roosevelt was what the novelists call tropism, all those other vibrations—other than how you look and how you sound—that one person sends off to another.

Of course, he did have a strong, compelling voice. And sound is still underestimated as a television force, so distracting is the picture. But the voice can make a difference. FDR's voice, his words, had the power to move men forever.

It is true that today we are more aware, more open and tolerant about handicaps and afflictions. In the 1940's some people still hid retarded children in the attic. Would they have been uncomfortable—if TV had been available then—with the sight of the President of the United States in a wheelchair with a blanket over his knees? I don't think so. We do know FDR was sensitive about his crippled legs. But there is a difference between a still photograph and the live television picture. With frequent coverage, his wheelchair would have been accepted as just another interesting way to get around.

Harry Truman had a potential for disaster on television. He was unhandsome, with a shrill voice, the language blunt but not graceful. We know that when he first took office he lacked confidence that he could handle the job. He would have come across that way on television and it would have hurt him.

Yet I believe that by 1948, with television, a feisty Harry Truman would have beaten Tom Dewey more handily. Dewey's shortcomings, his image as "the little man on top of the wedding cake," would have been given even greater exposure. He was a cold, stiff, hesitant campaigner.

The legend of Dwight Eisenhower's fractured syntax was, I think, exaggerated. It is fair to say that he was not as articulate or as thoughtful as Adlai Stevenson, twice his Democratic opponent. But Ike was a man of action, incisive, and more people would have seen those virtues.

I traveled around the rim of the Far East with Eisenhower in 1956. I thought then, and still do, that he used the twisting language, at times, to lose the press and avoid the question, as Kennedy used his humor, and LBJ used the stare and the blowtorch phrase, and Nixon used the waffle.

One had the feeling Eisenhower did not choose to retain all the answers in his head. He could be snappish and impatient. With subjects that caught his interest he rambled on and on. The atmosphere was grandfatherish. That fits the cliché image of Ike but happens to be true. His look said, I'm uneasy here. You know it and I know it. Let's get on with it.

Yet part of the dynamics of an Eisenhower news conference was the press corps' great respect for Ike as a person. Certainly this feeling reflected the view of the American community: his record as a war hero, the awareness that in important ways he *had been there*. It was not unlike a good university class where the professor has a track record a mile long, and you walk into the room knowing you can really learn something if you can only stay awake.

There was a different kind of respect for Kennedy. You knew he liked words, admired a well-turned phrase when he heard one. This is part of the meat of being a journalist. So the challenge sometimes with Kennedy was, if one could ask a question in a certain way, he might be able to turn it into an answer that was not only instructive but fun.

I was not an uncritical observer of the Kennedy presidency, not a willing buyer of the Camelot myth. In the early months of the Nixon Administration, well before the ultimate sourness set in, that belief became a recurring topic among Ehrlichman, Ziegler and Magruder. Their view was, "You guys in the press really got suckered in by Kennedy." In some ways we did. The Nixon crowd saw JFK's strength as a communicator and performer. They tended to attribute this strength to his youth, his physical attractiveness, the shag haircut. They saw it in superficial ways.

But his success with the press, and the public, went deeper. Had Nixon's men been the students of news techniques they claimed to be, they would have seen the great power of admitting a mistake, which is well apart from whatever you looked or sounded like, whatever your grace or wit or language. There is a power in saying, "I blew this." Kennedy understood. He was careful, when he could, to admit errors on small things. It created a feeling of, look, when the guy boots one he is willing to admit it. That approach helped him overcome the Bay of Pigs. It proved disarming, but few politicians ever have that much security.

It pleases me to imagine what Abraham Lincoln would have been on television. I suspect he would have been superb. He had the wit, the power of language, honesty and humanity, and all that would have shone. Lincoln held news conferences, although they were not given that name. He simply kept an open door.

You have to pinch yourself to remember what the presidency was like in Abe Lincoln's time. No fence around the White House. People coming off the street, lounging in the hallway, waiting to see him and frequently doing so. He walked the grounds freely, often accompanied only by his secretary.

It is not possible, nor desirable, to go back to 1861. But stripping away some of the royal trappings around the presidency would be helpful. Whatever its faults, and they exist, television is one of the tools.

There is no cause to get emotional, but I *am* an electronic journalist. I think in those terms, and I like what I do. Ed Murrow once said, "Unless you care about it, unless you really work at it, all you have is wires in a box."

Out-Take

13

THE IMAGE

For years I heard people who feared and opposed George Wallace argue, "You don't want to put Wallace on television because you are afraid he will fool people and his support will increase."

The same was said about the late Senator Joseph McCarthy of Wisconsin. I am not trying to equate the two. The reference is meant only in the abstract. But I would say to the critics of Wallace, "If he's as bad as you say he is, you ought to be *buying* him time on television."

Without the Army-McCarthy hearings of the 1950's where might Joe McCarthy have gone? His words read well in print. His positions were certainly not unpopular. But when he appeared on the home screen he came off as the demagogue we now know him to have been.

There will always be those people who feel that the camera has a potential for evil, for a kind of national hypnosis. Consider Adolf Hitler, with his sense of timing and his powers as an orator, his ability to mesmerize a crowd, so evident in newsreels. What would he have done on television? My guess is that if TV had been in use then, the United States would have gone to war long before we did. Hitler, in a you-are-there, the camera-never-blinks way, would have been so frightening that the message who he was and what he was about would have traveled fast.

It has been said that those who control the language control the images, and those who control the images control the race. It was said in a context that had nothing to do with television, but certainly the thought applies. The key point here is language.

But eloquence alone, the power of speech, will not sustain a bankrupt politician. An honest man doesn't always come across well on television. But his honesty usually does.

Time and again we have heard the same weary argument against televised public hearings. Put a camera in a room and whatever goes on in there "will turn into a circus." Yet the Watergate hearings did more for the reputation of the House of Representatives than anything in my lifetime. Yes, the hearings could have turned into a televised circus. If foolish people had led those hearings, their foolishness would have come through. But without exception, those who did resort to demagoguery lost in the public mind and at the polls.

To follow those deliberations, and discover the quality of the people, had to create new faith in the Congress. One had to be pretty hardhearted to hear the eloquence of a Barbara Jordan and not feel one's eyes moisten, knowing what and where she came from. Barbara Jordan fought her way out of the ghetto in Houston, up through the state legislature and the state senate and on to Congress, always the first, or among the first, to sit there as a woman and a black. What a thrilling moment when she talked, so movingly, of her love for the Constitution.

One had to be aware of the quality of these people, these members of the House Judiciary Committee, who were judging Richard Nixon. In style and appearance they ran the gamut, some of them not very attractive. But their conduct said volumes about the Congress. And about television. Both systems worked.

Chapter 14

THE CELEBRITY SYNDROME

I STOOD SHIVERING in the damp, morning cold of a January day in 1969, outside a church on Fifth Avenue in New York, watching my breath form into puffs of vapor. There was the usual crush of news people waiting to record the arrival of the new President, Richard Nixon, and his family as they walked into services led that Sunday by Dr. Norman Vincent Peale.

I had arrived an hour and a half early in a grumpy mood. I was also wearing a pair of shoes purchased the day before. Ordinarily that would not be worth mentioning, but for me it was a major event. My wife had nagged me into buying them.

"Your shoes look awful," she had said, "all scuffed and worn down at the heel."

"Listen," I replied, "if you ever see a reporter and his heels are *not* worn down, you know he is spending too much time in the office with his feet propped up on the desk."

That approach never worked with Jean, so I had bought a new pair of Florsheim Imperial Wing Tips, a heavy number that year, as I recall.

But it did not please me, or make me feel pious, to be standing outside a church in my new shoes early on a gray and chilling Sunday morning. It was one of those days when I am saying to myself that this is no work for a grown person. I had made a point of getting there around 8 A.M. to stake out a favorable position. I knew that for security reasons a bullpen area would be roped off for reporters and photographers. Experience taught me it was best to get there early. Otherwise I would be stuck behind four or five waves of people. Our pictures would not be as good as the competition's and if the President did stop to talk, I would likely miss him.

I had been among the first on the scene, but as time passed the New York version of the paparazzi appeared. It got to be quite a shoving match to hold my ground. My irritation was building. Here I am, I thought, having to elbow these guys out of the way and where the hell is my cameraman? He was twenty minutes late and the reporters behind me were now five deep.

At that moment I was aware that, from way in the back, someone was torpedoing toward the front at about knee height. I sensed it before I actually saw the ripple of movement in the crowd. I said to myself, I don't know who this miserable thudpucker is but he's about to get crowned. If he thinks I'm going to stand out here in the cold for an hour and a half and let him cut in front of me, I am really going to brad his head.

Just as I figured, this intruder wriggled through the crowd, straightened up out of a kind of Vietnamese crouch and stepped on my new shoes.

It was Barbara Walters.

Immaculately dressed and coiffed. She caught me by surprise. For one thing, I would not have expected her to be in that place, at that hour, on that kind of assignment. But it says much about her that she was.

I did not brad her head. But I looked at her with something less than a pure heart as she stood beside me, smoothing her dress. With what I thought was commendable restraint I said, "Madam, I have been here since eight o'clock, and if you think you are going to stand *there,* and do *anything,* I must tell you, it ain't going to happen."

She smiled brightly and said, "Dan, you seem to be in a remarkably bad humor this morning."

I said, "As a matter of fact, I am."

She said, "Oh, come on, it can't be that bad."

Now she proceeded to con me a little, which she does beautifully. For all her toughness and ability to be aggressive when she has to—sometimes when there is no call to do so—for all her support of women's rights, Barbara knows how to use her femininity.

She was saying, "Oh, come on, what the hell, I don't take up much space." She gave me the standard "It's-us-against-the-zoo" bit. And, in so many other words, she said, "Don't be an ass. So you've been here since eight. There is still room for both of us."

By then it was nearing 11 A.M. For the next few minutes she tried to pacify me and hold her position, which was, of course, exactly what she should have been doing. As a reporter, once you have elbowed your way into a situation you try to make peace with everybody and then work your claim.

Finally she said, her eyes still amused, "I'm sorry, but I don't understand what you're angry about."

In a burst of frustration, having exhausted all of my arguments, I said, "For one thing, you are *ruining* a pair of forty-two-dollar shoes." And I pointed to her heel, spiking the wing tip of one of my Florsheim Imperials.

Instantly she said, "NBC will pay for them."

If that was my problem, that was Barbara's solution. As a point in fact, she held her ground and NBC did *not* pay for my shoes. When the President-elect stepped out of his limousine he did not stop, did not talk with Barbara Walters or anyone else. We got maybe eight seconds of film of the Nixons walking into church. An hour later we picked up another eight seconds of the Nixons leaving church.

But I learned something about Barbara. She got where she did in 1976 by taking on all kinds of stories. And where she is now is at the top, at ABC, making a million a year, if the newspaper accounts are to be believed, co-anchoring the evening news. If you can't believe the newspapers, then what can you believe?

Our paths did not cross often. I ran into her again in 1972 at the Republican Convention in Miami. This was during the period when she was struggling—and I admired her for it—to become established as something other than "That Woman on the 'Today' show." In the end, I think it was clear, this was the reason she left NBC. She felt that getting to anchor the evening news would be the culmination of her struggle. ABC was willing to let her have that chance.

We had just been thrown together on the convention floor when Barbara was surrounded by a group of people who knew or admired her, or both. This was one of those situations I have never learned to handle well. Barbara does with grace. I have always felt trapped by a social situation in which people who have never seen much of one another, and none of each other lately, come together in a teeming room and give it that oh-how-have-you-been-dear treatment, with a kiss on the cheek. And you can't think of the other person's name and you're not even sure you know them.

The scene was ludicrous. We were on the floor with the balloons, the bands, the posters, in the midst of this sideshow collection of people. We both had on these silly, UFO-looking rigs, with the antennae sticking out of the top of our heads and small microphones curved in front of our mouths. (This was a slight improvement, however, on the headsets of other days, which made us look as though we had little helicopters on our heads.)

We had just said hello when the others fluttered over, and it got into one of those hugging and kissing things. I tried to bow out but Barbara drew me into the circle in an effort really to be courteous.

She said, "Let me present my colleague from CBS, Dan Rather. As a matter of fact, I was just saying hello to him." And she leaned over to give me a kiss. Now, understand, that was her way of putting me at ease. She had kissed everyone else, and she saw me shying away and wanted to be nice.

As we bent our heads together my microphone hit her in the mouth.

I wince even now when I think about it. Barbara had been smart and experienced enough to turn toward me with the cheek that was uncovered. But of course klutzy ol' Rather turned the side that had all the mechanical gear. There was an audible *clank* as my mike struck her teeth. It was an incredible feeling. And, understandably, Barbara did not take to it kindly. I had almost given her a harelip.

I found myself slinking away, and thinking, You know, Rather, there are some things you are cut out to do, and some you are not.

It was like two high school kids getting their braces caught. But can you imagine what the orthodontist's bill would have been for fixing the teeth of Barbara Walters? Luckily, she was unhurt. But it did startle her and did offend, I'm sure, her sense of dignity.

Four years later, without waving a banner, without being pious, Barbara struck a great blow for women's rights. Journalism, in general, has been laggard in bringing along minorities *and* women. There is a distinction. Women are not a minority.

But broadcast journalism has been ahead of print, particularly in the hiring of blacks and chicanos. I like to think CBS was a leader in doing so. Having said that, I fault all of us, myself included, for being far too slow to take what is now called affirmative action. The phrase has a bad connotation with some. I take it to mean being alert.

When I was in Houston I tried to hire a black newscaster. I was no crusader. What I proposed was someone to report on issues directly affecting the black community. No one called it tokenism then. I only knew that a part of the city was not represented, in or outside the studio. I discussed this idea at length with the management. Everyone agreed the proposal had merit. But nothing happened. The risk was considered too great.

That was sixteen years ago.

With hindsight, where one's vision is always 20-20, I know now that the risk was not too great. The move was right, needed to be done, and would have helped the station.

The danger today is that everyone will think the battle is over. Blacks and women are on the air, to a sometimes comic point where local stations have gone overboard to *balance* the team. Their idea of a good mix would be Tony Orlando and Dawn.

The next stage—we are not there yet—is to judge people on the basis of ability. Even then, we need to temper the search with an attitude of, look, if we don't have a black or a chicano who meets our standard, then we better get out and find them.

The disorganized, pell-mell quality of journalism has contributed to this exclusion but does not excuse it. Time and again I have seen a black or a woman put on camera, and if they do not impress, the reaction is, well, we tried and it didn't work. What needs to be said is, "We will help this person and make it work."

These changes are not made overnight and I do not mean that in a patronizing way. There has been no backlog of blacks educated in journalism. There was no backlog of women trained to do television. Such trials produce tension and, too often, the tendency is to let the reporter sink or swim.

Believe me, no one in the trade missed the irony when television news produced its first million-dollar baby. The baby was a girl.

When the Barbara Walters auction came along in the late spring of 1976 it brought into question again the entire issue of the newsman (or newsperson) as celebrity. Now keep in mind that no one is paid a million dollars just to do the evening news, not even in these inflated times. There are specials and other obligations involved.

When I stopped to think, the first question I asked was: What will this mean for my profession? The next question, if I was at all honest, had to be: What does this mean for my pay check, if anything?

So much of this business is related to luck—being the right person, in the right place, at the right time, doing the right thing, with the right people watching. The fact is, the ratings on the "Today" show had slipped a bit before Barbara made her decision. Panic had not set in at NBC, but concern certainly had. Another six months and Barbara might have had trouble getting her contract renewed at NBC at the level where she was. I give credit to her and her agent. They created a competitive market. This is a business where there are only three bidders and she had two of them. Luck was riding with her.

Long range, for the profession, I can't believe the heist helps. That is no criticism of Barbara. Offered a million dollars, who could refuse? But I fear that it will lead to more of what is known in the industry as the "quick fix." If your ratings are in trouble, just go across town and hire the other station's anchorman. In that case the big salary is an attention-getter in itself and becomes a part of the box office hype.

Ideally, if you are a purist, you hope the fellow whose ratings are suffering will decide that what he needs is a better product; more people on the street reporting, more thought to what they do. It is expensive to retool a news operation, but more than that it takes time, which in television is beyond price. The temptation will be stronger now to hire someone else's talent. It is more food for the star system, the feeling that what counts is the name on the marquee, not the integrity of your news.

I don't believe we have reached that point. But it is getting close. What would be the next step? What if Paul Newman decided he was bored with the movies, went to the networks and said, look, I don't want to do dramas, or made-for-TV pictures, I want to anchor the evening news. I'll tell you, I would hate to anchor the news opposite Paul Newman. Over the long pull the good professional would win. Part of the problem is, the long pull keeps getting shorter.

There was a time when, if you came aboard as the news director of a station in a major market, you needed two years to turn the ratings around. Today if the numbers don't move in three or four months, it is not uncommon for heads to roll.

A television critic once suggested to me that we will go through at least a period, and it may last, where the *entertainment* aspects will be tried, increasingly. The choice is not just between the newsman and the public figure with a built-in audience, a Paul Newman or a Spiro Agnew. Do you spend your money on a set or two new cameramen? On an animated intro to the news or a mobile unit? In newsroom after newsroom these are the questions being asked, and in too many cases management is going for the set, the intro or the "star." That needs to be thought about. Is it a fad or a trend? If it is a trend, we have reason to worry.

No one I know on the journalism side of television is comfortable with the reality of ratings. That is, based on what amounts to a microscopic sample, enormous decisions are made on which programs stay or go; on which personalities become rich or wind up selling insurance.

There is no dodging the fact that ratings *are* a hard reality. What many viewers don't understand is that they matter a good deal more in a local newsroom than at the network. No local anchorman I know can survive if his ratings are low. At the network if the numbers are down and the anchorman is out, they can always find a warm bed for him. At the local station he and Mama pack and go to another town.

The answer is not complicated. Most local programming is in news and public affairs. The station can be sitting on a gold mine. The higher the ratings, the more they can charge their sponsors, the bigger the profit. The network will carry the news as a loss leader. The higher the ratings, the smaller the loss. The income is less important than what the network sees as a residual benefit of having a prestige news operation.

There are no islands of time in television. The twenty-year dominance by CBS of nighttime TV—high ratings for such shows as "Mary Tyler Moore," "Gunsmoke," "Movie of the Week"—built a solid ratings base for the local stations coming off that block into their ten o'clock news. The more money the affiliates made at ten, the more they could plow back into their six o'clock news. When ABC turned out a stronger nighttime product in 1976, their stations down the line were helped in the same way.

You may conclude that ratings and money go together like lox and bagel. But the network correspondent is less likely to feel the pressure. I don't want to kid anyone, including myself. The first day I return to the office after anchoring the Saturday Evening News, my opening words are: "How'd we do in the numbers last week?" I am elated if we did well, deflated if we did not. I have to believe the same holds true at NBC and ABC. I'm sure Tom Brokaw and John Hart walk into their offices and ask, "How'd we do in the numbers last week?"

All of which has to be laid against the knowledge that the ratings will make no real difference in that day's work or our approach to what we do.

Unlike entertainment shows, news ratings are not volatile. Among the networks it is understood that it may require four to five years to change the ratings. In the hiring of Barbara Walters the thinking at ABC seemed clear: Okay, we're third. But if we can just make ourselves a stronger third we will help our stations down the line. And if we hope to effect a major change in the next four to five years, we have to start now.

Understandably, everyone has an eye on the fight for first place. CBS became a solid Number One after the Apollo moon shot in 1968. If you are a CBS person, you tend to say our coverage of the lunar landing tipped us over. If you are an NBC person, you tend to cite the breakup of the Huntley-Brinkley team as the key factor.

But if you want to enjoy a ratings war, the fight to watch is when Number Two tries to keep from being overtaken by Number Three. A fall to third is more cataclysmic than the drop from first to second. The two leaders both fare well in terms of prestige and balancing what they spend against what they bring in. The battle between Two and Three is where the going gets tough.

Then there is the domino effect. When Barbara Walters left the "Today" show NBC replaced her with Jane Pauley, going on twenty-six, with two years in the business. Such moves have begun to follow a pattern. The network generates a tidal wave of publicity, spending a fortune to launch the new talent, who then protests modestly about all the attention being paid to her.

Is there a meaning to this madness? A gain of one ratings point would be worth one million dollars in new income to ABC, or so the wizards tell us. Some Chinese bookkeeping goes on at the networks, but a point can make a difference.

The reaction to Barbara's big score was instructive. She was seen by some as a female Catfish Hunter, taking advantage of a fluke in the market to dredge millions out of a new team. I thought she handled herself well through all the commotion. For those who are bothered only by the money and not by the larger, moral issue—meaning, why couldn't it happen to me?—there are two points that time will answer: one, will she be worth it to ABC? And, yes, she will if her presence brings up the ratings, as ABC clearly expected; and two, will she be worth it compared to what her associates are being paid?

It is true Barbara came out of what is basically a variety show, not news. But she is a gifted interviewer and no one outworks her. If anyone comes close to being worth a million, she may. But in my own view no one in this business is, no matter what or how many shows they do, unless they find a cure for cancer on the side.

For a lot fewer dollars, I had to make a decision about going the other way early in my career at CBS. Blair Clark flew into New Orleans, where I was covering the civil rights story, and offered me a job on the CBS Morning News when it first started.

I said, "You're offering me this assignment, but do you think it's a good idea for me?"

Clark frowned. "Now I have to take off my hat as an executive," he said, "and talk to you as an ex-correspondent. It may not be. It may be too early. One of the things we are pleased about is that you are willing to stand out in the rain. Over the years that will be valuable to you, and to us. But I have to tell you, this is a helluva break. You would be anchoring a major news broadcast. There is more money in it. If it catches on, in terms of being a celebrity, a TV personality, you'd be on your way."

When I could talk with Jean she looked at me hard. "You told me," she said, "that when you went to work for CBS this was a career decision. This was the chance to do what you wanted to do with your life. Be a reporter. Now you're talking about going to New York, for double the money you've been making, to read the news. Either this move is wrong, or else you are not what you said you wanted to be. Which is it?" Then she added, gently, "You know what you have to do."

The offer did not prove that difficult to turn down.

But one does go through stages. It helps to have a roommate who has come along in the business, and whose head is as clear as Jean Rather's. You *must* have someone who will talk straight to you. I have benefited from Jean's candor and honesty beginning with the time she marched to the closet, pulled down a suitcase and announced, "Listen, you're getting big-headed and we are going to take two weeks off and go to Texas."

You have to know that with the Rathers, going to Texas is considered the cure-all for everything, the way some people go to the springs to take the mineral baths.

There is always that trapdoor through which the reporter can fall and emerge, in his own mind, as a media folk hero. But the fall is long and the way back is hard. I had my first exposure early, in Houston, in the aftermath of Hurricane Carla. Our coverage had amounted to a blitz. I was on around the clock. People got to know me. That was to be my first strong lesson in the impact of television on an entire community. As a family, the attention hit us as a storm of its own. I was unprepared and I made mistakes in trying to cope.

Up to a point praise, even criticism, can be mighty pleasant. Having strangers stop me on the street, phone me for help, ask to use my name in one cause or another, usually their own, is a big ego rub. But after a while I had to develop a set of reflexes.

We had two babies in the house, and with all of the other problems of getting a family started I had my own growing up to do. My solution was to overreact one way or the other. I went through a period of trying to accommodate everybody. If I was stopped on the street or cornered at a party, I reacted with so much friendliness as to turn a small courtesy into a kind of reunion. Then I went through a period of trying to ignore people.

All through this time, but especially during the first wave, Jean watched me very carefully. If she thought I handled a situation poorly, or rudely, she would tell me so in no uncertain terms. She knew I was groping. "If this is going to be your life," she would say, "you have got to find a better way to handle it than you did just then."

As my accountant friend and longtime advisor Richard Leibner has helped me to learn, one cannot retreat from the curiosity of the very people whose interest your job depends upon. One cannot become a Tibetan monk. What you think of as your right to privacy others mistake for snobbery. But it is important to keep your pulse, not to kid anyone, including yourself, about who you are and what your business is.

Often during the Watergate months as I was pulled along by tides that were strange to me I kept coming back to what Hugh Cunningham used to pound into us during my student days. He was death on first-person reporting and he would say, with scorn, that such journalism was for amateurs. "Nobody gives a shit about you," he preached. "You are not the story."

I worry now because I see young people leap right out of college into the twenty-one-inch jungle. We must find a way to give them bench marks. What will they use for integrity? When they say to themselves, What am I doing here, what answer will they get back? I'm here, glorifying my name, making my mother proud of me. They have to know the glory doesn't last.

Part of this business of the newsman as media star has been a phenomenon of the intensely human stories of the years since 1960. Suddenly, during the Nixon tenure, you had people writing letters about the arch in Walter Cronkite's eyebrow. Some of my own mail was along the line that "Rather telegraphs how he feels by how grim he looks." It was a lunatic time. You found yourself defending the natural habits of a lifetime. I am not, never have been, a natural smiler. I wish I were. I watch Jimmy Carter and wonder how he does it.

Possibly a psychologist could make something out of that. Who knows, maybe in the forgotten mists of childhood someone told me I did not have a good smile.

Actually, it is not a bad demeanor for a reporter to have. There is nothing more painful than smiling in the wrong place. People often unconsciously smile in situations where they are nervous or unsure how to react. I go the other way. My expression freezes. If I don't know how to act, I attempt to keep a neutral look on my face. But I began to get criticisms about being grim. I would look at myself on a strip of film and think, hell, I didn't look grim that day. That's just the way I am.

If newsmen became celebrities in those years, certainly one has to acknowledge the role of the carefully orchestrated Nixon-Agnew campaign to turn media people into public targets. I suppose one can attribute both fairness and irony to that campaign. I remember reading once about a professor who operated a flea circus. After each performance he would take the fleas out of their box and let them feed on his arm. In that way they lived off each other.

The Nixon-Agnew pitch was timeless. The problems of society were not war, corruption, the economy, racism. The real problem was the fact that the media kept publicizing all the bad news. The country was fed this rich load of fertilizer and soon letters were pouring in about Cronkite's eyebrow and the curl in Eric Sevareid's lip and Rather's stoneface.

Having isolated television as the primary enemy, Nixon and Agnew and their people scouted tirelessly for whores among the press. They always kept an eye out for those who, by their definition, were conservative, middle American, silent majority types. What time and Watergate proved was that they sought anyone who would slant the news in *their* favor. They would take advantage of their beliefs or prejudices, use them, and then do whatever was necessary to keep them as their allies. If you look hard enough, you will find a few as they did.

In one or two cases the Nixon White House played on the resentment of some newspaper columnists against the money and attention lavished on television reporters. That resentment is not unfounded. One syndicated columnist, with a record of rocklike integrity, became a target. They worked on him. Finally when they reached him it was through his belief that television is the root evil of society. To him TV was just show biz, pretty faces and animated cartoons. He could not imagine anyone in television giving a damn about journalism, in the way that newspaper people do.

The administration sold him a bill of goods about CBS faking an incident in Vietnam, staging, or recreating, a battle scene. I took it as a personal affront because I knew the people involved in the original report, among them Don Webster, one of our more experienced correspondents.

I made it a point to challenge the columnist after his writeup appeared containing the charges furnished by the White House mill. I said, "I know Webster, and this guy is out there where he could get his ass blown off at any time. This is a political maneuver to discredit him and CBS, and I would have thought you'd be smart enough to see it."

But he didn't or wouldn't. He bought the whole bundle and, to his everlasting embarrassment, the story later proved to be based on outright lies.

There is little real awareness in this country of the breadth and depth of a President's public relations and propaganda apparatus. Within the White House itself if he chooses to do so—and President Nixon did—he has the power to mount a campaign to wipe out anyone or anything. There are tremendous resources to be summoned.

I can't think of a clearer example than what was done to Daniel Schorr. To some, Dan Schorr has an abrasive quality that sends off sparks. They would see his stuff on the air and say, "Hmmm, there is something about that guy I don't like." But he is a fine, no-nonsense, incisive reporter. And this was what brought down the wrath of the White House. President Nixon had gone to New York and delivered a speech, before the Archbishop, in which he talked about increasing federal aid to parochial schools.

Schorr promptly ran a piece saying, in effect, that what the President had proposed was unconstitutional on its face and simply was not going to happen.

Immediately a campaign began—get something on Dan Schorr and destroy his career. The effort involved Haldeman, Fred Malek and the FBI. There is no point in dancing around that fact. Schorr's phones were tapped. The FBI grilled his friends and neighbors. They dug into his past. Once exposed, the Nixon people tried to lie their way out of it. The story was peddled that Schorr had been investigated by the FBI because he was being considered for a post in the government. That was the explanation offered by Ron Ziegler on behalf of Fred Malek, who knew it to be untrue.

If people with that degree of public trust, at that level of power, can say, "We're going to fix Dan Schorr," they can try to do the same against anyone. And that, in no small way, is what Watergate was about.

If possible, Schorr was even less popular around the White House than

I was. I remember once asking John Ehrlichman why he kept referring to Schorr as "Daniel P." I knew that his middle initial was "L." One day I inquired of Ehrlichman what the "P" stood for.

"Prick," he said.

Certainly, it became a status symbol to be on Nixon's enemies' list as opposed to being a White House pet. There are fewer favorites today than at any time in my memory, one of the small pluses of Watergate. There was no way you could read the Nixon transcripts and say, "I am a journalist," and be comfortable with what went on in the White House.

Still there is a kind of notoriety no reporter wants or can afford. You are always conscious of what happens when you *do* become a part of the story you cover, like it or not, and I didn't.

I am a guy who is accustomed to having his family pay a high price for what HE wants to do. It is fair to say that it became very difficult for them toward the final months of the Watergate crisis.

My daughter, Robin, probably the most sensitive member of the family, came home from school one day and said, "Dad, I know you're tired of talking about it. But I have to tell you it bothers me when somebody at school asks me why you hate the President."

Well, try sitting down and explaining to your fifteen-year-old daughter that you don't hate anyone.

And there was pressure from the other side, well intended though it may have been, adults who would come up to our children, Robin and Daniel, and say, "Tell your father he's doing a good job. I hope he *nails* that blankety-blank." I don't know which was worse.

My children had lived in Washington long enough to know that people took sides. Even so, this was a unique experience. None of us had ever been exposed to the depth of bitterness the Nixon crisis produced.

It was unavoidable, I suppose, that Watergate would engulf us socially. Jean had always struggled very hard to have and develop friends for us. That was never easy, given my pace and schedule. She prided herself on having friends on both sides of the aisle. It occurred to me during this period that we had as many, if not more, Republican as Democratic friends. But times got to be tight and we lost a few. We could say to hell with them, but it hurt. It was a shock, the first time I noticed someone I liked glaring at me across a room, and when I walked toward him he moved away.

The point is this kind of notoriety begins to weigh fairly heavily. There comes a time, if you are human, when you suspect that it might be nice to be less visible. Your wife says, "Hey, I hope you know what you're doing, because I have a feeling we're out there pretty far." And you talk that through.

Others say, "You're playing into their hands."

"How can I not do that?"

"Just ease up for a while."

It is stated just about that directly. But in the end the answer boils down to what you have to do. Not in any grandiose way, just, "Look, this is the only way I know how to do it and there is no use trying to change now."

What this tells you is that the White House is not just another beat. Any mistake on a story is apt to be a big one, pressure of no mean proportion in itself. You don't live with someone who is under that lid and not be aware; it comes through by osmosis. The pressure placed on me was felt by my family.

It is a humbling, sobering experience to go through one's mail and realize there are people who despise you. No one likes to think about having enemies. But if you test life at all you will make some, even by accident. At least, one would like to think it was accidental. Yet I know there are those who believe I was unfair in my coverage of Richard Nixon. I think they are wrong. As Marlon Brando said in a scene from *The Godfather,* "It's important to know who your friends are, but it's more important to know who your enemies are." I wondered what kind of a person would sit down and write a letter threatening to harm the family of someone they had never met.

Once, a lady braced me on a flight from New York to Atlanta. She walked back from her seat to confront me at mine. She was well dressed, in some kind of fur, not mink but definitely not just a good Republican cloth coat.

She created what in polite circles is described as a scene. She let fly a string of fairly colorful names. She went on to accuse me of disrespect to the President, if not treason. And she charged me with being a ringleader of the eastern, liberal, slanted news conspiracy. There is no place to hide on an airplane other than a lavatory, which would involve an inconvenience to others. I felt trapped.

Much of what she said was vile and I took it as long as I could. The plane was crowded, the passengers for eight rows around us tried not to stare. Then I said, in the polite, teeth-clenched tone that for me conceals the worst anger, "Madam, enough is enough. You must return to your seat now." I gave her my best I'm-not-kidding-you look. As she turned to leave, she said, "Somewhere you are going to get yours. If I have to arrange it, I will."

No cold chill shot through me. I did not take her seriously. But, of course, things happen and words echo. A car would jump the curb and I would scramble to get out of the way. I would open the door of my home to see a man loitering across the street. I would read the mail and see the looks and take the calls at midnight and know if someone wanted to run a car up my backside, there was not much I could do to stop him.

I tried to fight against a tendency to get paranoid. There was a time when I thought we leaned over too far *not* to be careful, to convince ourselves that we couldn't live in fear. It is a subject that, with regret, I must talk about. Jean and I did so during the civil rights story in the South, again when I went to Vietnam and once more during the worst of Watergate.

We had to recognize that the world is a tough neighborhood. If we forgot that, we were in peril. We wouldn't, and didn't, live in a fortress, with burglar alarms and floodlights and triple locks and nobody goes anywhere without a nanny. But we didn't want to be foolish either.

Our approach was to be ourselves and not to overreact, yet to be alert when there was a good reason. A voice on the phone says, "I'm gonna blow your ass off," click; that is a specific reason. My experience as a reporter tells me that the people who called were not the ones who would act, but I preferred not to test my theory. As calmly as we could, Jean and I would tell the kids that there had been a threatening call or letter.

The last thing we wanted to do was to instill a sense of terror in our children. On the other hand, we did not want to be careless or silly. At the peak of Watergate I would guess there were two or three such threats a week, most of them by mail. They rose in proportion to how much I was on the air, and the importance of the story. The mail was heaviest in the week after the incident in Houston.

I do not want to make too much of all this; I would prefer to believe that the calls and letters represented a flyspeck of people with muddled minds.

The bad part is reminding myself that the good journalist does *not* become a part of the story he covers. A newsman does not make news. The idea of the reporter as *pop media star* is offensive to me. It becomes a form of advertising, as harmful in its way as a doctor buying space to promote his transplant-of-the-month.

We may be at a turning point in television. I fear the consequences if it becomes a celebrity business. That way is simply not compatible with the vision Ed Murrow had of the scholar-correspondent, a vision still good enough for me. Keep in mind that in the beginning, in radio, you had mostly men who were newspaper-trained, if they were trained at all. Murrow was not. He was trained as a scholar, through education, books, experience.

One correspondent who came out of that process was Eric Sevareid, a man of class and inherent shyness. I cannot explain how a man can be in this business for so long and remain so shy. I only know that he is shy and his shyness is frequently mistaken for aloofness.

Eric feels strongly about the journalist as a "celebrity." He has been helpful to me and to others, not only by warning in strong terms of the dangers but by example.

The story is told around CBS that once on a visit to Hollywood, where else, Eric went with friends to a restaurant picked specifically because it was out of the way. They took a table in a quiet corner because Sevareid had long since eschewed the center table. They had ordered drinks when a young man appeared.

"Pardon me, Mr. Sevareid," he said, "I don't mean to interrupt." What goes through your mind at such moments is, well, if you didn't mean to interrupt, then why did you?

But the young man was nice about it and went on to say: "In this town I can see Cary Grant and Raquel Welch and I'd never do this. But I have been an admirer of yours for years. And, more importantly, I'm out with a young lady who is so excited she can't eat because she's in the same room with you. I'm seated by the door and if you would be kind enough on your way out simply to stop and say, 'Hello, Bob,' I'm telling you it would make me forever."

Sevareid didn't quite know what to say. He mumbled something non-committal and the young man smiled and left. Eric wrestled with himself. This is the kind of thing he simply never does, but the others at the table encouraged him. "Aw, go ahead, you were young once, Eric, help the guy out."

So, against every instinct he had, he stopped on his way to the door, held out his hand and said, "Goodnight, Bob. Nice to see you."

And the kid looked up from his plate and said, "What the hell is this? On your way, old man. Can't you see we're trying to eat?"

Out-Take

14

FACES

Perhaps an entertainer, with good lines or the right music, can appear on television one time and become that rare article, the overnight hit. In television news no such lightning strikes. The newsman must be on the screen night after night, long enough for the public to decide if the personality is hollow.

To a degree TV news is built around the star system. Far less than the rest of the schedule, but inescapably based on it. Yet search as I might, I can find no pattern to the success of the most visible faces in the industry.

Walter Cronkite. David Brinkley. John Chancellor. Harry Reasoner. Mike Wallace. Edwin Newman. Eric Sevareid. In looks, voice and approach no two are alike. But there is a common denominator. They are believable. No machine known to science can measure the human waves that come across the screen. But believability is the test.

Local stations have tried bringing in an actor to read the news, with consistently poor results. On the other hand, if Walter Cronkite walked into a local newsroom today and said, "Hello, I'm applying for a job as your ten o'clock anchor person," I have an idea how the management would react. They would say, "This guy has to be kidding." Walter might be hired as their news director or even to manage the station. But not to appear on camera. What made Walter Cronkite a star, at the network level, was not his physical appearance but his inner integrity. Over the years the viewers came to believe him.

Television is a copycat medium. What works in one place is soon tried in another. The impression is heightened by the fact that on any night the network anchor teams are working with generally the same bulk of news. The nuances of staging and direction are lost on the viewer. He knows he can change the dial and hear the same story three, or more, times.

So, conditions being equal, the contest often comes down to a quality easily named, hard to define: believability, charisma, personality, warmth.

I have no intention of compiling a list and analyzing the weaknesses and strengths of my colleagues. On the one hand I am not a critic. On the other, nothing could be more boring than a string of paragraphs, each beginning, "I admire this one because . . ."

What I will do is offer a thumbnail impression of the broadcast journalists I am most often asked about; I consider it important for the viewer to know that the people who bring them the news are not machine-stamped. I hope the names I omit—or for that matter, the ones I include—will not ask for equal time.

HARRY REASONER, ABC—His career has been built on a superior writing talent. Harry has an overlay of wry humor that tends to mislead people and conceals a determined nature. I have heard him described as diffident. Not so. I worked with Reasoner long enough to know he is demanding of himself and those around him. He falls into that category of making the tough play look easy. In his own way he cares very much about what he does, his way being a little lighter than many journalists'. That touch is evident in his description of the anchorman's primary duty as to "not interfere with your understanding of what we can find out."

JOHN CHANCELLOR, NBC—At a time and in a place when Jack had no reason to be, he was helpful to me. I ran across him in Europe in the mid-1960's on my way from Brussels to Paris. He was big in the business and I was still getting my feet wet. He asked what I was working on and I told him, a meeting between Charles de Gaulle and the British Prime Minister, Harold Wilson. I admitted to Jack that I did not know my derriere from third base when it came to French politics. Quickly, he said, "Unlike our State Department, their foreign ministry, the *Quai d'Orsay,* is not a bad place to begin. They are very helpful."

I said, "Jack, I don't quite know how to put this, but number one, I doubt I can find the place. And I couldn't pronounce it if I did."

He laughed and said, "Don't worry, they all speak English."

I believe Chancellor worked hard at one point to analyze what it was that made Cronkite successful. He worked to give himself a different style and succeeded. He is a good drawing room man. A Washington correspondent may come across as terrifically knowledgeable, talking about politics on your screen. But at a party you may find he can't talk about anything else. No one has to worry about Jack Chancellor's range. His interests vary from fashion to archaeology.

MIKE WALLACE, CBS—He raised TV interviewing to an art form in the 1950's on a show called "Night Beat." Sitting in a chair opposite his guest, firing away, Mike pioneered a style of tough questioning and spawned a legion of imitators, some of whom confused toughness with nastiness. Wallace was denounced in the early days of "Night Beat" as a hatchet man, a rap I regard as unfair. But he outlasted his critics. He has stayed around long enough to see the trend turn his way.

Wallace was influential on a generation of younger reporters, among them Dan Rather. There may be such creatures as natural interviewers, but I am not one of them. I never felt gifted at asking a politician what he did with the money. When I came to CBS I knew I had to improve that part of my game. I studied Wallace, how he asked a question, the turn of the words, the tone of the voice, the way he leaped on an answer to forge the next question. I picked him out in the same way I looked for good writers and came to Charles Kuralt and Harry Reasoner. They are still among the best lettered people in television.

A point ought to be made about Wallace. Some people have the same personality on the screen as off, Cronkite, for example. Mike Wallace looks competitive, and is, on television. He sometimes comes across as harsh and combative. In person, he is not. Mike has a gentle quality. I doubt that anyone who knew him only from television would use the word *gentle* to describe him. But those who deal with him on a day-to-day basis know his great capacity for gentleness. Aware of how hard he labored to develop a style and a reputation, I am not sure he would be eager to have that said.

DAVID BRINKLEY, NBC—There are some in broadcasting, myself included, who in a pressure situation may literally say to people, you just don't want to be around me today. Not Brinkley. Whatever is going on inside him, he always has time for people. David has a knack for doing something that eludes most people in TV news. He has the ability to sit back, read a great deal, observe from a distance and get the essence of a story without being there. I tried the Brinkley method once, couldn't make it work and nearly went crazy. I know in my bones I have to be at the scene to tell a story as well as I can.

ROGER MUDD, CBS—A playful sense of humor, especially about politicians, is one of Mudd's strongest assets. He is a master at writing an ear-catching close for the "stand-ups," short bursts of the correspondent on-camera reporting a story. He often seems to be barely suppressing a smile. Roger's off-camera style is that of a blunt-talking Southern gentleman. He does well the things that count for a TV newsman: report, write, interview, broadcast. No one has a better knowledge of the inner workings of Congress. When I was first assigned to the Washington Bureau, Roger accepted me faster and was personally kinder than any other correspondent. Like most of the people named Mudd in this country, he is distantly related to the doctor who treated the injuries of John Wilkes Booth.

EDWIN NEWMAN, NBC—No matinee idol, he is another who won by being up there night after night and coming through as someone people could trust. Newman is known for the precision of his language, about which he wrote two best-selling books. He also is about as low keyed as one can be in this business and survive. When I first started covering the convention floors I would be aware that Newman seemed to float while the rest of us tumbled. I thought he knew something the rest of us didn't.

ERIC SEVAREID, CBS—We have fished and hunted and walked the woods together, and if there could be such a thing as a guru in television then Eric would qualify as mine. I am always hesitant to go to anyone for advice. This is not a business in which people seek or give advice very readily. But I could go to Eric, as I did once in Saigon. The experience in Vietnam was to be extremely important to me, but I was then flooded with a sense of how little I knew, of not understanding what was going on. Eric assured me that no one knew what was going on. But he added, "You're right on the edge of being totally consumed by this job and that is not a good thing."

Months later he dropped me a note and I was grateful for it: "I have been thinking about our conversation, Dan. I think perhaps what you ought to do is take a sabbatical, try to get in a year of study at Harvard. Most of us don't think to do this until we're older. This is probably a good time in your life to do it." He was perceptive. And I should have taken his suggestion. But this was near the end of 1965 and something else came up. CBS asked me to return to the White House.

A final thought. NBC was on top in the news ratings during the heyday of Huntley and Brinkley. They caught on and everyone knows how well they blended. But often overlooked was the fact that a very strong team supported them: Chancellor, Sandy Vanocur, the late Frank McGee, Ed Newman. Just as Cronkite was to have a strong bench at CBS in Sevareid, Mudd, Wallace, Kuralt and Kalb. For the long pull, no matter how good Harry and Barbara turn out to be, the test is how deep a team ABC can develop.

Chapter
15

THE MIDNIGHT COWBOY

NEW YORK never became the symbol for me that it has for so many others in the arts. I first landed there in 1956, by thumb and by bus, on my first trip East. It was the summer of the all-star baseball game in Washington, my time to see the U.S.A., a couple of years out of college and still new in radio.

During that visit I wanted to see Broadway and the bright lights and Times Square. I mean, I had taken the Gray Line tour—which, incidentally, I strongly recommend—and now I was ready for New York in the raw. As I jostled my way through the crowds I heard the happy rhythms of Dixieland jazz blaring through the doorway of a place called the Metropole bar. I was like a hungry man who catches the scent of a roast escaping from a kitchen window.

I thought, that's terrific. I'll go in there. I was, needless to say, watching my money carefully. I had on a raincoat and the fellow at the door practically undressed me, saying, "Take your coat, sir." And I thought, well, it would be nice if he allowed me to unbutton it first.

He was a squat, chunky guy with a Dick Tracy hat and a cigar and an expression on his face that you see on the man in the constipation ads. I said in what I thought was a very decent way, "Okay, but does it cost me anything?"

He froze, looked over the top of his cigar and said, "Nah, I'm a gawddam Chinese coolie and I work for nothing."

Every stranger to New York I have ever known has a similar story to tell. In the Big Apple they just lay it on the line, and I like that honesty. Money jumps out of your hand, but you are paying for a sense of excitement that exists nowhere else. And I like the fact that New York does not suffer second-raters gladly.

I did not have difficulty communicating with and understanding New Yorkers. I discovered their pride and kindness, once I got onto the fact that though New York is a very big place, it is made up of small neighborhoods, each with its own character. Of course, the pressure to succeed is something else again. I don't know where you have been or what kind of job pressures you have felt, but there is no comparison. There is a feeling of everyone keeping score. You ride in an elevator and people are looking you over, making judgments: he's very strong today, but that one over there is slipping, and that fellow behind me is moving up and the one in the corner is a has-been.

Of course, I had no real impression of New York until my second trip, when I flew up to meet with my new bosses on what should have been one of the more exhilarating days of my life.

Riding in from the airport, my taxi passed two immense, sprawling graveyards of a size I had never seen before. It was not an eerie feeling, but I remember thinking, This is no big deal because *that* is how it all ends. I didn't smile then. I still don't when I think about fate, which I still do, in passing, when I travel that route into the city.

So whatever the reasons, and possibly they are too deeply rooted to sort out, New York was never the sum of my dreams or ambitions. The stars were there, the faces most of America recognized. But New York was not where the news was made. It merely held the funnel. I had to face those feelings when CBS asked me to move there after nearly eight years at the White House. The offer did not seem sudden or surprising. But the exact timing was suspicious, to say the least. Gerald Ford had been in the Oval Office for less than a month. The man he replaced was back in San Clemente, the first American President in exile. I was still a visible symbol of the hostility between the Nixon White House and the press corps. If my name had not led the enemies list, it was surely among the top five.

We had gone through all of that discord, and I do not mean Dan Rather alone. CBS. My family. We had fought off the pressures and the unpleasant sense of finding ourselves in a contest we had never meant to enter. In politics, to a point, I can subscribe to the practice of the ancient Egyptians who, when the Pharaoh fell, buried his servants with him. But I draw the line at applying that practice to the reporters who covered him.

In truth, my rotation had been overdue. Once it had been CBS policy to change the beat men when a new administration came into power. I had stayed on to satisfy my own objectives when Nixon took office. I continued to stay on in 1972 because I could not let the Nixon people feel they had forced me out. It is fair to say that their tactics probably kept me there beyond what CBS considered a normal tour.

That was the background when Bill Small asked if I could meet him in New York for lunch. As naive as it now may sound, I assumed we were to lunch alone, as much for social as professional reasons. We were, and are, good friends. We talked often. And, keep in mind, we had been together through an incredible chain of events. Bill had been the bureau chief when I arrived in Washington in 1964 to cover the presidency of Lyndon Johnson. He was in New York now, had not been there long, and it did not strike me as odd that he wanted to visit.

Of course, I should have been prepared. But I wasn't. My mind was on I know not what—Watergate, Nixon, Ford, the snows of yesteryear.

When I went to Small's office I found that we were to be joined by Dick Salant and Bill Leonard. On the way to Alfredo's, on Central Park South, I was feeling a little tight. These were three of the top executives of my company. That is a lot of artillery just for lunch and I knew it.

It was Salant who brought up the move, in an almost offhand way. He simply said he wanted to talk about the future, and when I heard him say "New York" I braced myself, just out of pure instinct. I thought, Okay, now listen to what they are saying, don't talk much, then get out of here and think about it, talk with Jean, before you say or do something ill-considered.

I was being offered the job of anchorman-correspondent on "CBS Reports," a job unfilled since the days of Edward R. Murrow. I should have been flattered.

But what I kept waiting to hear, and did not, was whether I had a choice. In the light of later conversations it is clear that I probably did. Apparently they did not understand then how important that assurance was to me. The whole tone of the lunch was friendly. There was little if any reason for them to believe that I was not ready to make a move.

But I had not exactly just walked out of a cold shower. This was a very difficult period, overall, for me. A tangle of thoughts and pictures flashed into my mind. The whole lunch was distorted in my mind. I don't remember what I ate or who said what. It was the feeling one gets just before he goes under the ether; one hears the voices, feels the eyes staring, but nothing is clear.

No doubt Salant thought it made sense to put the White House behind me, that a new assignment would be good for me and for CBS. He was making a case, not giving me an ultimatum. But that was not obvious to me then and I didn't press him. I probably should have. But my tendency when caught off guard is to listen and say very little.

I flew back to Washington that afternoon, a Thursday, and Jean and I talked far into the night. At one point she said, "Okay, believe the worst. For the moment, let us assume that somebody, somewhere, sent a signal to get you out of there. That doesn't necessarily mean you want to quit and walk away, does it?"

And that was the question I had to answer. There are, of course, a lot of ways to send signals. Politicians do so all the time. It is also true that, whatever the reason, your career can be manipulated in such a way as to coincide with what you know to be your own best interest.

If indeed that was the case, I know I still would have been obliged to look for a job elsewhere. We had been through too much, for too many months. At the risk of sounding overstuffed, there was too much riding to go meekly into the night.

I am reluctant to use the words that are so easily abused by politicians— honor, integrity and principle. But in any job, a man comes to a time when he faces a decision that deals with his vitals, and he just can't compromise.

I had vacation time coming and I decided to take it. The thing I needed most to do, literally, was to go fishing. I had been promising Daniel, then fifteen, that we would get off and for a lot of reasons I had kept postponing the trip.

So this seemed a good time and a good way to air out my mind. Then I made a mistake. Instead of going fishing, I called the office early the next morning hoping to catch Sandy Socolow, who had succeeded Small as the bureau chief. He was between his house and the office and I left a message with the deskman. I knew better. But I said, "Look, I won't be in today. Tell Sandy I'm taking my two weeks' vacation and I'll call him."

And . . .

What I didn't know was that news of the Big Lunch had already made the rounds of the CBS offices. The meeting was about as secret as Elizabeth Ray's sex life. Great waves of rumors were already crashing in. The mill was very busy and then I fed it some more: *Rather called in early this morning, sounded hurt and confused and said he was taking two weeks off.*

By Monday some of the rumors had hit the public prints and the situation was fast turning into a shambles. Of course, if I had stayed that Friday and talked to Sandy, I might have put a less dramatic face on it. But I needed some free time and space in which to think.

On Monday night I telephoned Jean. She didn't know exactly where we were, either. Daniel and I did that as often as my work habits allowed. We would hit the road, sort of test out one place and then another, maybe rent a motel room, maybe camp out. All Jean knew was which direction we had gone and that sooner or later she would hear from us.

I realized that when word got around that Rather had "gone fishin' " it would be taken by some as a euphemism for hiding out. But, dammit, I *had* gone fishin'.

Jean was relieved when we called. Bill Small had been trying to reach me, she said, and it sounded important. He left word to call from wherever I had gone, at whatever time I received the message. We had driven to a lake about one hundred miles north of Washington. I called Bill from a pay telephone at a gas station on the highway. Whenever one of those huge diesels roared by, the booth trembled. I had a symphony of sounds behind me, trucks rumbling and sports cars whining past, as I tried to shout into the receiver.

Small's tone was considerate, but he said, "The story has gotten out. The newspaper people have jumped on it and we're going to need an answer. What have you decided?"

I flattened myself against one side of the booth and cradled the phone. "I don't know," I shouted. "I really don't know what to do about it."

He said, "Well, we're going to have to step up the decision because it has a potential for getting out of hand." Bill said that he and Salant were coming to Washington on another matter Wednesday, and could I meet with them? I must say, I strongly suspected they were *not* coming on another matter. I told him I wanted to fish a while longer, but if he felt it was necessary I would return to Washington. He said I should.

Between Monday night and Wednesday I got on the phone. I had some research to do. I guess, one of the lessons driven home to me from hanging around Presidents was the importance of talking to other people. There are not that many people with whom one can discuss a private decision, but sometimes those few are worth an army.

One of my first calls was to Don, my younger brother by six years. He has always been a good sounding board for me, an absolutely straight talker who is simply not capable of dressing things up. He is the toughest member of the family.

During that year and a half when Watergate was breaking loose I would call Don and say, "Look, I'm not sure I'm right about this. What do you think?" Now, his life is not made up of sitting around the television set watching what his brother does. But his judgment is precious to me. I wouldn't say he is apolitical, because he cares about politics. But he is not a party man. I knew I could rely on his ability to be fair.

Actually, my job, my exposure, what people thought I believed, on occasion made matters awkward for Don. When he accepted a high school head coaching job in Austin, which he had really labored to get after six or eight years at a smaller school, a number of people said, well, Dan Rather is in with Lyndon Johnson and Johnson got him the job.

Knowing my erratic relationship with LBJ, that idea was laughable. But not to Don. The real world for him was having to face such gossip and he was awfully good about it.

I laid out the bones of information as simply as I could: It is a good spot I'm being offered, one I want to consider seriously. But there is this problem of possible pressure, and whether CBS has yielded. What do you think and how does it look?

Don gave me a hard-nosed answer. First I had to decide whether the network was, in fact, buckling. If I could not satisfy myself, then I ought to quit.

For one of the few times in my life I was having trouble sleeping. I am famous for being able to sleep anywhere, sometimes on my feet. I went to the track at Georgetown University to run off some of the tension.

I placed calls to four friends in Houston, people I went to college with, Bill and Carolyn Johnston, Jerry and Eunice Martin. I needed to talk with old friends who knew my roots. All of them, coincidentally, had supported Nixon. I don't doubt that they had voted for Nixon every time he ran. I no longer remember what we said, but it helped. After a day or so Bill Johnston called back. "Hey," he said, "I'm not bugging you. But I've been thinking about what we talked about earlier. I don't have anything new to add, but I just thought you might like to discuss it some more."

I telephoned veteran CBS writer Charlie West, and a couple of old New York friends, David and Susan Buksbaum.

Other calls were coming in, one from a television writer I respected. He was calling on the record, as a reporter. I told him I wasn't in a position to talk, a reply he didn't take kindly, as no reporter does. But I did seize the moment to say, "I want to talk to you on a personal basis. It would be a help to me. If I do take a new assignment, whatever the job, whatever the reason, how is it going to look?"

He gave an honest and harsh reading. He said he was, first of all, suspicious. And whatever the facts, this was the way it would play, that I had been pushed over the side.

So be it.

Small and Salant came out to the house on Wednesday. By that time the gossip wasn't helping anybody. Questions were being raised and CBS wanted to get the matter settled. The stories and rumors generated a pressure of their own.

Fortunately, Small and Salant were no strangers to me. I trusted them. Everyone ought to be skeptical of his bosses some of the time. In a broad, philosophical way I am. But more than that I had been to the well with these two a number of times. All through the Watergate bombardment Small and Salant had never given an inch. "Look, I can't keep the pressure from you," Small had said at one point. "You and I know it's there and I'm not going to sit here and tell you it doesn't exist. What I am saying is this: I get paid to handle that sort of thing. You get paid to do the job that has to be done." That kind of support was invaluable to me.

The only way you could get through a hellbox of that kind was for Nixon, and his people, to know I was there yesterday, I am here today, I will be back tomorrow. In 1972, when I had raised in a tentative way the subject of my being rotated, the question had been brushed aside quickly. "Whatever you may be thinking," Salant said, "you have to stay. We can't be in the position of appearing to yield to White House pressure."

And now that was exactly the impression being circulated, partly because the change had not been well handled, something for which I was also responsible. In the end I said, "I'm asking you, on a man-to-man basis, to level with me. Have you seen anything, heard anything, that would suggest to you that there are any kind of politics behind this move?"

Salant and Small knew me well enough to realize I would quit if that were the case. And anyone who knows me and how I feel about CBS and the people who work there would understand how painful that would be. But Salant put the doubts to rest. He said, "Dan, it's your choice. You can stay at the White House and continue to do what you have been doing.

You can take what we have offered. Or you can suggest to me whatever else you might like to do."

I had satisfied myself that it was not a matter of anyone caving in to pressure. In the end I only had one skeptic to convince and that was me. I could not control the shop talk or the printed stories that speculated on whether I jumped, was pushed or fell. This was a new experience for me. In the past my job changes had been of interest only to my family and a few key contacts, such as the milkman. Now they were news. At such times it is easy to magnify whatever has happened to you. You just try not to lose radio contact with earth.

My detractors, went the story in *Newsweek*, "were finally given something to cheer about. With a flourish of press releases extolling Rather, CBS announced his transfer to New York."

Whatever was being said or written, only one rumor disturbed me. It soon reached me that some of the owners and managers of the CBS affiliate stations were claiming, boasting, that they had pulled the strings. It was true there had been complaints, but they had come from a small minority of stations, many of them from the deep South. That clique was hardly a secret. As many station managers, or more, were determined not to allow those few to have their way. I will be forever indebted to those who supported me. Some of them spoke up and said, "I am neither negative nor positive about Dan Rather. Sometimes I like what he does and sometimes I don't. But it is crazy to talk about taking him off this run at this time."

In late August, 1974, when I accepted the move to "CBS Reports," I found myself still thinking, dammit, one thing I am not going to do is give the "get-Rather" clique any satisfaction. But obviously I did. My critics accepted the announcement that I was leaving the White House as a victory. In the weeks that followed, I heard some of the station managers had taken credit for whatever it was they thought had happened. On the country-club veranda or at the Chamber of Commerce meetings, they were saying, "Well, we managed to get that s.o.b. Rather." On the other hand, I don't believe I should have stayed at the White House another eight years just out of spite. That would have been too high a price to pay.

Others rose to my defense. The wife of a friend volunteered, "I don't know what the situation is, but I know how to organize a mail campaign. If one will help, I'm here to tell you that I can put it together."

I threw up my hands. "For God's sake," I said, "I don't need that. I don't want it. But thanks for the thought."

Networks tend to take the mail seriously, and for that reason it does matter. The count ran between eight and nine thousand pieces, they told me, in the weeks after CBS announced my reassignment. The letters expressed three sentiments. There were those who thought I got my ass kicked and were glad; those who thought I got my ass kicked and were sympathetic; and those who saw it as a promotion and were happy for me.

From my standpoint two out of the three categories did not exactly lift my spirits.

· If there had not been quite so many elements aloft, I might have seen more clearly that the New York transfer was my chance to go to graduate school. I had done documentaries before, but not in this league, with these resources, bringing my full time to bear. This was an opportunity I welcomed to treat in depth subjects that left an imprint on the American condition. And we would tackle a wide range of them. There were the four assassination shows (the Kennedys, King and the Wallace attempt). There was an hour called "The American Way of Cancer," on the environmental causes of cancer. Another called "The I.Q. Myth." One of the first we did dealt with the influence of special-interest money on congressional elections: "The Best Congress Money Can Buy." The ability to handle that kind of subject in an hour showed me the potential of "CBS Reports." And I was excited.

After the self-winding deadline pressure of daily journalism I found it a luxury to be able to study and reflect and write with greater care. Not long after I had slid behind my new desk my mind flashed back to a country road in Georgia. I was bouncing around from one tank town to another with Wendell Hoffman, the cameraman, who was then in the process of teaching me a great deal about a side of television I did not know—film making. Of seeing each piece as a little picture show. To an Antonioni that would seem ridiculous. But not to us. In our own small world we felt we were turning out forty-five- and sixty-second movies.

That afternoon he was harping on how much I had to learn and I had heard all I could take. Finally I got so mad I pulled the car over and jumped out and had to walk around for a minute or so to cool down. "All right," I said. "All right. What else do I need to know?"

"For one thing," he said, "you need to learn how to write."

I said, "I can write."

He said, "No, you can't. You can put a declarative sentence together and that's good enough for the AP and the UP. But if you are going to be a correspondent, with all that is supposed to mean, you have to know a helluva lot more than you know now. And you have to be able to *really* write."

Wendell was prodding me. He wanted me to think about doing better than just getting by. And so I did, all the more when I landed at "CBS Reports." For one thing, there was again the presence of Edward R. Murrow. Not as strong as in London. But given how long he had been gone from that show and those offices, it was astonishing how often his name and work came up. To someone outside CBS it is probably hard to believe. But true it is.

Time and again I heard someone say, "Ed wouldn't have done it that way." I found myself asking, and not in a calculated way, "I'm having trouble with this. How would Murrow have done it?" And the answer often was surprising.

John Sharnik, who was there in those days, said to me once, "You know, Murrow's broadcasts were extremely well written for television. I believe that is what set them apart. If you go back and look at the scripts as a piece of literature, they may not say it to you. But for television they were marvelous."

In an hour show you have to build to certain curtain lines. Murrow was a master.

I made it a project to go through the film library and look at every show Murrow did. You tend to forget how many there were. After a year and a half I had to give up. I had seen most of them, but not all.

Mainly, I reminded myself of something I already knew. That experience drove home the final nail. I was able to say, You're not that good and you are never going to be that good. But console yourself. Neither is anyone else.

In the summer of 1976 I took on another assignment, joining Mike Wallace and Morley Safer as the anchors on "60 Minutes," a show then moving into prime time. The producer was Don Hewitt, a genius at what he does, who had been with CBS for twenty-five years and whose name figured prominently in the telecast of the Kennedy-Nixon debates. Hewitt produced the first one. He was alarmed at how ashen Nixon looked on camera, and before they went on the air he argued, to no avail, that Nixon needed something on his face other than Shavestick.

As the first news broadcast to fight the entertainment hours for ratings, "60 Minutes" is a different art form. It falls between the banzai charge of daily journalism and the thoughtful, reflective, one-hour-to-do-it of "CBS Reports." And I love it. With a short time lag, on every week, reaching a large number of viewers, there is an opportunity on "60 Minutes" to produce the so-called "exposé."

We did break one such story, a case of irresponsibility by a company that turned out a deadly chemical, called Kepone, at mortal risk to their workmen. The impact of that story was as great as anything I have ever done. The case resulted in 153 indictments. That might have happened without the broadcast. But, at least we were able to make sure the situation would not be ignored.

For the viewer the success of "60 Minutes" will bear watching. Other such broadcasts will follow, testing whether a newscast can compete in so-called "entertainment" time and not lose its journalistic integrity.

The result may shape the development of video news for the rest of this decade and into the 1980's. One theory offers that television, with its voracious appetite, will repeat the pattern of national magazines. The popular magazine of the 1930's was filled with fiction, but fact overcame it. *Time* and *Newsweek* need no fiction.

Whether the basic hours of television will ever go in that direction, I am not prepared to guess. But TV has the capacity to devour plots and ideas. The only self-renewing source is fact, reality. The trend may be to *docudramas,* the reenactment of historic and romantic events, with creative license. I would be remiss if I did not point out that Ed Murrow gave us a taste twenty years ago with a program called "You Are There."

A young person who wants to get into the business, who wants to do what Dan Rather does, needs to know that in addition to a lot of luck, a variety of experience helps. And more than one set of reflexes. It does not necessarily hold that because you can read the news you can master the short, visual essay of "60 Minutes," or the documentary style of "CBS Reports." The leaps are not unlike those of the writer who wants to go from newspaper articles to magazines to books.

If you ask me where this training leads, I can't honestly say. I don't think in those terms. People, mostly TV columnists, keep asking who will be the next Walter Cronkite. The answer is easy. No one. It would be foolish to believe there is going to be another Cronkite or Eric Sevareid. My job is to make myself a pretty good Dan Rather. Sure, I have fantasized at one time or another about anchoring the Evening News, socking away the money for a few years and then returning to what I do best—reporting. I have to believe that if Ed Murrow were alive he would not be doing the news at seven o'clock.

The curious part is that I am a fellow who has been happy at every job he ever had, who would be happy if he were still doing the drive-time news on radio in Houston. I didn't really want to leave the White House. It startles me to realize I felt that way but the point was made when the time came to go.

I had spent eight of the past ten years there, had arrived too soon and too young and then overstayed my time. I had seen one President driven from office by war and another by scandal.

Yet when my tour at the White House had ended I had few personal effects to show for those years and those events. My office, a hutch actually, was in the rear of the pressroom in the White House basement. It didn't take long to clean out my desk and I didn't even do the chore myself.

I'm not sure I like this about myself. But I did not go back, purposely, once the move to New York became final. Part of that was a small defiance. I would not give the few old Nixon hands who were still there under the new regime, the satisfaction of my saying good-bye. In the pressroom I knew there would be questions and I wasn't sure I wanted to hear them. And I do believe in clean breaks. My job belonged now to Bob Schieffer and Phil Jones and I really had no business there.

Of moments and memories and friendships I had a few, but of tangible things far less. So I asked a friend to clean out my desk, and there wasn't much. I always did work lean. But one of the items I salvaged was my first pocket notebook, the original one I had the day I came on the job in January, 1964. It was just a small, spiral notebook, not anything of quality, the kind you buy in a drugstore. I flipped through it for the first time in years.

It was filled mostly with notes about my first day, when I interviewed President Johnson. He had walked out to the lobby to meet me, which was no big deal. But I had a sentence on the first page to remind myself that *"A political reporter's contacts are everything."* I wrote that across the first page, underlined, three times, the way a schoolboy would write a sentence on a blackboard.

I do not collect souvenirs, but I did want to keep my White House press pass. A lot of people who worked at the White House saved theirs. I simply remembered how proud I was when mine was issued, and I was reluctant to give it back. I hoped that while I was in transition between New York and Washington the White House would forget about mine and I would just hang onto it. But CBS had new people coming in and they needed passes. The White House press office said, "We're not giving out any new ones until we get Rather's." They got a little tougher than

I think was necessary. I know the standoff led to a bemused conversation in the CBS bureau.

One of the fellows said, "Well, who's going to call him? I mean, who is going to call Dan Rather and say, 'Hey, we want your White House pass.'"

Sylvia Westermann, a CBS friend who had just moved from Washington to New York for the company, finally gave me the message. Even then I held out a few more days. In symbolic terms I just did not want to let it go. Finally I drove to the CBS offices at 2020 M Street, laid my pass on the desk and said, "Here it is, I don't give a damn, just close the file."

Bill Headline was on the desk that day. He picked up the card and turned it slowly in his hand. Bill is a sensitive guy and he understood. He wanted to keep the tone light. He grinned, looked up at me and said, "From the picture I would never have known it was yours." Then he opened a drawer and dropped it in and said, "On the other hand, Dan, I wouldn't expect them to have a good picture of you."

Out-Take
15

SOURCES

When journalists grow emotional about such matters as protecting the public's right to know, we need to acknowledge that the public isn't all that hot to be protected. Many Americans really do not want to be told what their government is doing, any more than they would want to know what went into the grinder to make the hot dog they are eating.

Unfortunately, we have done a poor job of explaining why we feel so fiercely about the freedoms granted the press under the First Amendment. Among these freedoms is the protection of our sources, a principle tested in the fall of 1976 by what became known as the Daniel Schorr case. At the time, I regretted that so vital an issue had to be tested in so cloudy a case. But lawyers tell us that bad cases make good law.

The Schorr controversy was hardly clear-cut. The case involved other, complex issues that had to do with the relationship of a reporter with his employers and colleagues. In some ways the arguments became bitter because of the subsidiary issues. These are important questions on their own, but they pale beside the cause of protecting sources.

I am eager to argue, as Schorr did, that such a right is provided under the First Amendment. Not all newsmen agree. Some feel the issue is not big enough to make a stand on the Constitution but falls more properly into the category of a lawyer's relationship with a client, or a doctor's with his patient. The important point is to understand why journalists defend this right so strongly.

Any working newsman can cite clear and compelling examples. I can describe one from my police-beat days in Houston: Some cops are skimming narcotics. The operation is set up in such a way that no one knows for certain who, or how many, are involved. But one of them is stricken with conscience, wants to end his involvement, wants to stop the graft. He is looking for a way to expose it, but suspects he has nowhere to turn.

He can't go to the police chief, or even the district attorney, because he can't be sure how high the payoffs reach.

Where can he go? The policeman looks around and says, I know this one reporter with a reputation for never breaking a trust. He goes to him and says, "Look, I'm into something I'm ashamed of. I'm powerless to stop myself but it ought to be stopped." And he lays out the rough outline of the activity. The reporter takes it from there.

This isn't a script from "Kojak" or "Baretta" or "The Blue Knight." That scenario happened, and in some form still does in virtually every major city in America. Not very often, but often enough.

Exposing graft among cops may seem a long way from the leaking of state secrets. But we are talking about the working level of government, of our system of checks and balances. No one wants to sound pompous about it, but the press has a role to play in this process. For someone who wants to see corruption uncovered, and has nowhere else to plead, the press is a court of last resort.

Certainly there are going to be abuses, as there are among doctors and lawyers and in every profession where a privileged relationship exists. We need a press sensitive to its responsibilities but not intimidated by them. The role of the press as a watchdog is critical to making the system run.

Some of these elements were at the heart of the Daniel Schorr case. The issue was not his personality nor his politics nor whether his own ideology got involved in the story. The charge that Schorr had a personal, ideological blade to hone is, I believe, unfair to him. Set those factors aside. The core issue was whether a reporter has the right, indeed, the obligation to protect his sources.

Congress attempted to force Schorr to reveal who had leaked to him the so-called Pike Report. The House Select Committee on Intelligence, headed by Representative Otis Pike (D-N.Y.), had investigated abuses covered up by the CIA. The Committee voted to make the report public and, at that point, copies were leaked to Schorr and an unknown number of other reporters.

After the document had been passed, the House voted against releasing it. The other news people returned their sets. Schorr made a Xerox copy. He now had reason to believe that this was the only liberated, unedited copy of the secret report. Eventually he turned it over to the *Village Voice,* which published the report intact.

Meanwhile Schorr had broadcast over CBS virtually every item that was newsworthy. Excerpts from the report already had been carried by *The New York Times,* all of which got lost in the rush of the House Committee to make Schorr the focal point of its hearings. He was held accountable for having the full report put in print.

His decision to do so, Schorr insisted, was based on conscience. The Committee made some ineffective efforts to find the source and improve its own security, but concentrated on putting Schorr on the griddle. All wrapped up in this case, in my opinion, was a belief by some of the Committee members that these were inviting targets: Schorr, a newsman not especially popular; a newspaper, the *Village Voice,* unrelated to the national press establishment.

Schorr himself argued, and I am not sure he is wrong, that the move against him was in part an attempt to settle grudges that dated back to Watergate and the Pentagon Papers.

After Schorr refused to identify his source, the Pike Committee backed off, voting 6 to 5 not to cite him for contempt of Congress. The right of a reporter to protect his sources was hardly resolved forevermore.

For many years journalists assumed that, in the end, the bench would defend this principle. But there is beginning to build a body of court cases that leave the issue as unsettled as ever. What makes any reporter bristle is the reluctance of the courts to give this relationship the same legal standing already given the doctor-patient and the lawyer-client. And, after bristling, I can only lament that apparently we have not stated the case as clearly and as forcefully as we feel.

One result of the Schorr case was to revive the charge that some reporters regard the First Amendment as a license to steal. No one would argue that a government must have the power to conceal certain of its actions. But one has to know how selective that process is, and how much hypocrisy is attached to the subject of state secrets. For example, Henry Kissinger could classify a report as *top secret* for decades to come. Then, when it suited his purpose—if someone was writing a long assessment of his record for, say, *Foreign Policy* magazine—a leak of material previously classified as secret would develop, flattering to Dr. Kissinger. The same sort of thing happens regularly with the military, the CIA, the FBI, even the Agriculture Department.

Frankly, I try not to get too outraged by such self-serving diplomatic tricks of the trade. But if you are going to have a committee of Congress hammer down on security leaks, I would think a good place to start would be in the office of the Secretary of State. Or at the White House. There you are dealing with leaks from the highest windows of government, not the treachery of some film clerk.

Dan Schorr did not walk away untouched. Paid by CBS but taken off his beat while the case was under investigation, he later resigned. Schorr is shrewd, abrasive, sometimes calculating. He has an outsized ego, as many of us do in this business. His would manifest itself in myriad and mystic ways. We were not close and I don't want to mislead anyone. Trouble sometimes developed between us. But he could be and often was an excellent reporter. And on the principle of protecting sources, Schorr was absolutely correct.

Without such a right, few major investigative stories of our time—including Watergate, My Lai or the Pentagon Papers—ever would have seen the light of day.

THE MISTRESS

I WAS ONCE INVITED to speak to a journalism class at a university in Arizona. I expected an audience of perhaps thirty-five people—there had been six in my class at Sam Houston State—but instead I found myself facing an auditorium packed with hundreds of students. In *Arizona,* mind you. I guess I should not have been surprised.

Journalism has become one of the glamour professions of the 1970's. In no small way that status was due to the heroics of Woodward and Bernstein, not to mention Redford and Hoffman. But I applaud the new wave they represent because all of us, television included, are the beneficiary. We need to remind ourselves that the maverick journalist frequently breaks the big story: My Lai, Watergate, the early Vietnam record.

Too often the errors I have made occurred because I followed the herd. There is always a temptation in journalism as in society to graze with the sheep. As Americans, we proudly boast of our independent streak. We say to ourselves and to our children and to people elsewhere, Look, we are not a flock of turkeys heading off in one direction. We ask questions and we demand answers and we make our own decisions.

But the line gets harder to hold, in journalism, as the industry grows in size and power and in the number of people who want a piece of the action. The new reporter, the one on the front edge of his career, has to know that he pays a price to make his own way. But the joy of the craft is not in following the herd.

They say that the law is a jealous mistress. I can only say that journalism is just as jealous and keeps longer hours. For those who want this life, and those who see it as some kind of glamour factory, here is what they have to know: It is a business that consumes you. You become addicted. At times I think you *have* to be addicted to do your job well. There is always another deadline, another story. You find yourself wanting to be there. And it eats at you.

I have said to myself any number of times, hey, I'm going to take Saturday and Sunday off. I surely don't need another weekend in Albany, Georgia. I'm going home and spend it with my family.

By Friday morning a rumor would circulate that *something big* was going to happen the next day. Now I found myself thinking about how much time I had invested in a story about to reach a climax. "I can't be away from here." And there went my weekend at home.

I wouldn't argue that in most cases I made the right decision. To do the job well calls for a total commitment. Once a reporter has made what Jean Rather refers to as "our pact with Lucifer" he may get out of it what he wants. But he pays a price.

The young journalist has to know what an irregular world this is. Colossal egos are at work, including his own. Stresses and strains and pressures are placed on his relationships with everyone, but obviously none more than his wife and children. The road is littered with the bones of marriages that did not make it.

We moved from Houston to Dallas to New Orleans to Washington to London and back to Washington in less than two years. Our daughter, Robin, attended four schools in the first grade. Fortunately for her, I think she came out of it with a stronger character. Not every child would.

But you make the first move and you say, Gee, that one was tough but we rode it out. Then another move. And another. At one point Jean nailed a sign to the wall of one of our homes, a sign we had inherited years before from a minor league baseball player.

That was the year I broadcast the Houston games in Triple-A ball, and we traveled to Florida for spring training. We became friendly with a journeyman player hoping to stick with the club, whose chances were not exactly golden. Over his locker he kept a sign that bore the legend: "DON'T SEND OUT THE LAUNDRY." It was a way of reminding himself that this was a pretty dicey business at best. When the Houston Buffs cut him, he left the sign with us.

In the years to come Jean too often was required to be not only wife and mother but daddy as well. I was working, traveling, fulfilled. She was back there with the kids and the broken washing machine. In today's climate I can well see how someone with a feminist point of view would ask: How could you do that to another person? And I have to say, I would not have left her so much alone if I had been smarter and more sensitive.

Robin grew up seeing her father on television. She knew and understood what I did for a living. While we were overseas Daniel was too young to know or care. He was six or seven when we settled in Washington for the second time, and the experience of seeing his father on TV was new to him. And, again, I was on the road a good deal.

I came home one evening to find Daniel entertaining a small friend in the living room, sprawled on the rug in front of the set. I stuck my head in and said, "Hi, son," but I could see that he was involved in whatever show he was watching.

As I turned away to greet Jean in the kitchen, I heard his friend say in a quizzical voice, "Who was that?"

And Daniel answered, without looking up, "Oh, that's Dan Rather."

That will make you laugh. But it should also make you cry.

If you are going to stay in television, you need to have a philosophy. Mine isn't finished yet, but I am working on it. I keep reminding myself that the people who first came into radio were newspaper-trained. The traditions of the newspaper business clung to them. When television came along even those who had been raised in radio still had that set of journalistic principles to guide them. Today, if you are lucky, you may wind up a small-bore celebrity, but I don't kid myself, and I try not to kid anyone else, about what I am and what I want to be, which is, in caps, a JOURNALIST.

A special vigil is required if you are to resist becoming something else—a showman, an actor on a 21-inch screen, a *personage*. In ways varied and subtle, a reporter can be led down those paths.

I dislike deference even when I am the beneficiary of it. But this is not a business where restraint and understatement thrive. You slide in behind a desk on the newsroom set, catch a draft of air, flap your lips in an almost involuntary "brrrr," and the next thing you know four workmen with wrenches are standing on ladders with their heads in an air-conditioning duct in the ceiling.

A producer will ask what is going on and one of them will say, "We were told Mr. Rather was cold."

There is, or seems to be, a law of compensation at work in television—for every handful of moondust thrown in your eyes you will catch a handful of something else. For myself, I have found this to be a fair deal and a helpful one. For every moment of glory, I can recall a humbling experience.

This balance was much on my mind in the last days of 1976. CBS was preparing to introduce a weekly, prime-time news program called "Who's Who," with me as anchor and chief reporter. In such cases they literally build a set around you, custom tailor one as they would a suit. The elevation of the stage, the size of the chair, the dimensions of the desk, all are designed to order. You have to go back for two or three fittings, all of which can be a fairly heady exercise. I imagine the sensation is not unlike what the astronauts must have felt, when the couch in the spaceship was measured and contoured to their very own bodies.

I had to admit the set of "Who's Who" was a long way from sitting atop a light pole and broadcasting a college baseball game. The first time I walked in for a "fitting" I could not shake my self-consciousness. I had on shoes with leather heels. As I made my way across the studio, the click-click-click of my heels against the tiled floor echoed in my ears. And I laughed to myself, remembering other echoes, from other rooms.

In 1962 CBS sent me to California to work as a "gofer" under Stu Novins, a top newsman for years, who had come along in the third wave after Ed Murrow's original group. The effort that goes into a national political campaign actually begins two years ahead, with the mid-term elections. Novins was covering the West, everything beyond the Rockies, twenty states including Alaska.

One day there was an earthquake tremor in Southern California. CBS had film of some mudslides in the hills outside Los Angeles, and New York wanted to do an insert on the Sunday night news. When they called Novins was out to dinner, and they reached me in my room, doing my homework, trying to fathom what was going on in twenty states west of the Rockies. Never mind who the candidates were, I was trying to memorize the capital of Wyoming.

Arrangements had been made to interrupt a rehearsal of the Red Skelton show at Television City, the CBS studios in Hollywood. We didn't have a news set and Skelton's producers had agreed to call a five-minute break and move a desk onto the floor so I could narrate the film of the earth tremor and mudslides.

This may not sound like a breakthrough, but in 1962 I was new to the network, and it didn't take much to excite me. We were on a hurry-up basis from the start. I had to write a piece quickly about a story I hadn't actually seen. There was just enough time for a couple of phone calls to verify the information. All we had was a small window in the Skelton show. I remember being told to go up to Studio 42 and be on my best behavior. We were imposing on Mr. Skelton's kindness and I would have one take only.

The studio was large and I walked across it while the entire Skelton crew stood around—chorus girls with legs as long as doors, guys in bunny suits, a full orchestra and Red Skelton himself. There was almost complete silence, except for the metallic sound of the taps on the heels of my shoes. Taps had been big around the Heights, in Houston, in the late 1950's, and I still had mine. They saved your heels.

A steady "click-click-click" marked my progress across the room. I thought to myself, geez, I don't guess a CBS News correspondent ought to have taps on his shoes.

The last few yards I tried to walk on my toes, all the while taking in the dancing girls and the guys in the bunny suits and hoping to meet Red Skelton. I did the piece and there was a little light applause at the end. A show-business courtesy. Skelton himself came over and said in a bright, friendly way, "I hope you're through with that foolishness so we can get back to the more serious things."

I never wore taps again.

There is a saying in football that some pass receivers, when they are at the point of catching the ball, hear footsteps—real or imagined. You hear them in television, as well. Sometimes the footsteps are your own. But not always.

One such time dates back to the 1968 Democratic convention in Chicago. This has never ranked among my five favorite memories, but it may be worth retelling if only to set the record straight. Some political background is necessary here. I thought then, and will go to my grave believing, that Lyndon Johnson was hoping against hope that he would be able to sweep into the convention and somehow win the nomination again. Furthermore, I believe he intended to name Nelson Rockefeller as his vice-presidential running mate in a coalition ticket, his way of uniting the country, and assuring his victory, in the face of a destructive foreign war.

You would have had to know Johnson to understand how he could nourish that dream right up to the last. As a consequence, he needed to have the convention in a city where he could exercise some control. The

Democratic National Committee wanted to go anywhere but Chicago. The decision was LBJ's. He gave it to Mayor Richard Daley, with the guarantee that Daley would not let the convention get out of hand.

Daley had said, in effect, "By God, I can run my town and I'll prove it." Part of the arrangement was a very stiff security both inside and outside the hall. There was an elaborate credential system, gates people could exit through but not enter, all designed to maintain control. No one fully understood the security system and they didn't mean for you to understand.

The floor assignment in Chicago was about as tough as any reporter is ever likely to have. Within the hall the mood was mean, the party clearly split, the Gene McCarthy antiwar faction versus the established wing. One of the unforgettable scenes at the convention came when Senator Abraham Ribicoff criticized Daley for the repressive atmosphere around the hall, and Daley stood and gave the "cut" sign to turn off his microphone.

Outside, hippies, yippies, students and other demonstrators were getting clubbed and gassed in the streets and parks of Chicago, in what the Kerner Commission later would label "a police riot." Federal troops camped outside the city like an invasion force, ready to move into action. Anger spilled into violence. The Conrad Hilton Hotel had to be sealed off by police in blue helmets wielding nightsticks. Among the madness there was melancholy. Supporters of the late Robert Kennedy wandered through the crowds in a lost and aimless way, still mourning the death of their candidate to Sirhan's bullets.

At one point the bus, taxicab and telephone unions were on strike. All of Chicago seemed to have come unglued. It was as though Typhoid Mary had showed up at a banquet.

Against that backdrop, the Democratic party went about the business of rejecting a peace plank, nominating Hubert Humphrey and tearing itself apart. In his acceptance speech, Humphrey promised to bring back the politics of joy. But there was no joy in Chicago.

Two nights before the convention ended, I noticed a tussle going on across the floor. Four or five very tough-looking characters, in plain clothes, were trying to hustle a man wearing a delegate's badge out of the hall. They literally had him in the air, by his elbows, his feet barely touching the floor. He was struggling. I intercepted them as they passed near my area.

I stuck out a microphone and asked the basic reporter's question: "Pardon me, sir, what's happening?"

Very gruffly, one of the men in the suits said, "Get the hell out of here."

They physically brushed me aside. It was obvious to me that they were trying to rush him out one of the gates where no one could reenter. So I circled back around and met them again, walking backward in front of them. I asked the man who he was and the name of the delegation he was with. He said he was from Georgia. All the while we were getting closer to the exit and the guys in the convoy were not treating me gingerly. They had no identification of any kind on their clothes. I genuinely could not figure out what was going on, but I knew they were removing a delegate against his will. I also knew that once they passed through the gate I'd never find out the answers.

So I made one more maneuver and got back in front of them again. I stopped backpedaling this time and just planted myself in their way. At that point one of them grabbed my arm and threatened to have me arrested. I told him, "If you're an officer of the law identify yourself. If you're going to arrest me do so. But don't put your hands on me."

Walter Cronkite was talking about other things from the CBS aerie high over the convention floor. But others in the control room were monitoring this scene and wondering what I had gotten into. Finally, the men in the suits rushed me in a kind of wedge. I yelled out, "This man is a delegate and I have a right to talk to him." I squeezed inside them, held up the mike and said, "Sir, stop for a moment and tell me why these men are treating you this way?"

He had blurted out a sentence or two when a member of the convoy caught me with a punch to the solar plexus. He knew what he was doing, not as a security man but in using his fists. He kept his elbow close to his side and really drove the blow in, off his foot. He lifted me right off the floor and put me away. I was down, the breath knocked out of me, as the whole group blew on by me. I not only could hear footsteps, I heard chimes and a few bars of celestial music.

In the CBS control room, they had switched the camera onto me just as I was slugged. I was getting to my feet when Walter came to me with a question. Still gulping for air, I explained what little I had learned. Some people who acted as though they were part of the security force had hustled a Georgia delegate off the floor because he had tried to demonstrate. Walter had apparently trained his binoculars on me and seen a little of what had happened. He was shaken. He made a reference to "a bunch of thugs down there" and suggested, on the air, that I get some medical attention. I remember throwing a very weak line back to him: "Don't worry about it, Walter, I'll answer the bell."

We did have the scuffle on videotape. We were able to stop-frame it and pick out the one who hit me. The tape was replayed two or three times during the night and Walter was hotly critical of the convention security, charging that "they're beating hell out of reporters on the floor." By then the Democratic National Committee was alarmed.

A Secret Service agent came around. Keep in mind, they are responsible for the security of office holders, not reporters. But they looked at the videotape. Two days later, a friend of mine in the agency came to me and said, "We found your friend. As a matter of fact, he's seated in the back of the hall. What do you want to do?"

I said, "What are the options?" To be honest, it was not my desire to go back and get in a fist fight with this fellow. He had already established to my satisfaction that he knew how to use his hands.

I discussed the matter with CBS officials and decided the matter was best dropped. Although no one said so directly, the inference was strong that the man was part of an ad hoc security outfit hired by the Daley machine. The balcony was stacked with city employees and people holding "We Want Daley" signs. This one was someone's brother-in-law. He had no security experience. He was probably paid twenty-five dollars a night.

A reporter usually can tell when he is being roughed up by amateurs. The police have ways of edging you out with no fuss. Like Edgar Bergen, their lips won't even move as they tell you, "Don't futz with us right now. We'll answer your questions later."

The fellow who slugged me was questioned by the Secret Service. He told them his orders were not to allow incidents on the convention floor. When I got in the way someone said, "Take him out," and to him those words had only one meaning. I was lucky he didn't have a steel pipe on him.

By the end of the week the story had been embellished to the point that I had either single-handedly stood off eight of Daley's "goons," or been plowed under by a like number.

Getting kicked, stepped on, punched or otherwise caught in the middle of someone else's argument are among the risks a reporter takes in the heat of an election campaign. This does not often result, I might add, in an outpouring of public sympathy. But the risks are often worthwhile. The main thing is not to get beat up on company time.

A close presidential election is a little like Christmas Eve. No one can go to sleep while the packages are still under the tree. As we did in 1960 and 1968, millions of Americans stayed up until the small hours of the morning in 1976, this time to learn that Jimmy Carter of Georgia would be the new President of the United States. We can be sure, on such occasions, that roughly half of those who go to bed early will wake up mad.

I have one other lasting and instructive, but less painful, memory of 1968. I was assigned for the first time as a CBS analyst on election night, always a special moment for television. A national election is one of the ways we mark time. This is our Olympics.

The coverage involves frequent rehearsals, especially for people new to the run. I had been in New York all of the final week, rehearsing, meeting people, getting myself up for an assignment I couldn't blow. Frankly, I was nervous, and I decided to fly home to Washington the night before our final rehearsal. I wanted to be with Jean, which for me is always therapeutic.

Our producer was Bobby Wussler—now Robert Wussler, the president of the CBS Network. He was understanding, if not enthused, about my leaving. He emphasized that I had to be back by ten the next morning for the start of rehearsals.

I decided to make the 7 A.M. air shuttle out of Washington to allow myself a little margin. I got up at 5:15 and in order not to wake Jean I groped around in the dark, dressed, left a note, kissed her on the cheek and headed for the airport. I congratulated myself on such thoughtful planning. A fog cover had begun to move in and my plane left just ahead of it. We landed at La Guardia at twenty minutes to nine and, enjoying the leisure, I bought a copy of *The New York Times* and decided to get a shoe shine. I was reading the paper when I heard the shine man say, "*Ummmm-ummmm,* been a lonnng time since I seen that!"

I peeked over the top of the paper and said, "What's that?"

He shook his head. "One black shoe and one brown shoe. Yessir, been a lonnng time since I seen that." Not a dark brown shoe, mind you, almost a tan.

I said, forget it, handed him a dollar, raced out of the terminal, jumped into a cab and blurted, "Get me into Manhattan and stop at the first shoe store you see." Instead of being way ahead of time I was now fighting the clock.

It soon became clear that no stores were open until 10 A.M., which was exactly when I had to be in the studio. I thought to myself, there just isn't a lot that can be done here. I'll go to the rehearsal, try to sneak behind my desk, maybe no one will notice I have on different colored shoes, and at the first chance I'll run out and buy a new pair.

I went up the back way of the CBS offices and walked off the elevator at two minutes to ten with only one thing on my mind. To get to the desk as inconspicuously as I could.

When I opened the door to the studio I saw Wussler waiting with four other men. They were Dick Salant, the president of CBS News, Jack Schneider, the president of CBS Television, Frank Stanton, the president of CBS, Inc., and William S. Paley, the chairman of the board. According to company tradition, the top executives always visited the set before an election. At the door I froze like a rabbit.

Wussler spotted me and sang out, "I see you just made it." They were standing near my booth and Bob motioned me over. Again, I had to walk the length of a studio floor and all I could hear was the echo of my own footsteps. I wondered how anyone could fail to look at my shoes.

Either Mr. Paley did not notice each shoe was a different color, or he had too much class to say anything. He asked me how I was. I gulped and said, "Fine, Mr. Chairman," as I sort of stood on one leg, with the other foot behind me.

Whenever I begin to feel any confusion about who I am, or I find myself taking the star treatment seriously, I remember the black shoe and the brown shoe. And the feeling always passes.

INDEX